The Trial of Hatred

Incitements

Series editors: Peg Birmingham, DePaul University and
Dimitris Vardoulakis, Western Sydney University

Editorial Advisory Board
Étienne Balibar, Andrew Benjamin, Jay M. Bernstein, Rosi Braidotti, Wendy Brown,
Judith Butler, Timothy Campbell, Adriana Cavarero, Howard Caygill, Rebecca Comay,
Joan Copjec, Simon Critchley, Costas Douzinas, Peter Fenves, Christopher Fynsk,
Moira Gatens, Gregg Lambert, Leonard Lawlor, Genevieve Lloyd, Catherine Malabou,
James Martel, Christoph Menke, Warren Montag, Michael Naas, Antonio Negri,
Kelly Oliver, Paul Patton, Anson Rabinbach, Gerhard Richter, Martin Saar, Miguel Vatter,
Gianni Vattimo, Santiago Zabala

Available

Return Statements: The Return of Religion in Contemporary Philosophy
Gregg Lambert

The Refusal of Politics
Laurent Dubreuil, translated by Cory Browning

Plastic Sovereignties: Agamben and the Politics of Aesthetics
Arne De Boever

From Violence to Speaking Out:
Apocalypse and Expression in Foucault, Derrida and Deleuze
Leonard Lawlor

Agonistic Mourning: Political Dissidence and the Women in Black
Athena Athanasiou

Interpassivity: The Aesthetics of Delegated Enjoyment
Robert Pfaller

Derrida's Secret: Perjury, Testimony, Oath
Charles Barbour

Resistance and Psychoanalysis: Impossible Divisions
Simon Morgan Wortham

Reclaiming Wonder: After the Sublime
Genevieve Lloyd

Arendt, Natality and Biopolitics: Towards Democratic Plurality and Reproductive Justice
Rosalyn Diprose and Ewa Plonowska Ziarek

Worldlessness After Heidegger: Phenomenology, Psychoanalysis, Deconstruction
Roland Végső

Homo Natura: Nietzsche, Philosophical Anthropology and Biopolitics
Vanessa Lemm

Spinoza, the Transindividual
Étienne Balibar, translated by Mark G. E. Kelly

Uncontainable Legacies: Theses on Intellectual, Cultural and Political Inheritance
Gerhard Richter

The Trial of Hatred: An Essay on the Refusal of Violence
Marc Crépon, translated by D. J. S. Cross and Tyler M. Williams

Visit the series web page at: edinburghuniversitypress.com/series/incite

The Trial of Hatred

An Essay on the Refusal of Violence

Marc Crépon

Translated by D. J. S. Cross and Tyler M. Williams

EDINBURGH
University Press

Edinburgh University Press is one of the leading university presses in the
UK. We publish academic books and journals in our selected subject
areas across the humanities and social sciences, combining cutting-edge
scholarship with high editorial and production values to produce academic
works of lasting importance. For more information visit our website:
edinburghuniversitypress.com

L'Épreuve de la haine: Essai sur le refus de la violence
by Marc Crépon © Odile Jacob Publishing, 2016

English translation © D. J. S. Cross and Tyler M. Williams, 2022

Edinburgh University Press Ltd
The Tun – Holyrood Road, 12(2f) Jackson's Entry, Edinburgh EH8 8PJ

Typeset in Bembo
by R. J. Footring Ltd, Derby, UK, and
printed and bound in Great Britain

A CIP record for this book is available from the British Library

ISBN 978 1 4744 8025 3 (hardback)
ISBN 978 1 4744 8028 4 (webready PDF)
ISBN 978 1 4744 8026 0 (paperback)
ISBN 978 1 4744 8027 7 (epub)

The right of Marc Crépon to be identified as the author of this work
has been asserted in accordance with the Copyright, Designs and Patents
Act 1988, and the Copyright and Related Rights Regulations 2003
(SI No. 2498).

Contents

Acknowledgements

This book owes much to the collaboration of friendship and teaching. Thanks are therefore due to Steven Ecovitch, Marc de Launay and Jean-Yves Le Corre, who accompanied me these past few years along the book market stalls in search of unfindable volumes by Romain Rolland or out-of-print editions of Martin Luther King, Jr; my friends at Northwestern University, Michael Loriaux, Nasrin Qader and Samuel Weber, as well as their students in the Paris Program; friends at DePaul University, Michael Naas, Pascale-Anne Brault and Elisabeth Rottenberg; friends at the University of California Irvine, David Pan, John Smith and Jane Newman, who lent me their magnificent hilltop house while finishing this book peacefully among the flowering cacti, hibiscuses and palm trees; David Johnson and Donald Cross at SUNY Buffalo; and, lastly, my colleagues and students at the École normale supérieure who have, for these past few years, attended the courses and lectures that prepared the material for this book. Finally, my gratitude goes to Perrine Simon-Nahum, who believed in this project, and to Odile Jacob Publishing, which welcomed it. Its completion owes much to their confidence. Nothing, however, would have been the same without the constant support and affection of Rodica, Elena and Stephan. I dedicate this book to them.

Translators' Note

Wherever available, we use existing translations of the works cited throughout this book. Where no translations exist, we ourselves translate the cited passages. Wherever Marc Crépon's analyses lead us to modify an existing translation, we signal the modification accordingly. The unique status or history of several works will influence either Crépon's comments or our translations, but we reserve more detailed comments for the end notes.

Wherever Crépon's own lexicon poses problems, we offer explanatory notes, but we attempt to keep these brief and to a minimum. When certain words or formulations force a decision on our part but nevertheless do not inhibit the passage's intelligibility, we gloss the French term in editorial brackets. One such term, the only we will mention here at the outset, occurs in the title itself: *L'Épreuve de la haine*. The French term *épreuve* has no strict equivalent in English. Although we attempt to keep translations as consistent as possible, we render the term variously as 'trial', 'test', 'ordeal', 'challenge' and so on. For more details concerning this word's semantic spread, we refer the reader to our Translators' Note in Crépon's *The Vocation of Writing: Literature, Philosophy, and the Test of Violence* (2018). While, in the subtitle of *The Vocation*, we render *épreuve* as 'test' due to the book's general direction (and the title's syntax), we felt 'trial' to be the most suitable option in the context of *The Trial of Hatred*. Nevertheless, while legal procedures play an important role throughout the book, the 'trial' is not limited to a strictly juridical context.

We thank Marc Crépon for his enthusiastic support of this translation and his timely responses to our queries. At Edinburgh University Press, Carol Macdonald, Kirsty Woods and Sarah Foyle have made every step of the publication process both painless and rigorous. We also very much appreciate the hospitality with which Peg Birmingham and Dimitris Vardoulakis have welcomed the project in their Incitements series. If one risks becoming burdensome by asking friends or colleagues to help track down obscure works, one risks outright audacity by doing so during a pandemic, but Alejandro Orozco Hidalgo in Paris did not hesitate to help us find some of the works that were not readily available to us in the United States and Chile. We also thank Shaun Irlam and Eric Lynch for input on some difficult passages in Chapter 5 of Part II, 'Exiting Apartheid'.

Preface to the English Translation of
The Trial of Hatred

From Murderous Consent to the Trial of Hatred in the Vocation of Writing

> I had plague already, long before I came to this town and encountered it here.
> Albert Camus (1975: 245)

I

In Albert Camus's *The Plague*, which has been frequently cited these past few months, during the time of a pandemic that renders fragile all our reference points, there is a passage worth rereading for the sake of renewing the critique of violence. Jean Tarrou, Dr Bernard Rieux's medical assistant and one of the most enigmatic characters in the novel, finally opens up and, confiding at length, begins with the memory of a scene in which the fate of a life comes to be decided. He recounts the trial [*procès*] of a man and his death sentence: the unbearable contrast between the pitiless generality of the judiciary machine, embodied by his own father, and the singularity of the condemned, the irreplaceable character of his life doomed to disappear by a death sentence. That day, Tarrou recounts, a horrified indignation gets lodged in the heart of his existence, an inextinguishable revolt against death sentences and executions. Just as it will have precipitated others onto the paths of philosophy and writing, the scene was an initiation, he specifies, because it placed him on the path of a politics that he hoped would be driven by the refusal of violent death, in other words, the refusal of all 'murderous consent'. "'To my mind'", he confides, "'the social order around me was based on the death sentence, and by fighting the established order I'd be fighting against murder'" (Camus 1975: 250).

If this passage should hold our attention, it is because, over the course of the self-narrative, in the secret of an avowal, the metaphor of the plague surges. Short of providing a key to the novel [*une clef du roman*], the metaphor at least signals its double scope – ethical and political: "'I didn't want to be pestiferous'", Tarrou confesses; "'that's all'" (Camus 1975: 250). For what, then, is the plague a metaphor? Of nothing less than contagion of the 'consent to murder', in which, throughout his life, Camus saw and combatted the most durable and dreadful sign of the nihilism of our times. Nothing is simple, however, for it is not easy, in these times of ours, to avoid being 'pestiferous' in the sense Tarrou gives to this word. Who can claim that, albeit unwittingly, one will not have consented by silence, indifference, cowardice, resignation or political choices to violent death, exemplified by the many tragedies of the twentieth century and the compromises with murder that accompanied them? Is this not the trial [*épreuve*] that all political commitment faces when it accommodates itself to the death of some in the name of the life of others? Tarrou admits to having had this painful experience.

'And thus I came to understand that I, anyhow, had had plague through all those long years in which, paradoxically enough, I'd believed with all my soul that I was fighting it. I learned that I had had an indirect hand in the deaths of thousands of people; that I'd even brought about their deaths by approving of acts and principles which could only end that way.' (Camus 1975: 251)

This issue concerns the articulation of ethics and politics on the scale of our belonging to the world. If it is true that the solidarity between humans and their necessary complicity rest upon the responsibility for the care, help and attention demanded by their vulnerability and mortality, every political compromise – more or less fraudulent, more or less explicit – on this demand makes anyone who surrenders to it actively or passively 'pestiferous'. Some are no doubt more 'pestiferous' than others – and one should always draw distinctions. To participate directly in murder, as a cog in the murderous machine, is not the same thing as resigning to it by closing one's eyes and plugging one's ears. Nevertheless, as soon as one consents, as soon as one compromises even once, there are no longer limits to what one is ready to tolerate. As we inherit them today, Camus's whole experience and tragic vision of politics, perhaps also his melancholy due to history, are concentrated in the bitter observation that his character makes about his era:

> 'My reply to this was that if you gave in once, there was no reason for not continuing to give in. It seems to me that history has borne me out; today there's a sort of competition who will kill the most. They're all mad over murder and they couldn't stop killing men even if they wanted to.' (Camus 1975: 251–2)

II

There are thus two good reasons for rereading *The Plague* now. First, taken in its proper sense, the epidemic that constitutes the story's plot finds a troubling echo in the pandemic that has struck populations very disproportionately throughout the entire world in recent months. The epidemic emphasises the variety of emotional, intellectual and affective reactions engaging the idea that each of us has of our individual responsibility when the illness [*le mal*],[1] an invisible virus, might come from anywhere at any moment – from the spaces we cross, from the beings we meet, from the objects we touch and even from the air that we breathe. It recalls in the same stroke the vanity of wanting to confront on one's own, without worrying about others, the disorder caused by the contagion in existence and calendric reference points, habits and projects. Yet, as Tarrou's confession suggests, the epidemic's proper sense is not the final word on the disease. Understood in a figurative sense, the 'plague' refers us, moreover and more generally, to the way in which – faced with a crisis or catastrophe of any order whatsoever: sanitary, to be sure, but also climatic, migratory, political, economic and social – what I designate with the name 'murderous consent' is at work.[2] These individual and collective trials contaminate us, in the sense that they push us to say and do violence, to accept compromises with violence, to which we never would have imagined it possible to accommodate ourselves. Such is the 'sedimentation of the unacceptable', which paves the way for a thousand and one murderous consents that weave the web of our existence.

These consents, then, constitute our belonging to the world insofar as they are each time the symptom of the abyss that separates our responsibility, defined theoretically, from its practical exercise. This was my point of departure. From a theoretical point of view, if one will merely admit that this re-sponsibility is defined by the care, aid and attention demanded for everyone everywhere by the vulnerability and mortality of the other, it is uncompromising, radical, perhaps hyperbolic, and it brooks no exception, accepts no concession. One cannot distinguish *a priori* those to whom this responsibility would apply and those whose lot – that is, the violences they suffer – does not concern us. It knows no belonging and no border. From a practical point of view, by contrast, in the ordinary course of life we ceaselessly make compromises on the principle of this responsibility. This principle wants nothing of what damages or injures the world to remain foreign to us, no unjust and violent death to be indifferent to us, and yet the exact opposite happens. Everything contributes not only to installing and justifying these compromises but also, perhaps, even to calculating them: partisan politics, economic wars, the interests of which – albeit unwittingly – we endorse. We close our eyes and plug our ears to what we prefer not to see and not to hear, or we see and hear it only in passing and indirectly before moving on to something else. This is precisely how violence lodges in the heart of our existences.

In this sense, in the case of the pandemic, this form of 'letting die' is murderous: the cynical calculation that, in trying to save an economic system (itself synonymous with injustice), deliberately chooses to defer as long as possible the guided and controlled organisation of individual and collective protection against the contagion, thereby abandoning through its negligence the weakest and most defenceless, those deprived of access to health care, to the pandemic's lethal ravages. Just as murderous is the refusal of sceptics (anti-mask militants) of various persuasions to implement the protective measures and bend to that form of auto-hetero-protection according to which everyone recip-rocally assures the protection of everyone else by protecting themselves. Thus, the two senses of the plague (the proper and the figurative) join together, and the configuration leaves no doubt about its deadliness when one merely thinks of the particularly devastating effects of the coronavirus in countries where the leaders adopt this sort of discourse and encourage this sort of attitude. And it is true that consent to the worst produces its most perverse effects when – as was the case in the United States, Brazil and Mexico – it benefits from an irresponsible political injunction. But the list does not end there. Murderous too, in another vein, are Europe's immigration policies, which have for years exposed thousands of men and women to attempting the impossible, risking their lives, in order to flee their country, where life has become unliveable for economic, social or political – if not military – reasons. Murderous, finally, are the industrial and agricultural practices and the exploitation of the oceans, forests and mountains that destroy the planet, along with the economic and political forces pushed by short-term interests into shamelessly siding with long-term destructions, with no regard for future generations.

III

At stake is our relation to violence. The thought of murderous consent makes sense only insofar as it calls for a philosophy of the refusal of violence. To consent to violence, one way or another, always in effect amounts to finding excuses for extreme violences, inventing good reasons for them, producing justifications while inscribing violences in the programmatic order of history, economy or education as an inevitability or a necessary evil. This never happens alone. The reasons are all the more acceptable in that they draw upon negative passions, beginning with hatred, in the very place where it articulates a culture of fear with an enemy culture.[3] On the other side of this inscription, which many philosophical and literary texts have supported (when they have not themselves constructed or represented it), this is why the refusal to back murder (and all forms of violence applied to bodies and minds) calls for critical, ethical and political exit ramps to escape, not so much murderous consent itself, but rather the nihilism resigned to and satisfied with it. In a general way, Camus's entire oeuvre exemplifies the invention of the means that everyone must find to tear free from the plague's grip and the weight of its contagion upon bodies and minds, to escape this paralysis of heart and action that would attest to the victory of disease, to recover – lastly – the minimal confidence and hope in a complicity to come, without which life is unliveable. The response unfolds on several registers.

First, an ethical register. In *The Plague*, the character Tarrou exemplifies two forms of extrication for leaving the particular form of nihilism constituted by, in the case of contagion, resignation to letting-die. The first form consists in inventing gestures of goodness that side with victims as a principle:

'I say there are pestilences and there are victims; no more than that. If, by making that statement, I, too, become a carrier of the plague-germ, at least I don't do it wilfully. I try, in short, to be an innocent murderer. [. . .] That's why I decided to take, in every predicament, the victims' side, so as to reduce the damage done.' (Camus 1975: 254)

This active benevolence is the inverse of abandoning victims to their dire lot; it is an act of resistance against the pitiless calculations that, in difficult times, would see saving oneself and protecting one's loved ones as most essential. The second extrication from the tangles of nihilism is shame.[4] Shame explains *a posteriori* Tarrou's commitment to coming to everyone's aid alongside Dr Rieux, as if the feeling of never denouncing violence enough had created a lifelong debt – a debt of attention, care and help for which the victims of violence effectively call:

> 'For many years I've been ashamed, mortally ashamed, of having been, even with the best intentions, even at many removes, a murderer in my turn. [. . .] Yes, I've been ashamed ever since; I have realized that we all have plague.' (Camus 1975: 252)

Shame is not nothing! The shame one feels for the suffering that humans inflict upon each other is the expression of a refusal, if not a revolt against the contagion of illness and evil [*mal*]. It manifests the insufficient but necessary will, often desperate, to uncouple from violence, to do nothing and say nothing that might give credence to the idea that those who perpetrate violence have good reasons for destroying what they destroy and for taking the lives they take.

IV

Next, extrication is critical and political. Thought demands, indeed, a reflection on the mechanisms engineered to produce and maintain support in hearts and consciousnesses: the factory of discourses and photomontages, which one must therefore learn to dismantle. At the heart of this construction, one feeling dominates: hatred, which one will always be surprised and troubled to see how disconcertingly easy it is to incite. One needs next to nothing to enflame a society, a community, a family, any human group whatsoever, to awaken collectively the taste for blood and death sleeping in each individual. This is why no refusal of violence holds up without an uncompromising deconstruction of the forces that provoke hatred. Nothing is harder, for these forces are armed – and their first weapon is language. These forces know how to make use of all the artifices of rhetoric to instil in hearts a dreadful enemy culture nourished by the bacillus of fear. Thus, they must be combatted in two ways. The first way consists in critical vigilance. Once ways of speaking, describing or judging inject their murderous poison into bodies and consciousnesses, their dangerousness – made of falsifications, lies and insidious caricatures, but also of dissimulations and sometimes even veritable calls for murder – must be brought to light and denounced. Consequently, this denunciation does not suffice; it also calls for – this is the second combat – a counterword, which must first of all show another relation to language, freed from the murderous bogs of ideology. What relation? The relation distinguished by a singular inventiveness [*inventivité*] and creativity, borne by new work of the imagination. Ordinary language is a habituation. It brings us to announce, without paying further attention to it, what we can no longer imagine. We satisfy ourselves with counting the deaths. Disease and evil [*le mal*] become banal. To use the imagination otherwise is to find the courage to see and in the same stroke to think what, while caught in the cogs of violence, one did not know how or no longer wanted to see; it is, through a singular word or writing, to contribute a refusal to ways of denying the gravity of violence, minimising it or hiding it, ways which prepare the path for murderous consents.

Only thus does one move the threshold of tolerance in societies to the forms of disease and evil [*mal*] that they ended up tolerating or allowing to carry out destructive work without resistance.[5] This is undoubtedly not the only vocation of literature and philosophy, but one such vocation is surely to make this counterword heard wherever literature and philosophy answer together for the future.

Marc Crépon
Paris, October 2020

Notes

1 In French, *le mal* means both 'illness' and 'evil'. – Translators
2 See Crépon, *Murderous Consent* (2019).
3 The French formulation – *culture de l'ennemi* – would be more literally translated as 'culture of the enemy', but this formulation too readily suggests a culture belonging to an enemy is at stake rather than a culture defined by its relation to an enemy. The formulation 'culture of enmity' more accurately portrays Crépon's sense, but it loses the focus on the association of the 'enemy' and the 'foreign' since enmity is also domestic. The formulation *culture de l'ennemi* is the first heading in Chapter 2 of Part II of the present volume, 'Of Hatred', where we have also rendered it as 'enemy culture'. It is also worth indicating that the twin formulation, *culture de la peur* ('culture of fear'), refers to Crépon's eponymous two-volume work. – Translators
4 Shame is the common denominator between *Murderous Consent* (Chapter 5), *The Vocation of Writing* (Chapter 4) and *The Trial of Hatred* (Chapter 5).
5 See Marc Crépon, *Inhumaines conditions* (2018) and *La société à l'épreuve des affaires de mœurs* (2020).

Preface to the French Edition

I

On 7 and 9 January 2015, then again on 13 November and 14 July 2016, violence irrupted into our lives.[1] We undoubtedly did not have to wait for these days to have either a direct or indirect experience of violence. Whether familial, scholarly, professional, moral or political, none of the relationships that comprise the fabric of individual existence escape violence. But the violence on these dates was an immediate trial [*épreuve*] for at least three reasons.

The first reason is that the proper of a terrorist attack pertains to the obsessive fear [*hantise*] of its repetition. Beyond the victims that an attack instantaneously creates, victims who arouse our indignation and compassion, we immediately dread that the attack will recur. This is the very essence of terror. This irruption was not momentary, limited to a certain time, but rather lasting. It installed the prospect of its reiteration within the horizon of existence. On café terraces, in a concert hall, on public transportation, at a sporting event or a festival, we know it can return at any moment. Nothing could persuade us of the contrary, and nobody would dare guarantee it.

The second reason that makes this violence a trial pertains to the negative passions that these attacks provoke: fear, certainly, but hatred as well. Because terrorist violence proceeds from a mad hatred, constructed and fostered, repeated during its exercise in murderous camps and on each of its propaganda channels, it gives birth in everyone to the pressing need for a response in which – however legitimate and comprehensible this need might be – justice, vengeance and protection merge. We want *to finish* with what we perceive as a radical evil and what we identify as its source. How could it be otherwise? And who would blame us? Yet, the risk is then the fiery words, the hasty judgements, the reckless actions and the blind decisions to which the hatred awakening in everyone exposes us in turn. The risk is even higher in that, prisoners of their electoral calculations, the responsible politicians do not resist indecent escalations for their own benefit. Beyond the victims that the spectacular violence creates, the trauma it engenders offers choice terrain for simplifying all thought, as well as reducing analyses, when it does not require confiscating all investigation and reflection, as if required by the memories of these same victims. It favours false evidence. From this emotionally overloaded perspective, how can one resist the weighty idea and feeling that *violence begets violence*, demands it, and that this rejoinder should be denied nothing, no legal or policing method refused to it, so as to track the criminals in the broadest possible way and punish their crimes, even if certain shared freedoms would have to be infringed? And how can one avoid the conviction that nothing, absolutely nothing, should keep us from *hating* those who sow terror?

The third reason that makes these terrorist attacks a trial is that they unquestionably change the perception we might have had of our belonging to the world. Crushed by bombings and subjected to routine attacks, the people of Syria, Iraq and Libya have for years suffered the violence from January, November and last July every day. We had hitherto been distant and, if not indifferent, at least resigned spectators. For many, by the force of things, this violence came from that form of murderous consent according to which we see without seeing and hear without hearing, compromising on the responsibility for the care, help and attention for which the vulnerability and mortality of every other nevertheless calls. Whether one acknowledges or denies it, the mass murders of the Syrian regime and its supporters affected us from afar. They took up so little space in our lives! The influx of refugees who, risking their existence, have been knocking on Europe's doors since last summer, along with the origin and circulation of terrorists, has made this violence catch up to us. We can no longer ignore what binds together the fate of peoples from both sides of the Mediterranean. No border, no barricade, no barbed wire, no wall will be able to erase this community. It is a challenge for thinking. For there again simplifications lie in wait for us, like the simplification that would interpret this common exposure as the sign of an inevitable clash between two opposing civilisations: 'Islam and the West'.[2] But the Islamic State is not a civilisation! It cannot even be identified with the religion it proclaims, and nowhere does it create more victims than among the populations that nevertheless define part of their identity on the basis of that same religion. Violence seeks division, for which hatred is the most effective instrument; this is its culture and work. Violence needs hatred to justify and maintain itself! And nothing sustains it more than taking it to be definitive by essentialising it. Is it nevertheless certain at this point that, between the two shores of the Mediterranean, no form of understanding or solidarity remains possible that can oppose this hatred, no common reason that can unite the shores? The ravages of hatred and the destructions engendered by violence are nevertheless common. Breaking all the dams that bind them to the rest of humanity, those who have chosen hatred and violence as their *raison d'être* create victims on both sides. How could one imagine, then, that *the refusal of violence* might be the privilege of one shore or the other and does not constitute the principle of their confluence?

II

Thus, we need to know what we are talking about, and we need to find the method to get there! Whenever violence is in question, the snare consists in approaching it via its causes, endlessly disputing the reasons that explain it. Regardless of what anyone says, this does not necessarily amount to justifying violence, finding excuses for it or minimising it, although this is sometimes the case, as seen in so many speeches delivered in support of certain regimes of terror. Nevertheless, this in no way accounts for the experience of violence. Although universal, the experience of violence remains impossible to comprehend as long as one does not start from the one point of view that escapes all complacency, namely, that of *its effects*. It is important to describe and analyse the way the experience of violence transforms our relation to the world, brutally or surreptitiously affecting our relation to time, space and – more generally – the totality of what surrounds us. Assuming one wishes to make the refusal of violence a principle of judgement, thought and action, one must know precisely what one opposes, all the more so when this same violence finds support in a factory of hatred. Part I of this book is devoted to this comprehension.

But the method does not stop there. Once the articulation of violence and hatred is brought to light, one must also show that this articulation is not inevitable, that one can avoid the former and overcome the latter. It must be shown, consequently, that the double refusal of violence and hatred can be the object of a principle: the principle of non-violence, which has its own efficacy. Henceforth, a second conviction comes into play. The first was that violence should be analysed by way of its effects, which can alone constitute the lever of a critique that transcends divisions and awakens indignation, shame and revolt in everyone. The second conviction concerns the living memory of speeches and actions. We are always less abandoned, less disoriented than we think when we just remember that others, in other times and other places, have weathered the trial [*ont fait l'épreuve*] of this violence that seems inexorable to us, this hatred that we think is inextricable, and what they said then about violence and hatred – the terms with which they described, thought and opposed them – is an inextinguishable source of clarity. Part II of this book wagers the supposition that, despite everything that separates the contexts (the war of 1914–18, the rise of European fascisms, the struggle for civil rights in America, the end of apartheid, the Rwandan genocide),[3] it is possible to believe in and revive their help or support in the space of a few quotations and analyses. This book's second part thus solicits the great voices of, among others, Jean Jaurès, Romain Rolland, Martin Luther King, Jr and Nelson Mandela.

Still one final point remains, which pertains to the necessity of mobilising against hatred and violence resources that – spiritual, moral or other – are radically foreign to political strategies and calculations but capable of commanding them. It is no coincidence that Rolland, King and Mandela all drew decisive inspiration from Gandhi's commitment [*engagement*]. What they found there was not only the illustration of remarkable powers of non-violence, capable of bending the British Empire, but also the force of a moral and spiritual injunction. For at least two reasons, however, the articulation of morality and politics is far from evident. First, morality's power of conviction appears *weak* in the face of political interests and the means politics implements in defence. This is why recalling morality's principles often seems like wishful thinking, and we doubt such recalling will ever be able to curb or stop any destruction whatsoever. Second, morality itself is not exempt from compromises with violence, especially when it remains particular, linked to a determined denomination that has its own interests like, for example, proselytising. But can one dispense with such a command? In order to escape the nihilism of our times in the sense Camus gave to the word, namely, the proliferation of a generalised murderous consent, a response to this question is not the least of this book's goals.

Notes

1 References to – respectively – the Charlie Hebdo attacks, the coordinated attacks on the Stade de France in Saint-Denis, the Bataclan and restaurants throughout Paris, and the truck attack in Nice. – Translators

2 See Part I, 'The Experience of Violence'.

3 By design, this book contains no substantial developments on either the Stalinist terror or Nazism, the Second World War and the extermination of European Jews. These forms of extreme violence occupied two of the preceding volumes of a trilogy, of which *The Trial of Hatred* constitutes the third and final installment: *Murderous Consent* and *The Vocation of Writing: Literature, Philosophy, and the Test of Violence*.

Part I. The Experience of Violence

1

Intimacy

Violence is invasive. Wherever we look, it seems to merge with the real. We know it to be hidden in family secrets, as if every intimate relationship were contaminated in advance by the probability of violence's irruption at one moment or another of its history. Every attachment – between a man and a woman, between two men or two women, between parents and their children, between brothers and sisters – harbours the threat of being rendered fragile by hurtful and offensive words, inappropriate gestures, the thousand and one possible forms of brutality introduced into the relation, wearing out over time or destroying in a single stroke the fiduciary confidence that supports it. Friendship itself does not resist its spectre. In all the moments of sharing that we invent in order to maintain friendship, it is always possible to invite violence into the encounter, casting a chill between friends who hoped for something entirely different from it. In a general way, not one of the relationships comprising the intimate fabric and history of all existence remains unaffected by both violence's original possibility and the recurrence of its imminence. It would be futile to deny it: violence belongs to the essence of what binds us to others in existence.

Is this to say that a principled refusal of violence is illusory? Does this mean that there is no sense in wanting to think the means and conditions necessary for resisting its grasp or suspending the course of its manifestations, escaping its machinations, re-establishing or restoring the bonds it has undone? The necessary acknowledgement of the unavoidable role that violence plays in existence undoubtedly exposes us to the intellectual and affective temptation of a disillusioned cynicism that refuses to lull itself with illusions concerning the nature of the relations that bind us to others. But if we had no chance of escaping it, would we still seek, as we so often do, to protect what attaches us to others from disaster each time we fear an irremediable rupture? Love and friendship, before being characterised by the violence that threatens to separate the men and women whom they unite, are distinguished by the force that makes violence unimaginable for a time. When we love, we begin by believing violence to be impossible; we refuse to think that the destructive possibility of violence secretly inhabits the bonds being built. This is why, if one must know how to recognise at the heart of every relation the existence of forces that, even if unconscious, threaten to destroy that relation, it is equally necessary to recall that each relation is defined by the singular invention and repetition of gestures and words, of a care and attention that are all ways of countering violence, keeping it at a distance and sometimes even forgiving and forgetting its untimely manifestations. Consequently, it could very well be the case that *countering* violence belongs just as much to the essence of life: in what binds us to others, there would be the possibility of violence's irruption just as much as its leveeing, its repression, its correction and its refusal.

2

Countering Violence

The question, however, far exceeds the limits of the intimate and
private sphere, and there thus exists a second way to interrogate,
sceptically, that which seems to come down to an injunction,
imperative or exigency in the preceding expression (*countering
violence*). Draped in the comfortable garb of what Hegel called
a 'beautiful soul' or, no less suspect, a foolproof 'good conscience', does one not to lack lucidity and realism to want 'to
counter violence', to oppose it or to refuse it in principle? Is the
aforementioned, invasive violence not only ineluctable, since it
belongs to the essence of life, but also, what is more, necessary?
We should pause for a moment on this necessity, which serves
as an argument in at least four domains: the thought of education, the pronouncement of moral prescriptions, the thought of
history and political philosophy. This necessity comes down to
maintaining, pell-mell, that we do not do much in the world
without violence, that we do not advance or progress in individual or collective life without violence either and, consequently,
that the refusal of violence not only comes from a refuge in an
ideal world that wants to know nothing of the harsh reality of
human nature and the world men have fashioned but is also,
additionally, a synonym for *both* stagnation and immobility *and*

cowardice and conservativism. In this way, the refusal of violence in principle would be condemnable, at least in a paradoxical way, for both anthropological and political reasons! To refuse violence would thus be to fail to see that it is indispensable not only for the development of individuals but also for the becoming of 'peoples', if only they take their 'due' place in history – indispensable as well for the progress of societies, to say nothing of the propagation in the world of particular religious faiths, from Christianity to Islam. Better still: one might hastily affirm, not without nonchalance toward the physical and moral suffering that this amounts to accepting, that neither social justice nor the emancipation of peoples nor equality of rights and conditions would have been won in the long struggle without *granting* violence *its due* [donner droit].

These arguments cannot be neglected. They have in their favour, first of all, solidly established philosophical – but also literary and scientific – traditions, and one could cite a thousand works in literature, history and philosophy that conjugate them in every form. Without being analysed for itself in its most concrete and universal effects, violence has ceaselessly engendered everywhere, in every domain, discourses that justify it. One might even say that thoughts that do not recognise the necessity of a minimal 'dose' of violence are rare. Let us return to the domains evoked above. Innumerable, first of all, are the treatises on education that call for rigorous discipline and construct the catalogue of brutalities necessary to make it respected. School itself took centuries to shake the idea that a minimum of physical violence was indispensable for making students work and for obtaining from them the expected results. And, if it is true that corporal punishment now belongs to the past, its legal sanction nevertheless has not abolished the physical violence or the public and no less destructive humiliations that certain teachers still authorise themselves to inflict. Hence, it is not surprising that the dogma of this necessary dose is also found in all sectors of the work world when so many managers, imbued with the power that their directorial function gives them, imagine that verbal violence and all the forms of moral and physical harassment that accompany it are indispensable for carrying out the task of supervision or direction that has been bestowed upon them. With respect to moral principles, whatever catechisms are given with the vocation of remembering them and drawing rules of conduct from them, not one dispenses with a doctrine of punishment, that is to say, not one avoids imagining or having imagined, at the limits of cruelty, forms of salutary suffering in order to impose these rules upon individuals and communities. Similarly, every moral denomination, with its great priests and catechists, can be retraced at one moment or another to its taste for blood or sentencing – as all magnanimity assumed that one does violence to *oneself* or that one accepts violence from those who have, recognise they have and are recognised to have the authority to wield it. Finally, concerning speculations on history and politics, I will say only a word to begin. Both history and politics make violence the means judged necessary for an end that they take as imperative. The nature of this end matters little. Whether a question of the arrest, imprisonment and elimination of opponents, the massacre of ethnic or religious minorities, civil war or the terror exercised against populations, all of this violent action has been justified for centuries by the conservation or the restoration of an old order, as well as by the establishment of a new order. And there is nothing in the final analysis that reactionary, conservative or revolutionary ideas [*pensées*] share more than this obsessive justification of violence that they accept, encourage or organise.

3

Levees that Break

These intellectual and scholarly traditions would have no weight if they were not supported by false evidences that seem to come from common sense in each of these four domains. One would be tempted to say, at the risk of appearing disillusioned before the surprising convergence of ordinary language and scholarly discourse, that one knows the tune when it is a question of granting violence its due. Men are warped wood,[1] corrupted by an original fault that must be straightened. Nothing great, elevated, sublime or transcendent is achieved without one of the passions (ambition, pride, greed, jealousy and – why not? – hatred) that one would try in vain to imagine without violence. Happy people, those who would imagine themselves capable of escaping the miseries engendered by war and terror, have no history. The ends adopted by political action (justice, freedom, emancipation, independence, equality, etc.) justify the means, even if that action must make a few concessions to murder as the price for the efficaciousness of those means. These discourses are undoubtedly known. Readers familiar with philosophical texts will have recognised in them many theories; interlaced with evidences from common sense, one cannot tell if common sense is the source or the unwitting inheritor.

However, one cannot minimise the attractiveness of these theories or the seductive power of their apparent simplicity. These theories, as well as these evidences, are the ordinary regime for the justification of crime. And yet, they are only the abstraction of what they justify and do not say much of the consent that they organise. Their common point, indeed, is to analyse violence by its causes and to be selective with respect to the comprehension of its effects, which they globalise. The benefits that they recognise in violence, as well as the reasons that they find for it, are in fact always general. They are not interested in the nevertheless irreducible singularity of what violence reaches or destroys. This is the decisive point that will serve as our guiding thread! It pertains to the fact that the explication of violence by its causes and its ends always ignores the singular. Better, this ignorance supports violence. Each time someone might have gone astray in order to justify, in the name of a given cause, recourse to any form of violence whatsoever – revolutionary, conservative or other – it is the level of generality of his or her comprehension and perception of these effects that has made it possible. Such is the price paid in order to be able to maintain, without qualm, the establishment of fascist regimes, as well as Stalinist terror, the Chinese Cultural Revolution or the regime of the Khmer Rouge. This is why these theories and evidences raise a whole series of questions. What 'warped wood' do we mean when straightening it translates into the enslavement and humiliation of singular beings, one by one? What is this 'greatness' that demands the abasement of those who supposedly bear it? What of these 'passions', the murderous madness of which would have to be recognised as a motor of history, at the price of so many broken lives? What is this 'progress', which we make the law of becoming, when it implies so many regressions with regard to the acquisitions of 'civilisation'? And this 'individual happiness', which one wants to consider an inconsequential factor, with all the forms of security necessary for it – why would it be contemptible? With respect to the 'ends' valorised to the point of conceding every means to them, is one so sure that they keep the value accorded to them when so much blood stains their achievement?

This series of interrogations must be taken seriously. First, it means the justification of violence is always a dreadful construction around the most common notions. It mobilises a powerful rhetoric; it makes use of 'magic' words that make it effective. When interrogating the subject, it will always be possible to find anthropological, historical or sociological reasons for it, like those that Françoise Héritier gathers in her seminar.[2] One could also give a psychoanalytic explication, like the one proposed by the Freudian theory of primitive drives in *Totem and Taboo* and the death drive in *Civilization and Its Discontents*. One could therefore just as well find a natural ground for human aggressiveness as, inversely, think that there is nothing innate about violence and that it is futile to look for a genetic or biological origin. It nevertheless remains the case that, whatever the pertinence of the schema recognised for accounting for the causes of violence, thinking stumbles over an enigma: it cannot *thoroughly* account for the mechanism that makes *acceptable*, in the eyes of a given set of individuals, the passage to action that destroys the other by denying at once and simultaneously that which constitutes his or her irreplaceable singularity and that which attaches him or her to a common humanity.

It is important, in other words, to recognise the part played by an irreducible lack of understanding. Who would deny it with respect to the terrorist attacks that struck Paris, Brussels and so many cities in Africa and the Middle East in recent years? One can advance all the explications of their extreme violence that one wants. These explications will all have their legitimacy, whether they retrace in detail the historical genealogy of the jihadist movements[3] or the sociological reasons for the radicalisation of a part of the young generation resulting from emigration. No explication will suffice to confront the inexplicable: the murder in cold blood of dozens of targeted and slaughtered individuals, not to mention the decapitations staged by the Islamic State, actions for which the word 'barbarity', which comes spontaneously to the tip of the tongue, indicates above all our inability to name them. Let us admit that men have a predisposition, whether natural or not, to exercise violence. Let us recognise that there exists something like a 'thirst for blood' inscribed in human nature at the beginning or end of a long history. Let us duly grant the hypothesis of a death drive that civilisation would have the task of repressing. One will still have to understand – and the task is infinite – how the levees break and why, how, by what means such discourses contribute to exploding these floodgates, including discourses belonging to the domains of morality and religion that should prevent it. In other words, one will always have a partial, lacunary and unsatisfactory explication and comprehension of violence as long as one has not confronted the complex mechanisms of its provocation, acceptance and justification that are therefore constructed with the help of variable techniques that are ceaselessly renewed: the press, the radio, television, the internet. So let us say it again: whatever the images that henceforth support it, violence is invoked and guaranteed by words that become its motor and remain so all the more insofar as considerable forces – in particular the force of images, their framing and their montage – are mobilised to engage the mechanisms that unchain it.

If the idea and the injunction of 'countering' violence is to make any sense, one must thus task oneself, in more than one language, with these words and the semantics that organises their use. One must mistrust them with an exercised ear that they alert and worry when they surge in discourse and invade public space like an infernal and interminable ritornello offered in all languages on the web, a murderous Tower of Babel. Let us risk a non-exhaustive series that would accompany, as the shadow it casts, the course of violence during the last century. These words are capitalised: Fatherland, Revolution, Civilisation, Race, Identity, Separation (Apartheid), Faith. One will be surprised that they can be placed in a series, and the reaction will be correct. One must measure the irreducibility between discourses. Demanding that one 'give' one's life for the fatherland [*la patrie*], which was required to a nauseating point in so many idioms during the First World War, is not the same thing as preaching violence in the name of the Revolution or in defence of Civilisation or the same thing as advocating a war of extermination in the name of the superiority of this or that 'race' over others or to save or restore vengefully this or that supposedly threatened or besmirched 'identity'. Truth nevertheless demands recognising a common denominator to all these forms of injunction. If one surrenders to the images that haunt collective and individual memory, the question that then arises, reanimated by so many stories,[4] is the following: beyond the violence common to all of them, is it necessary to redirect them without distinction to what I will term, at least provisionally, a call for blood? Does 'countering violence' thus amount to anything other than thwarting the snares of this call and deconstructing each time, with new arms, its syntax and semantics?

Notes

1 For this formulation, see Kant, *Political Writings* (1970: 46). We thank the anonymous reviewer for pointing this passing reference out to us. – Translators

2 See Héritier, *De la violence* (1996). In this priceless volume, Héritier gathers interventions from philosophers, anthropologists, as well as historians of law and religion, united on the occasion of a seminar held at the Collège de France.

3 See Kepel, *Terreur dans l'Hexagone* (2015).

4 See Crépon, *The Vocation of Writing* (2018b).

4

Broken Confidence

Let us stop for a moment on what links the justification of violence and the call for blood. At times, violence undoubtedly knows *whom* it destroys. This is certainly the case for the majority of the manifestations that I evoked at the beginning: everything unchained with infinite refinements of cruelty behind closed doors at home, out of sight, in the silence of stifled cries. Yet, at times the turmoil [*égarement*] is so powerful that the murderous madness – the murderous madness that, for example, strikes women and children day after day – no longer knows what it does and forgets, has long forgotten, what it devastates. Most of the time, however, the justification is unaware, or pretends to be unaware, of the harm it does. Every time it authorises itself with one of those magic words that I recalled above, violence is *indifferent* to [*n'a rien à faire de*] the person whose destruction it encourages or pursues. For it is confronted only with anonymous abstractions that, without exception, conjugate in the plural: Enemies of the people, Jews, Kulaks, Blacks, Tutsis. This is what distinguishes the call for blood: it always presupposes the erasure of names; it is constructed in the eclipse of all singularity. Violence certainly murders, wounds or kills singular beings; the thirst for blood is quenched through singular murders, but it never sees these singularities; it wants to know nothing of them, because it takes aim as such only at the particular. Once again, the beings at whom violence takes aim do not exist for themselves, like a world unto themselves, unsubstitutable, irreplaceable. They are good only for the imagined [*fantasmé*] *particular* that they represent, that they incarnate and symbolise.

The following, then, is the first thing that one must oppose to this denial like a counterword raised against violence: the victims are and are not this particularity that they find themselves forced to incarnate, with which they are identified *through force* and to which they are reduced *by force*; they are *infinitely more* and *infinitely less*. National, 'ethnic', confessional, professional, communitarian, no belonging whatsoever exhausts anyone's identity. Everyone's life is *infinitely* more mysterious and complex, his or her opinions more diverse and his or her beliefs more dispersed [*partagées*] than any abstract category could summarise. Thus, his or her life should, in principle, escape all definitive 'judgement'. Similarly, one should be able to recognise a 'belonging', to give 'content' to his or her identity without, however, confusing or being confused with the description imposed by those who believe themselves authorised to impose it. Yet, violence implies the complete inverse; it blindly judges or condemns only by knowingly abstracting from this *infinity*. In the eyes of their murderers, who, if not an abstraction, were those men and women killed at the *Charlie Hebdo* offices on 7 January 2015, and in Hyper Cacher at Porte de Vincennes two days later? What did the murderers know of their lives, of their peculiar thoughts, of their most intimate convictions? What could they have known of the infinite fabric of relations that made the existence of each of their victims unique and incomparable? Nothing, absolutely nothing. For this was not their problem. Thus, violence turns against life not only because it mutilates or destroys life but, more essentially still, because it denies, in its very principle, what distinguishes the life of everything living, which is its *infinite* singularity. Violence reduces the irreducible. It abstracts that the significance [*signification*] of which no abstraction could exhaust.

This is why, *contra violence*, what I will never recall enough pertains to what violence *is* and what it *does* very concretely. The diverse manifestations of violence are of such different natures that it is difficult to give a definition of it. What is common among a child mistreated and harassed on the school playground, a beaten and humiliated woman, a being who is insulted, outraged and assaulted in the name of the community (of language, of culture, of mores, of religion) with which he or she is identified, and others threatened with death for their opinions, their beliefs, their writings or their intentions? What is the common denominator of all these forms of violence, which allows one to identify them, but also to denounce and combat them as such? Unable to respond from the beginning in an absolutely univocal way, I will advance at least the following. These forms of violence produce the same effect; they result in an interruption in the ordinary course of life, an interruption that even happens to be originary at times, when one is born *with* and *in* violence without ever having had the chance to recall a time when it would have been spared. This interruption is a rupture, and *confidence* is broken first and foremost. On several occasions already, I have defined existence as a fabric of relations. Every instant, it results from a history that is essentially relational and, thereby, constitutive for everyone's identity insofar as it is plural. Each of us is at each instant defined, sometimes even unwittingly, by the set of beings and things with which we have *once* entered into and continue to be (or not) in relation. These relations, in which everything that

17

has happened to us and continues to act upon us is condensed, distinguish us from every other; we invent ourselves in these relations, becoming who we are; these relations make each of us a world by and unto ourselves.

It is therefore important to understand the temporality proper to these relations. Every instant, they hold together the past, present and future. What retains us in the present, through memory as the case may be, projects us into the future. We expect this form of continuity, maintenance and prolongation that renders life liveable. This is why the relation that we have with beings, things, a place, a space, everything to which we are attached, must first be thought as helpful [*secourable*]. It sustains us in time because it gives form to the course of life. If these relations are disturbed, however, if help [*secours*] can no longer be expected from them, if on the contrary everything proves to be a threat, the intimate sphere, the space occupied, the places visited, the beings we cross, our familiar reference points merge with violence, and life becomes unliveable. It is not a coincidence that violence [*la violence*] resonates with rape [*le viol*] and violation [*la violation*]. Both exemplify what makes it intrusive and invasive. Concerning violence, they remind us that traumatised memory extends this invasion and this intrusion beyond brute facts and that, when confidence is broken, it takes an indefinite amount of time for it to return, for the relations to be reconstructed (supposing that they should be) and finally for the injured body, the familiar places and the thread of passing days to be reappropriated! One now understands why Françoise Héritier can define violence, along the same lines, as an 'effraction sometimes of the body conceived as a closed territory, sometimes of the physical or moral territory conceived as a dismemberable [*dépeçable*] body' (1996: 19).

And where things have never been otherwise, as was the case for slaves in the southern States, for African Americans in the 1920s or for Africans in South Africa during the dark years of apartheid, and like the everyday experience for so many men and women on all continents still today, it is because life was (has become or remains) intrinsically violent there, from birth to death, and because no relation was or remains capable of escaping violence. There are two long chapters Part II of this book: one dedicated to the struggle for civil rights led by Martin Luther King, Jr and another to the end of apartheid in South Africa orchestrated by Nelson Mandela and Desmond Tutu. They recount the history of this original rupture in confidence that is at the same time the work of hatred, its education, transmission and culture upon those whom it reduces to its object. How are hatred and violence articulated and how does one oppose them? What resources are at our disposal to confront them? One of this book's *raisons d'être* is to contribute a few responses that will unfold over the course of singular cases studied in Part II with the help of a few great voices whose destiny was to counter violence and hatred (Jaurès, Rolland, Gandhi, King and Mandela). But one can already contribute a few elements to clarify the articulation of violence and hatred in view of the preceding analyses. In whatever way it manifests itself, what constitutes the violence of hatred is the fact that it makes he or she who suffers it doubt him- or herself. For, however one explains it, hatred also retains an irreducibly incomprehensible character for the one at whom it takes aim in its repetition and obstinacy. One can follow the religious, theological, political and social history of anti-Semitism again and again; the hatred that nourishes anti-Semitism will remain no less untenably enigmatic for those whom hatred continues to target and attack in their

19

very existence. Existence goes without saying to such an extent that, indeed, it should never be the object of a *right*. This holds, moreover, for every existent who should never need someone to recognise its 'right to exist', *a fortiori* should never live with worry over whether this right has been accorded or refused. And it is true that, while existence is at least confident in the diversity of its projects and assured of itself independently of life's vicissitudes, wandering and accidents, the question is not posed in these terms. What existence projects into the future does not come from some right to exist, even if its projects would be stopped or thwarted. It is therefore hatred that, in its entirety, creates this right that has no place to be – and this is its very violence. And because, as soon as hatred creates this right, the vicissitudes of history make it such that hatred can both grant and deny it, like a sovereign grace taking pleasure in the power that it claims along with the refinements of cruelty that distinguish it, hatred breaks all self-confidence.

5

Hatred and Violence

Whence the link between hatred and violence! It is vital for everyone to be able *to trust* in what surrounds them, which is a part of themselves. This holds for everything: one's body first, integrity and health, the possibility to breathe and to move freely in a given space that is not perceived from the beginning as a threat, objects in that space, the close or distant beings encountered there, but also the institutions and their administration to which one is exposed. What constitutes the violence authorised by hatred is very simple, then. Whether in the intimate space of the home, on the playground or at the entrance to school, in the workplace, on city streets, on public transport, it attacks this relation of minimal confidence that allows us to live there freely, without excessive mistrust. What we so commonly call a 'feeling of insecurity', which would be wrong to minimise even if it lends itself to all sorts of manipulations, cannot be explained otherwise. Except that, by defining it in the terms just emphasised, appreciating such a feeling demands that one not neglect anyone for whom this confidence has long been interrupted or for whom it has never existed. It demands that we ask about the communities of individuals for whom the bundle of relations binding them to the quasi-totality of what surrounds them, in a given space, seems to exclude this confidence from the beginning. To what extent can the violence done to them by insecurity be perceived as society's hatred toward them? Supposing one wishes to speak of insecurity, one must understand the term in a general and plural sense by doing justice to all the forms that it takes. It is then that we are reminded of entire categories of the population who are its first 'victims': legal or illegal immigrants, refugees, but also all of society's outcasts [*laissés-pour-compte*], the men and women who do not have – or who lose – the means for this minimal assurance. Let us say a few words about the hundreds of thousands of refugees who have in recent months arrived in Europe on condition of having survived the dangers of their journey. One by one, European nations have complicated their entry; barbed wire has reappeared; borders have been closed. One can advance all the arguments one likes to justify it. Some will hold that Europe cannot take in all the misery of the world since it does not have sufficient means to do so – which remains to be demonstrated from a strictly economic point of view. Others, more controversially still, will affirm that this influx of foreigners from Muslim-majority countries threatens the Judeo-Christian identity that they attribute to European civilisation. It nevertheless remains the case that, no matter what one says or does in this sense, with or without good conscience one cannot remain unaware or pretend not to see the violence of this immurement and the hatred it sustains. Beyond the statistics brandished like a scarecrow, has one merely thought of what the feeling of total insecurity about the surrounding world might have been for those who find themselves crossing the Aegean Sea or the Mediterranean on the most unlikely boats and are stopped in their journey, stuck in Greece or driven back towards Turkey? And their absolute mistrust with respect to the future that awaits them? Who will dare say that the situation that each of them lives, in its own singularity, is not intrinsically violent? And who will dare say that one of the major reasons for this situation is not the hostility of a growing part of European populations and therefore the haunting of European governments by a rise in xenophobia's power, when the latter does not constitute a fundamental part of the commerce that led those governments to power, which is the case in Poland, Hungary, Slovakia? Sad Europe!

Let us pause a moment on the justification of this violence and hatred, which barely gets acknowledged insofar as xenophobic protests obscure it in the name of protecting 'European civilisation' from the threat of 'dissolving into Islam'! The first thing that distinguishes this justification is the impasse that it maintains on a few more or less recent pages in the history of Europe, as if these pages have had no influence on the identity attributed to Europe. For those who defend the fantasy [*fantasme*] of this Judeo-Christian identity with a tense nostalgia, everything happens, indeed, as if the distant Crusades, then the conquest of colonial empires, followed by the decolonisation and the displacement of populations that accompany it, have had no influence on that identity, which remains forever homogeneous and fixed. Yet, such a conception constitutes a denial of history. It forgets that, against all nostalgic or backward-facing [*passéiste*] representations of this order, what allows an identity to remain living pertains precisely to the principle of transformation according to which this identity never remains identical to itself. This holds for all identity, moreover, individual as well as collective. What would the uninterrupted succession of relations that put us into contact with an exteriority be if they did not have the power to change us?

One will recall, then, that Europe was constructed over the course of its history according to a twofold bundle of relations:[1] on the one hand, the relations that European nations have maintained with each other (the circulation of ideas, of knowledge, of practices, their exchange, their translations – all the bonds, in sum, that bear the name of Renaissance humanism, the Republic of Letters or Enlightenment thinkers); on the other hand, the relations that these same nations have constructed, unequally and concurrently, with the rest of the world. It therefore almost goes without saying that Islamic civilisation will have played an important part in their complex and conflictive history, the denial of which stems from a mediocre and subpar [contre-performative] ideology. Such a denial, indeed, does the opposite of what it says. It holds that Islam is foreign to Europe but, with this affirmation, inscribes itself in a tradition – of confrontations, of resistances, and also in the same stroke of interpenetrations, importations and translations – that proves the opposite. It would be a mistake to think that this is a distinctive trait of the relation between European nations and Islamic civilisation. It is proper to the majority of territories where several different linguistic, religious, cultural and indeed 'ethnic' communities coexist. In question even today is an essential dimension of the so phantasmagorical [fantasmatique] and potentially devastating relation between culture and politics. Many of the conflicts in the past twenty-five years (in the former federated republics of the Soviet Union, in the Balkans, in Rwanda, in Sudan) include a denial of this order. The misfortune, then, is that this denial is never complete without the simultaneously murderous creation and contestation of the right to existence.

This is why this fold [repli] in identity prepares the way for hatred and violence. It always presupposes that a given population in a determined territory lives with the recurrent threat that its 'right' to be there might be called into question. It denies this population the confident relation to space and time, the confiscation of which, as we have seen, is the first sign of a situation of violence. If one defines violence through the experience of its singular effects on the concrete existence of the men and women who are its victims, one should at every moment be able to ask who we, with our eyes closed and ears plugged, allow to live with the perennial feeling that their right to existence might be contested at any time. This contestation (this is violence itself) is the price of all exclusion and all discrimination. It is also, more or less directly, the price of all speculation on identity.

Note

1   See Crépon, *Altérités* (2006).

6

Terror

Just as violence must be analysed according to its effects, the understanding of terror cannot be reduced to the study of its causes. There again, one might find a thousand and one explications, following word for word the proclamations, declarations and pamphlets that call for and justify terror. To limit myself only to the explications proclaimed by the Islamic State, one will profitably analyse the logic, semantics and rhetoric in the propaganda of the caliphate.[1] Yet, however necessary these approaches might be, in the end one will still have said nothing of what constitutes the essence of terrorism if one has not shown the way it generalises the reversal of confidence into mistrust, which constitutes the essence of violence. What, in effect, is terror? First, the limitless extension *to everyone and everywhere* (or, if targeted, to a determined category of individuals) of the degradation and the compromise, if not the interruption, of the set of relations with the beings and things that comprise the ordinary course of life. Terror counts on the men and women it terrorises finding themselves without recourse [*recours*] and help [*secours*] and, everywhere it extends its grasp, on no one – nowhere – knowing in whom or in what to trust.

Let us recall what we have learned from stories by Varlam Shalamov, Eugenia Ginzburg, Yury Dombrovsky, Aleksandr

Solzhenitsyn and so many others! When a totalitarian system establishes a regime of terror, it makes the total control that it intends to exercise over the whole population depend upon a generalised surveillance by members of the population meant to affect all domains of existence. Because the denunciation can come from anywhere and anyone, on any pretext, and because care for the truth no longer has any currency, every relation of confidence is interrupted equally in family circles and in the neighbourhood or at work.[2] Nothing can resist. Mistrust and fear colour time and space indefinitely. Thus, the strategy proper to the rupture produced by terror is always the same, which three terms summarise: division, isolation and abandonment. In the case of totalitarian systems, the strategy applies primarily to individuals. Each individual finds him- or herself alone with the feeling of having been left behind. But it is also at times entire 'communities' that terror separates, isolates and abandons. This is particularly the case with all the political regimes that systematise racial and social violence as discrimination, segregation or *apartheid*. The first three phases of rupture are then defined in the following way: separation consists in ensnaring everyone in his or her own 'identity'; isolation, in immuring everyone in the 'identitarian fantasy [*fantasme identitaire*]' that results for them and for others; abandonment, in leaving him or her neither chance nor hope of escaping this snare and this immurement. The first translates into the cartography of populations; the second, into the characterisation of populations; the third, into the oppression of and discrimination against populations.

It is undeniable that numerous States over the course of the twentieth century, and even still in the twenty-first have been, transformed into machines for terrorising populations, never short on inventions for tracking and breaking confidence in all the spaces in which it might still subsist – for example, the creative spaces. But terror today is not the exclusive privilege of the States that practise it as a technique of servitude within their borders and (relatively) protected from sight. Its acts are exported with the name of terrorism, whether orchestrated by the Islamic State or the doings of individuals or small isolated groups claiming association with the Islamic State, converted to its ideology and its bloody method. Thus, the new territory of terror, of its extreme violence and of the hatred it spreads has no border. To believe Philippe-Joseph Salazar and his reading of Islamic State propaganda, this unlimited extension is explained by the strategy included in the very idea of the self-proclaimed caliphate, namely, to propagate its influence everywhere in the world according to a triple movement: first, to destroy in its own territory 'everything that symbolizes apostasy or miscreancy (Western stores, churches, ancient statues)' (2017: 34); next, to make use of its territory as a point of departure for terrorising all non-Muslims in order to indicate that the right to possess the caliphate and its power extends to them; finally, to attract those aspiring to a decent life in order to convert them to a supposedly salvational terror, making them missionaries.

The result can easily be guessed: the extension and unlimited propagation, with the help of rhetorical resources and dread- fully powerful technical means, of an intractable call for blood in the name of an allegedly belittled identity that it would be a question not only of correcting but also, moreover, of restor- ing to its universal vocation: that of Islam. For the men and women whom this call fascinates today and carries away in mad murderous drifts, the first objective is, indeed, to immure each of them in an 'identitarian' or 'communitarian' affiliation that enjoins one to think of the other as an enemy. The proper of violence, then, is to be the cause of that which it claims to be the effect. It supposes an irreducible war between 'communities' that would be its *raison d'être* while, holding each person hostage to the hostility that it wants to impose upon everyone, it is violence itself that produces the war. Violence is associated with a 'clash of civilisations' that supposedly made it ineluctable, but this clash, which lends itself to so many confusions and simplifications, exists first and foremost as the object of an obsessional desire. One thus understands the snare set by this new form of terror. It consists in accrediting the terrifying idea that a clash of 'identities' is its historical reason, while the clash is the object of its imaginings [*fantasme*]: the murderous madness of the world of which it dreams. This is why the objective of *its* violence is always the same: to ensure that the state of the world and the state of society correspond to its desire. This is also what makes each attack a 'victory' that must be countered. For, each time, the credit accorded to this delirious correspondence (the world identified with the struggle of which terrorists dream: a frontal clash between civilisations engaged in a fight to the death that would justify the bloodiest loss of control) finds itself reinforced by the globally disseminated story and images of the attack as they play on repeat on the internet and in our heads. Indeed, if we add to the images of attacks the videos of throats being slit, beheadings and other executions staged by the Islamic State, today one must take into account the obscene publicity[3] of violence and measure the dreadful weapon constituted by new technologies of knowledge and information. To speak, as I am doing here, of a 'call for blood' or of the 'thirst for blood' that would make it audible to those who receive it, one cannot minimise the power of incomprehensible fascination that these images and stories have over the men and women who decide to join the ranks of the jihadists. It reinforces the untenable enigma of which I spoke above: the enigma of breaking levees, levees that we no longer know or have not known how to maintain. How are we to understand the fact that the sudden chill of horror that these images provoke is not unanimous? What resources must be mobilised, what discourse reconstructed, what force invoked for this to be the case? How to reach the end of the seduction of hatred and the taste for violence with which terror prospers?

Notes

1 See Salazar, *Words Are Weapons* (2017).
2 See Figes, *The Whisperers* (2017).
3 Not without reason, Salazar speaks of 'Islamic porno-politics'. Cf. chapter 9 of *Words Are Weapons* (2017).

7

Critique of Identity

So, how to counter violence and conquer hate when they are so
visibly articulated to each other? If one provisionally leaves aside
intimate violences, it seems indeed that the common denominator of the majority of the violences that outline the map of the
world – the common denominator that associates in the same
group wars, discriminations, segregations and so many other
forms of intimidation, humiliation, exclusion and separation – is
the question of identity. From wherever it may come, identification is a poison. It is a poison when it is imposed from the outside
and merges with a simplifying and aggressive characterisation. It
is also a poison each time it translates into a system of constraints
imposed from within. For the violence of all proclaimed affiliation, whether adopted or contested, is double. Within the set
that it circumscribes, one can be immured by 'others' as well
as taken hostage by one's 'own' or, more precisely, by the men
and women who arrogate the right to define the obligations
linked to this identification. As is well known, these obligations
at times – even all the time – amount to a consensual hostility,
as if the proclamation of an affiliation demanded the designation
of an enemy. As if the recognition of identity passed through
the following adage: tell me who you hate, and I will tell you

who you are and if you are who you ought to be; I will remind you then, by force if necessary, if you are the one you are commanded to be by belonging to the (cultural, linguistic, religious, national, etc.) community that is yours, that you recognise as yours and that recognises you as its own. This is what is so hard to admit: whatever criteria one retains (or imposes) to define it (culture, language, mores, religion), identity is not a natural fact [*donnée*] or a value in itself; it is a construction that is always conflictive. Because it concretises in a system of constraints that presupposes allegiances, control over identity is the stake of a fierce combat between opposed forces attempting to grasp it.[1]

There is no collective, real or imagined [*fantasmée*] identity without a struggle for power. This is why the forces that arrogate the right to define identity, forces that would each want to be the only to retain this right, always carry a ferment of violence. Whether they lay claim to a glorified past by invoking the weight of history, deplore a present marked with the seal of threatening decline or project it onto an anticipated future as vengeance or revenge, reality never corresponds to the idea of identity that these forces have. The reality is prevented (this is at least what these contradictory forces imagine) by an external cause that they always understand as an ill will, when not the origin of a 'conspiracy'. The real's resistance is nevertheless the result of a complex history, the study of which would result in bringing the identity in question to light as more differentiated than the identitarian construction that the imagined [*fantasmées*] representations give of it. But nothing is more opposed to this step back for the sake of knowledge, to the distance of these conceptual mediations and the patience for reading that they require, than the impatience and precipitation of violence. For its logic and its temporality are entirely other: since identity – the identity of the people, of the cultural or religious community, of the nation, etc. – is not identical to what it should be, it must be changed *without delay*. And if violence is necessary to remove interior and exterior obstacles *as quickly as possible*, it will not only be justified; it will also be the object of a blind faith and a mad hope. Such is the terrifying *credo* that prepares terror, whatever its nature: reactive, restorative and even revolutionary.

How to counter violence? Once reality does not correspond to *its* mad and murderous idea – for example, the idea of a society homogenised by the alleged unity of a 'race' or 'ethnicity' from a common stock, the idea of an original culture preserved from all exchange and all translation or again the idea of a religion fixed in its dogmatic orthodoxy – the violent will to make reality correspond to its idea always presupposes the denial of that same reality in its historical dimension. In the radicalism proper to it, as in its fundamentalism, it refuses to see that the proper of an identity that remains living is its auto-transformation and that therefore, as I emphasised above, it cannot remain identical to itself. Now, no individual or collective identity can or should define itself otherwise than by its becoming: *a* becoming (*a* becoming among *many* possible becomings) that does not have its source in itself but, rather, in what happens to it. *Auto*-transformation is, indeed, always a *hetero*-transformation, transformation of the other or by the other. If one recalls that all 'identity' is relational, this means that the infinity of relations, which weave and unravel over the course of time and make the weft of all individual or collective existence and are its *very life*, have no other meaning than being precisely in the principle of this *hetero*-transformation.

Thus, the denial of reality always comes down to turning life against itself. It implies, by the force of things, an inexhaustible resentment and sometimes even a mad and murderous rage against its movement. This no doubt holds for the life of individuals, but it holds even more so for the life of every community based on culture, language and even religion. This is why identitarian fantasies [*fantasmes identitaires*] are necessarily deadly. Along with reality, they detest the life that frustrates them. One henceforth conceives what matters for countering violence: tirelessly opposing this denial and re-establishing the truth, beginning with the recognition of the vitally heterogeneous character of all identity. It is not true that 'cultures' can be retraced to one and the same origin (which would guarantee their purity and authenticity) and that they each developed separately from the others. They are always plural. They are without doubt plural from the origin on, which is to say, constitutively. Nevertheless, their plurality is ceaselessly modified over the course of their history, enriched by new imports that are always new translations. Those who advocate absolute separation, like the proponents of all forms of apartheid, or those who speculate on the difference between races, when not on their inequality, just like those who think religions have nothing in common, that they have exchanged nothing, shared nothing, that between them only war is possible – they all imagine [*imaginent*], no matter what they say on the matter, a reality that does not exist and fantasise about [*fantasment*] a world that has never existed. What, by contrast, is true and so difficult for them to admit is that there is and has always been *more than one culture* in each culture, just as there is *more than one language* in each language and perhaps even – but can we ever show it sufficiently enough? – *more than one religion* in each religion. And because this reality is intolerable to them, because it is not an accident of history and because there is randomness only in the rhythm of translations, importations and exchanges and in the resistances that constitute the life of cultures in their diversity and their immanent universality, they attempt in vain to bring to reality, in the bloodiest way, an impossible denial.

Note

1   See Crépon, *La Guerre des civilisations* (2010).

8

The Call for Critique

Take these magic words, which are ferments of violence: Fatherland, Revolution, Civilisation, Race, Identity, Separation[1] – words
for which, like murderous idols, we use capital letters! If it were
not for fear of being too schematic, one would willingly hold
that each of these words carries in itself a tension – the tension
in which we live – between two calls, the opposition of which
is irreconcilable and must remain so: the call for blood and the
call for critique. On the one hand, these words are animated by
an explosive force that, almost irrepressibly, galvanises bloodshed;
on the other, each time they irrupt in the public scene, each
time one has them in mind or on the tip of the tongue, the long
history of the bloody use of these words should incite a principled restraint, to say nothing of a distance and suspension that
are, as the time of examination, the first condition of critique.
But nothing is simple, for where one would hope to find clear
and precise distinctions, an assured line of demarcation between
two types of vocation, of very unequal power, the risk of their
confusion, contamination and mutual instrumentalisation is never
definitively discarded. Over the course of the twentieth century
and still today, countless are, on the one hand, the unjustifiable
calls for blood (all those with roots in racism, xenophobia,

anti-Semitism) that clothe themselves in the glorious fineries of a necessary critique of this or that form of imagined [*fantasmée*] oppression and, on the other hand, the calls for the legitimate critique of real dominations that have 'turned bad [*mal tourné*]' or have inverted [*retournés*] into the murderous backing of the most criminal regimes. Language itself – the language of literature and the language of the human sciences, history and philosophy – will have often lent itself to both these calls, hesitating between the two before finally capsizing into one or the other. Numerous are the poets, novelists, essayists, but also the philosophers who will have strayed in the adventure of this inversion, and the intellectual history of the past century cannot be separated from these multiple forms of 'consent' to murder. Brandishing these word-formulas all over the place, like a 'bloody flag'[2] or rallying cry, will therefore have too often constituted refuge for a form of impotence, as if the radicality of blood, which one demands or to which one consents, could *a contrario* offer the illusion of a hypothetical power of thinking over action.

Thus, all singular languages and resulting idiomatic inventions, more or less radical, demand that one know how to detect the snares that they harbour. They hide, as one will have understood, in the murderous power of these capitalised words around which we have been turning for some time: supposing that they have ever been credible (supposing, that is to say, that the belief that takes them for its object has not *always already* been an illusion), these terrible words should be prone to losing (this is the meaning of critique!) a part of their power of seduction and their illusory credit over the course of analysis. But nothing is simple. Indeed, confronted with the seductions and temptation of violence, what *can* critique *do*, when it sometimes means finding oneself alone against everyone, as Romain Rolland knew in September 1914 when denouncing the idolatry of the fatherland that put Europe to fire and sword [à feu et à sang]?[3] If it is true that critique has its ground in refusing violence in principle, several questions arise that will accompany us. The spate of questions should not be surprising; it is at the origin of this book and constitutes its object. It alone governs the detours that we will take while reading – each in turn – Jaurès, Rolland, King, Mandela and a few others. What are the nature and scope of this refusal? Is it a question of an 'ethical' or 'spiritual' principle that is (or is not) heterogeneous to the interested and potentially murderous calculations of politics? And, if such is the case, is it possible only (and to what point) to hold course in order to orient oneself in thought and in action or must one, on the contrary, do justice to exceptional circumstances that would imply compromise with its demand?

This first series of questions calls for another, like a shadow it casts. By refusing to concede to any call for blood, does holding to critique not always come down to guaranteeing the violence against which one refuses to take up arms? Supposing that the ground [fond] of history or the ground of being or nature, as you like, is intrinsically violent and that, consequently, as Merleau-Ponty held in Humanism and Terror, we have the choice not between violence and non-violence but, rather, only between one form of violence and another to which we are fated in the density of the present, is this refusal not always a synonym for complacency to some degree?

Notes

1 On the Fatherland, see Part II, Chapter 1, 'The Fatherland, a Murderous Idol?'; on Revolution, see Part II, Chapter 3, 'Non-violence and

Revolution'; on Identity, see Part II, Chapter 4, 'The "Snares of Identity"';
on Separation, see Part II, Chapter 5, 'Exiting Apartheid'.

2 A reference to a recurring line from *La Marseillaise* by Claude Joseph
Rouget de l'Isle: *l'étendard sanglant est levé!* – Translators

3 See Part II, Chapter 2, 'Of Hatred'.

9

Limits and Contradictions of Politics

Does politics impose such a choice? The essential relation of
politics to violence must be understood, indeed, in three ways.
First of all, all politics imply a right and institutions, the first
function of which should be to protect *all* the men and women
to whom they apply, *without exception*, from violence or to correct
its effects. This should hold in all domains of existence. The
army, the police, justice, education, health, the environment,
not to mention the economy – considered as sectors of activity
that engage the action of governments and opponents' protests
against them – all have in common the fact that they can be
related to determined forms of violence such that at stake, each
time, is the acknowledged or presupposed risk of breaching the
confidence invoked above and the means to avoid it, to attenuate it or to re-establish it. We expect healthcare politics to ensure
equal access to care and not to abandon the men and women
struck with illness to the violence that the illness does to them
when it is no longer possible for them to have with *their* body that
relation of minimal confidence that defines health. We count on
environmental politics, to the extent that it is capable, to end or
at the very least to diminish the violent effects of environmental
degradation; we count on it to prevent this degradation from

escaping all control and continuing indefinitely, abandoning future generations to the destructive consequences of a forecasted disaster. At stake, then, is the confidence we might keep in the air we breathe and the precipitation that irrigates the soil, confidence in the solicitous character of the progression of the seasons and the temperance of the climate, confidence in sustaining biodiversity and, finally, the survival of species. We demand educational politics to correct the inequalities of birth that are an unjust separation by giving everyone, without exception, the means to invent his or her own singularity with the help of knowledge. We ask educational politics to protect everyone from the evils engendered by ignorance, which are the risk of a triple poverty (material, spiritual and symbolic), and from their negative effects. And we know that one must include first among these poverties all the imaginable forms of a breach in self-confidence, the manifestations of a self-underestimation that raise doubt concerning what one is and what one could be to the point of intimate destruction.

What, then, can one say about economic politics, which we would be within our rights to expect to deliver men and women with vital need for work and a salary from the mercy of appetites for domination and profit, from calculations of interests and profitability, from the powers on which they depend to sustain their life? What can one say about the violence of this absolute breach in confidence signalled by the fact of living with the impression that one is worth nothing, that one is exploitable and disposable at will, because they no longer need you or because it is more profitable without you? Finally, we would like to be able to believe (but is it possible?) that the army, the police, judiciary institutions will know how to guarantee that minimum of peace that permits the space we share with others, from the city to the world, to avoid being given up to the violence of rival individuals and collective passions and the forms of hostility that they engender. Perhaps naively, we imagine that, for all the forms of relation that directly or indirectly bind us to others not to be perceived as a permanent source of mistrust and distrust [*méfiance et défiance*] in the spaces of varying natures and dimensions (a neighbourhood, a city, the country where we live, those we visit) and in groups of diverse organisations (neighbours, the 'community', the 'people' that we institute, the 'nation' that we form, the rest of the world), it is necessary that everything that might surge in those relations as an interest of violence be dissuaded by the threat constituted by the police, the sword of justice and the army. Whatever one might think of these institutions and their recurrent reversal into danger, we know indeed that life is unliveable everywhere in the world where populations are abandoned to the brutality and cruelty of criminal mafias, governmental or terrorist armed groups, self-proclaimed militia, etc., when that fragile and always reversible confidence that the institutional dissuasion of violence should in principle and in fact preserve disappears.

This, then, would be the first way to link politics and violence. The preceding developments in each of the domains evoked, and more particularly in the latter domains evoked, show that this *protection* is always at the same time an *exposure*. For politics to be able *to counter* the risks inscribed in the relations that structure existence, it must retain the monopoly of a legitimate exercise of violence, arrogate it, conserve and protect it with means that always threaten to turn the need for security that claims to justify it into a source of endless insecurity.[1] It is no coincidence if, in so many languages, the ambiguous and ambivalent concepts of 'security' and 'health [*salut*]' are found in the denomination of the most repressive organs, the very organs that, sowing terror, will have ruined all confidence. Because politics comes down to giving men and women the power to declare all the wars they wish, but also to multiply at will the possible and imaginable measures of control and surveillance, the forms of repression and the restrictions on freedoms that they judge desirable in the name of protection against violence, politics is at every moment prone to brutally becoming (and this is at times systematic) the first and most inextinguishable source of violence. One will have recognised here the logic of the state of exception or the state of emergency prolonged indefinitely as a new system of government.

Such is the second form of relation that links politics and violence. But this is not all. For, supposing that one wishes to keep the idea according to which the first function of politics should be to protect against the irruption of violence, one must rush to add, as a third relation, that this protection is always *doubly* selective, partial and partisan. This is so first of all because it is nowhere true that the law protects equally, *without* discrimination or segregation, those 'categories' of individuals whose denomination and characterisation amount to dividing the population into a plurality of opposing and rigorously distinct groups, 'classes', 'ethnicities', 'races' or 'descents [*souches*]'. This clearly was not the case in the southern states of the United States in the era of the fight for civil rights, and it is not certain that it is the case today if one judges by the distribution of death sentences between the white and black populations in Texas and elsewhere. This was not the case in South Africa either when, in the time of apartheid, rights were tarnished by a violence that respect for the laws amounted to promoting. And it is certainly not the case today in Europe and elsewhere when the majority of States strive to complicate the rights of foreigners infinitely, multiplying conditions and procedures, if not humiliating and degrading treatments, in those grey zones of bureaucracy where respect for human dignity no longer has currency.

Next, the State's protection against violence is selective to the extent that it is relative to the domains in which the State decides to ensure it. For every State, there are 'violences' and 'violences': more than one regime in truth. There are violences that the State chooses to recognise as such and over which it claims to concentrate its action, and there are violences that it deliberately forgets or of which it pretends to be unaware under the pretext that it can do nothing about these violences or that they are not within its jurisdiction [*ressort*]. At stake each time, then, is the determination of thresholds of tolerance that lead the State to judge, in this or that determined circumstance, this or that form of violence to be unbearable. It is up to the State to decide, for example, the moment at which it becomes the State's responsibility to act against this or that political formation, this or that actor in public life, this or that artist (or alleged artist), because freedom of opinion and freedom of expression – which are the protection that the State guarantees with priority against *its* own violence and the violence that *its* representatives might be tempted to exercise against thoughts that upset it – are inverted into a longstanding exposure to a xenophobic, racist and anti-Semitic violence and its heinous provocation. This is why there will always be some deception to be thematised in the link between politics and violence without interrogating those forms of *laissez-faire* that mean abandonment. Among those that I have just invoked, every domain demands this reminder: health [*santé*], when here or there so many men and woman do not have (or no longer have) access to the care that saves others; the environment, when economic interests trump the degradations that they provoke; education, when populations of children, girls first of all, find themselves deprived for political, ideological or fanatical reasons; economy, finally, when governments seem to reconcile themselves with the growing number of outcasts and rival each other in their inability to let what they call the 'lifeblood' of the nation (as if all the rest were dead) plunge hundreds of thousands of men and women year after year into an insecurity transmitted from generation to generation – 'poverty in inheritance'.[2] All these sectors of responsibility and action presuppose in common the attention, care and help that signal a demand that apparently neither law nor politics suffices to satisfy. They thus call for being 'oriented', 'inspired', 'clarified', 'carried' by a heterogeneous principle that escapes their selective, partisan and relative calculations. 'What principle?', one will ask. A principle of justice? But then what is its source?

Notes

1　See Crépon, *La Culture de la peur* (2008).
2　I borrow this expression from a book by Martin Hirsch and Sylvaine Villeneuve, *La Pauvreté en héritage* (2006).

10

The Voice of Conscience

As I recalled at the beginning, when one thinks of religions and moral catechisms, like those proclaimed in order to place disciplinary shackles on bodies and minds, one must admit that sacred texts, like the institutions they have inspired and those that have adopted the mission of watching over respect for the law, have never been outdone when it comes to imagining, with great refinement in cruelty, the punishments inflicted upon the 'sinners' who have allegedly broken the law. Supposing that one retains the opposition advanced above between the 'call for blood' and the 'call for critique', one must even recognise that, in history, the moral and religious authorities will have most often given in to the 'call for blood' more than they will have done justice to the 'call for critique'. Better, animating crowds with a bloody passion against those they anathematised, these authorities will have used the 'call for blood' to defend themselves against the 'call for critique' when critique – whether of a philological, historical, philosophical, even theological or scientific order – had the vague will [*vélléités*] to make its opposition and difference heard. But the analysis must be pushed further. For the most surprising factor is not so much the cruelty of morality and religion in themselves as the haste, taste or passion with which isolated individuals, constituted groups or entire masses of the population find in the name of morality and religion a reason for satisfying their desire to give 'the gift of death', to the point that one ends up no longer knowing if one must understand their dogma and catechisms as the 'ground', 'pretext' or 'alibi' for the call for blood to which they give free rein. Everything blurs, indeed, in both the murderous fanaticism of individual acts and in those moments of collective fury when an unchained crowd cries for vengeance because it considers morality and religion undermined or insulted. Everything merges, and everything gets lost, beginning with the historical knowledge of religions themselves and of the texts on which they are founded. Words lose their sense or are reduced to their explosive charge. Nothing but this 'taste for blood and death' remains as a hard kernel.

Nothing less is necessary to complicate considerably the function that we generally agree to recognise in the moral and religious doctrines at the heart of civilisation. Does not the worst happen to us through them or in their name, from the torture and the stake of yesterday's Inquisition to the immolations and decapitations of today, with war always in the backdrop? How will one escape the chaotic impression that nothing distinguishes these doctrines more than their deadly vocation since they *spontaneously* offer the death drive its most powerful sublimation? Moreover, must one recall that, despite the commandment 'Thou shall not kill', most of these doctrines, far from condemning the death penalty, have on the contrary codified, sustained and accompanied it without protest and often demanded it with the most repressive powers? While one would have expected religions to contribute to the progress of humanity, however one conceives progress (for example, as a quest for 'tolerance', 'fraternity' or 'justice'), they have ceaselessly given place to

47

regressions that could not be more opposed to every idea of a progression in this sense, to the point of having recalled, while one thought it stowed in the warehouse of outdated accessories, a concept as problematic and overcharged as that of 'barbarity'. From the moment religions seem to tolerate an irrepressible 'taste for death and blood' with such a *force* that no knowledge, no critique, no reason seems capable of opposing it, is there any way to take them for anything other than a poison that envenoms the totality of human, social, *inter*-communitary and *inter*-national (to say nothing of familial) relations, which it gangrenes so often with a system of suffocating constraints in all confessions alike? The prefix *inter-* suggests partaking [*partage*] and not partition [*partition*]. It is this partaking that one would be within one's rights to expect from religions because they all equally profess it. One has to admit that they impose partition in all its forms, including the bloodiest.

I started from the necessity of thinking the *principle foreign* to all political calculations of violence that might come *to counter* its call. Do the preceding reflections mean that 'religion' and 'morality', which so often, commonly and concurrently, seem *to poison* relations on all levels of existence, have nothing to do with such a principle? And if this is the case (but is it really?), is it a sufficient reason for renouncing this thought? It is not difficult to measure what such a resignation would imply. First, it would suspend all condemnation of violence. Crushing everyone under the double weight of history and politics, such a resignation would amount to holding that everything is possible, that everything can be justified and that perhaps in the final analysis – the ultimate triumph of nihilism – everything is a question of rhetoric. To justify murder, it would be enough to know how to make these explosive words speak, to link sentences that reanimate their force and give them new life, in every language, with the grandiloquence suited to the enthusiasm of crowds. And we would have no recourse, we would find help nowhere, no resource for countering the disorienting logic that imposes as evident murder in this or that determined circumstance (of health, preservation, progress, the future, etc.)! Supposing that this would be the case, what reasons would we have for preferring one political regime over another and, for example, for opposing an oppressive system? If violence does not enter into the question (for we have no means to denounce it in principle, no system of values to which we might refer in order to refuse it), it is difficult to see which motifs one might invoke in order to declare a regime unjust and to condemn the suffering that it imposes upon this or that party – when not upon the totality of the population – that it subjects to its law. Only the reign of strength would exist, and the violence that conserves the right would be 'just', necessarily, as long as it remained the strongest.

Even supposing that we must admit that one does not escape violence in the historical density of the present and that it is necessary, consequently, to choose between forms of domination that sustain it, would there still be a criterion that we could retain in order to decide whether all moral consideration had to be suspended? What is it that makes us *today* despise slavery, apartheid, arbitrary imprisonments and deportations with their parades of humiliations? What is it that pushes us *more than yesterday* to consider such things to be violations and unbearable attacks on human dignity? What is it that seizes us with horror (or at least should) when we hear of capital executions? How does the threshold of our tolerance recede? All these transformations do not operate by political calculations. Nor is it sure that the ideas of 'freedom' and 'justice' necessarily contribute to them. Such an explication is insufficient, for the invocation of either idea lends itself to interpretations and manipulations that will never have had any difficulties adapting to violence.

11

Necessity and Conditions of Ethics

We thus touch upon one of the most mysterious points of existence: the radical necessity of ethics, which is first of all, beyond all the denounced forms of morality and its catechisms, its *irreducibility*. As we have just seen, we have every reason to mistrust these forms, their inflation and their compromises with the law of blood. And, at the same time, it is impossible to forgo ethical principles in a *critical economy* of violence, whether the latter translates the absolute and intransigent refusal of violence in principle or offers itself as a choice between this or that particular violence. How to choose if not between the brutality of a domination, like that of the capitalist, imperialist or colonialist system, and the brutality that opposes to it the revolt of the oppressed or the rebellion of the enslaved? If one wants one's action and thought to agree with an absolute principle of non-violence, ethics is necessary to understand what *inspires* and *grounds* its radical and absolute opposition to all the seductions of violence. We need ethics in order to understand the origin of the force that enjoins us not to tolerate any concession, any transaction, and to make no exception. If on the contrary one thinks, like Merleau-Ponty and so many others after him, that the condemnation of all violence in principle is untenable and that one cannot escape indifference (which is never neutral) without making a choice between diverse forms of violence, then we must recognise that the commitment that results cannot ultimately be justified, no matter what the author of *Humanism and Terror* says, without at one point or another taking into account the moral criteria that determine the distinction made between *what is good* and *what is bad*, indeed, *the worst*. And without saying, in the same stroke, what this distinction authorises and what it forbids.

Otherwise, how to condemn all forms of terror, whatever the justifications to which it lays hold? How to explain to those who imagine that their political and religious project gives them every right, beginning with the right over the life and death of those they condemn or pardon, that their cruelty cannot be justified on the basis of any cause? If not by placing oneself on the fragile and uncertain terrain of ethics, by tirelessly recalling what it *means* [signifie], in the strongest sense of the term, to let oneself get carried away by hatred, to give in to the violence that nourishes it, to delete *a* life – to believe oneself authorised to do so! One will perhaps find some naïveté in taking such a position. It is true that the powers of ethics are weak, and one conceives that its admitted impotence is perplexing. Against ethics there are warrior moralities that support those who believe it just and necessary to shed blood, in Paris as in Brussels, in Ankara as in Bamako, in Iraq, Syria, Libya and so many other places. But ethics here is indissociable from a critical exercise that requires three steps. The first step, to which the preceding pages were dedicated, consists in a phenomenology of violence that does not analyse its causes, reasons or motives but rather its most concrete effects. The second step is to deduce from this phenomenology the principle of an absolute refusal of the justifications with which violence is authorised since these justifications always amount to denying, relativising or minimising the effects, when not adapting to them. To all these transactions, by which one can be so easily taken in, I have given the name murderous consent.[1] The choice of non-violence is one way of responding to it. The third step consists in the critical thought and action that such a principle makes possible. Their protest attacks constructions of violence.

The whole question henceforth concerns knowing what non-violence is capable of opposing to violence. Where does it draw its critical resources? It is then that we are reminded, exemplarily, of some great voices that found in its resources the force for a major commitment: the voices of Jean Jaurès attempting to oppose the First World War, of Romain Rolland denouncing its lies and its atrocities, of Mahatma Gandhi de-stabilising British domination by the mere force of non-violence, of Martin Luther King, Jr fighting for civil rights with the same 'weapons', of Nelson Mandela, finally, working toward a recon-ciliation without violence at the end of apartheid. Part II of this book will be dedicated to them, for at least three reasons. The first reason comes from an intimate conviction. When one is confronted with violence, as we are today, disoriented in the present and worried about the future, it is never useless to take the step back offered not by reading in general but, rather, by listening to the voices that knew this double ordeal [épreuve] of hatred and violence in extreme conditions. These voices still have much to teach us today about taking a stand, for they know better than anyone how to speak of the murderous consent into which they who cave too quickly to the tantrums of hatred or violence plummet. The second reason is that these voices are the voices of thinkers who placed their words in the service of an action concerned with leveeing violence. In this respect, their discourses exemplify, in another way, what I analysed in the name of 'counterword' in *The Vocation of Writing*. Excepting Romain Rolland, it is no longer literature (fiction, poetry or drama) that constitutes the resource of their opposition but, rather, other addresses articulated directly with a counter-practice: the counter-practice of non-violence, along with the protests that constitute its force. They invite us to think this counter-practice of non-violence. The third reason pertains to the fact that, in very different historical and political contexts, they all had to gather their strength in order to overcome the trial of hatred [*l'épreuve de la haine*] in the spiritual heritage that was the most familiar to them. It then appears that our moral and religious inheritance, plural and diverse, is more complex than it seems when violence is in question. On the one hand, our inheritance will have acted (and too often continues to act) as a *poison*; on the other hand, over the course of the century, it has been ceaselessly recalled, reinvested and reformulated in order to contribute a *remedy* for violence, not a consolation but rather resources that permit one to refuse violence as well as escape or exit from it. Such is the lesson full of interrogatives and ellipses that bring us the voices of Jaurès, Rolland, Gandhi, King and Mandela. A *remedy* and a *poison*: this is what gives transmission a pharmacological dimension! It constitutes the heart of this book.

Note

1 See Crépon, *Murderous Consent* (2019). – Translators

Part II. Vanquishing Hatred:
Jaurès, Rolland, Gandhi, King, Mandela

1

The Fatherland, a Murderous Idol?

We saw in Part I that it is important to concentrate critically on those words that, especially since their power to fascinate is real, constitute catalysts of violence and hatred. The first word that imposes itself is difficult to translate from one language to another, despite appearances, because its connotations, over-burdened with history, are different every time: fatherland, *Heimat*, *Vaterland*, *patrie*, *rodina*, etc. These translations neverthe-less have common ground: the sacrifice that, at least for the last two centuries, has been ceaselessly demanded as a sacred duty everywhere for its wellbeing [*salut*] and safekeeping [*sauvegarde*]. Rather than writing the history of sacrifice here, I will pause on a particular moment of its exaltation, to say nothing of its unrest: the First World War. In the years preceding it, the political and philosophical controversy over the invocation of sacrifice brings to light the growing unrest incited by the rise of international tensions. The controversy divides minds, tracing in France a dividing line between those who desire, if not demand, war to avenge the affront of defeat and to recapture Alsace and Lorraine from the Germans, and those who decry in the resultant patriot-ism a bellicose chauvinism that, associating the bourgeoisie with the army that they accuse of being exclusively in its service and under its orders, expresses nothing less than the interests of a dominant class. By 1 August 1914, the cards are on the table, and those who once saw in the idea of the fatherland one of the pedestals of bourgeois ideology do not take long to succumb to the contagion that makes the wellbeing of the fatherland the ultimate reason for the moral and political demands gathered to impose upon citizens the sacrifice of their lives as a sacred duty. This is why the first voices raised in denunciation of the war, beginning with that of Romain Rolland, have no concern more urgent than demythologising the notion of the fatherland and restoring to the proliferated experience of death its proper truth against the rhetoric that dissimulates it behind the glorious mask of a death to which everyone has universally consented. This is what makes the fatherland a controversial notion! It appears vital and sacred for some, liberticidal and deadly for others.

A whole series of questions follows. What sense did the notion of the fatherland need when, on the eve of war, certain people – like Jean Jaurès – hoped until the last moment that it would be possible to prevent it? What was throughout that century – and still is today – the role of its ideological 'uses'? What calculations hide behind its invocation? Can one reduce the 'fatherland' to the particular interests of those who speak in its name? I will pose these questions over the course of a reading that crosses three major figures in this controversy between 1914 and 1918 – Jaurès, Rolland and Alain – while taking care to show the extent to which the very terms in which they pose these questions have lost nothing of their interpellating power.

I. The Double Sense of Fatherland

On the occasion of a bill he proposed concerning the organisation of the army, published as an annex to the minutes of the 14 November 1910 hearing and, shortly thereafter, in the form of a work titled *L'Armée nouvelle* [*The New Army*],[1] Jaurès expounds his conception of the fatherland and his defence of a moderated and nevertheless necessary patriotism that owes nothing to the bellicose tantrums then shaking up a part of the political class. The facts of the question are thus as follows. On the one hand, the nationalist right has nothing but this word on its lips, which it declines in every mode; on the other, a party of socialists, headed by Gustave Hervé, professes systematic antimilitarism and anti-patriotism on the pretext that the proletariat cares nothing for the 'fatherland' in the hands of the proprietor class that exploits them with the support of an army, which suppresses the workers' movement as one of its privileged functions. All of Jaurès's work aims to escape this alternative by showing that there can be no social justice and reform of progressive society without assuring peace and security and that, consequently, the proletariat should not remain strangers to the concern for 'national defence'. Peace, in other words, is too necessary to justice for 'defence', 'fatherland' and, along with them, questions of international politics to be abandoned to the hands of a class or caste army and its chauvinist illusions. Thus, proletariat engagement in international and military questions is necessary to assure that war, if it must take place, is declared only upon fulfilling certain conditions. The first would stipulate that war cannot be the object of a hawkish political calculation; the second, that one be sure first to exhaust all chances of preserving peace, such that the 'fatherland', which would be resolved to war despite itself, would be covered, he writes, with a 'verdict of approval from the universal conscience' (Jaurès 1915: 3).

This is why the socialist leader calls for a new patriotism that one could call 'negative', even though he himself does not use this expression, to account for how he twists the idea of fatherland. First of all, one must note that, if the idea remains necessary, it is because it spares the nation not only the 'convulsions of war' but also, at least as much, the 'humiliation of servitude' (1915: 2). This is Jaurès's leading idea, which opposes him to the anti-patriots and antimilitarists of his time. Beyond the First World War, in all countries alike, this idea signals toward the partisan resistance to the occupation during the war from 1939 to 1945, and it recalls in advance the sense that will be given to 'patriotism' by the men and women who will not accept seeing their country invaded by foreign troops and enslaved to enemy law. It would be a mistake, in other words, to see in the attachment to one's own 'fatherland' only an artificial construction, an illusion, the effect of dreadful propaganda in the service of a chauvinist aggressiveness that ridicules peace, or to see in it only the Gordian knot of a fabric of lies orchestrated by warmongers. It is undoubtedly true that the concept has served as a pretext for cementing the 'solidarity of all powers of authority' and that, in the era of the Dreyfus affair, the thought of which never leaves Jaurès as he interrogates the place of the army in society, 'defence' of and 'love' for the fatherland, erected into an absolute principle to the detriment of justice and truth, were the inexhaustible source of a 'flood of lies, insults, and fanaticism' (1915: 352–3). Yet, the concept of 'fatherland' cannot be thrown into the dustbin of history, no more than one should bury it with the ashes of militarism. If, far from an exhausted idea, it is instead a question of an 'idea that transforms and grows', as Juarès writes, it is because, indeed, the proletariat – whose emancipation is in motion – are less ready than ever 'to suffer passively' the yoke of an external domination that they intuitively know very well can only mean for them an 'aggravation in servitude' (1915: 361–2).

> The truth is that everywhere there are fatherlands, that is to say, historical groups conscious of their continuity and their unity, every attack on the freedom and integrity of these fatherlands is an attack against civilisation, a relapse into barbarity. To say the proletariat, being serfs of capitalism, cannot suffer from invasion, from conquest, from an aggravation of servitude is childish. (Juarès 1915: 363)

This is the reason why, he continues, one must not take too seriously the sentence from *The Communist Manifesto* that states '[t]he working men have no fatherland [*Vaterland*]' (Marx and Engels 2010: 502, translation modified). If Marx could formulate such a statement, it is, indeed, without having understood that the fatherland does not necessarily reduce to the distribution of landed property. If such were the case, one could have agreed that the invocation of the fatherland and the concern for 'defending' it amount to maintaining this unequal distribution and the *de facto* domination into which this maintenance translates. The proletariat who subscribed to this 'idol' would have been nothing other than dupes of the oppressive regime that this domination legitimates. This is the theory Gustave Hervé defends during the same epoch, and a large part of *L'Armée nouvelle* is directed against his ideas. But the fatherland, for Jaurès, does not have as its ground 'exclusive economic categories'. 'It pertains by its roots', he writes, 'to the very ground of human life' (1915: 448). What is in question? Nothing less than what one would call today, in more contemporary terms, 'a psychic and collective individuation'. The belonging grounded by the 'fatherland' is undoubtedly transitory; in no case could it constitute the last word on the rules of solidarity invoked to bind men and women together. But internationalism could not exist either without recognising this form of intermediary collective individuation designated by the notion of 'fatherland'; or, rather, it could ignore the notion of the fatherland only at the risk of abandoning its use and invocation to the regressive, vengeful and reactive perception that the most virulent nationalism and patriotism make of its necessity. Thus – and this is not to deny but, rather, to admit its existence – one must recognise that class struggle is far from the only form of collective consciousness, far from the only form of community and sharing that regulates the lives of individuals, unless one satisfies oneself with the denial of reality and history. In the end, this is what gives sense to the notion of fatherland: it concretises in that passive synthesis that permits everyone to be an individual with and at the same time as others by attaching it to a language, to places, to common habits. Whatever ideology says about it, one cannot act as if this synthesis and the attachment that it produces did not exist, and one cannot minimise its force. This seems trifling, but it is 1910, barely four years before the spread of the idea, nearly everywhere in Europe, that it is just 'to die for the fatherland' – and to those who do not want to hear it, to those who still imagine that abstract principles will suffice to overcome patriotic contagion, Jaurès explains that, in the final analysis, nothing other than the dreadful and in part uncontrollable power of attachment makes war possible.

> The individual soul barely suspects everything that enters into it from social life through one's ears and eyes, through collective habits, through the community of language, work and festivals,

through turns of thought and passion common to all the individuals of the same group that the multiple influences of nature and history, climate, war, religion and art have long shaped. [. . .] It is the mystery, the prodigy, of individual souls to be at once impenetrable and open. The whole historical group of which they are a part, with which they are interdependent, ceaselessly affects them and move them, often without their knowing. Only in the great crises, when a great event stirs up the whole depth and the whole breadth of a human group, is this solidarity fully revealed to itself. (Jaurès 1915: 449–50)

It is an understatement to say that in the years preceding the conflict – and until 31 July 1914 – Jaurès would ceaselessly try to prevent the anticipated war from being this 'great event' that reanimates 'solidarity' on the grounds of the fatherland. For one must not be mistaken. If the author of *L'Armée nouvelle* does not speak the same language as Freud, who from 1915 onward will analyse with unparalleled lucidity the power of sublimation and idealisation linked to belonging, Jaurès leaves no doubt concerning the terrifying character of the forces at stake in attachment to the fatherland. They are, he says, 'forces halfway instinctive and, for that very reason, simultaneously immense and dreadful', and he does not hesitate to add, as a premonitory sign of all the bloody outbursts of the twentieth century, that 'they take hold of the human being through an insensible and everyday action', merging with 'organic habits themselves, with ways of speaking, looking, walking, smiling, thinking' (1915: 451). One could not be more precise or describe with more finesse the threatening and explosive aspect of every form of belonging, however necessary it is, moreover, in what constitutes its grandeur. What Jaurès explains with implacable lucidity is, at bottom, very simple. Before even speaking of internationalism or cosmopolitanism, before even idealising the international community, peace, belonging to a common world (the fatherland of the world or the world as the fatherland of workers), one must know whence one begins and recognise as a first and unavoidable fact (which is not merely a political construction or the effect of just any ideology) what he calls 'forces that are grandiose and good, but also full of perils and troubles' (1915: 451). The forces of attachment to the 'fatherland' are full of unacknowledged threats because, if there is nothing arbitrary about the origin of these forces in the passive synthesis of our collective individuation, it nevertheless remains the case that, as every war shows, they are infinitely manipulatable and prone to being instrumentalised for the benefit of particular interests. It is then that 'forces [. . .] of solidarity' (1915: 451) invert into reactive and murderous powers. As soon as 'solidarity' is instrumentalised under the guise of the 'fatherland', it becomes exclusive. As Jaurés does not hesitate to say, it is similar to 'a great collective egoism' – the very egoism that constitutes one of the most powerful motors of wars and that can be summed up, among so many 'blind rages' and 'brutal maxims', with the following lapidary formulation, which is a common ground for all consents and all complacencies with respect to crime: 'right or wrong, it is my country' (1915: 452).

One conceives in the same stroke the socialist leader's untenable wager and promise, of which the war will signify the most dramatic failure: they pertain entirely to the necessity of exceeding everyone's attachment to their own fatherland in the recognition of a common 'human fatherland', which he also designates with the name 'universal fatherland of liberated labour' (Jaurés 1915: 453). Love for the fatherland makes no sense unless it permits one to transcend every form of individual and collective egoism by extending beyond its borders. This idealisation of a belonging sublimated into a universal fraternity that exceeds this belonging and deports it outside itself is an absolute necessity. And it is important to recall it as the condition of all sustainable peace. But at the same time, having attained the international dimension of their emancipation, the proletariat – and this is a crucial point, which constitutes all the singularity and lucidity of the author of *L'Armée nouvelle* – cannot project this 'high ideal [. . .] into the void' or realise it anywhere other than in an 'autonomous nation' (1915: 453). Because socialism cannot be severed from the lives of those whose right to equal emancipation it intends to defend, it must not (this is a condition for peace) turn its back on this form of collective individuation, on this passive synthesis of terrible forces that the fatherland signifies. This is Jaurès's credo: it is not a matter of 'sanctifying' the fatherland like, shortly after, the hard-line war thurifers and, with them, those who demand that one 'sacrifice' oneself for it; it is a matter, rather, of recognising the fatherland as a vital necessity with which one must live and transform from within in order to allow it to contribute to the only idea that truly holds up: a transnational and, consequently, intrinsically and essentially *pacifist* 'solidarity'.

There is therefore 'fatherland' and 'fatherland' – and one must be clear about the watchword [*mot d'ordre*] that cries 'down with fatherlands'. When a revolutionary syndicalist takes up the word again, he or she does not call for the disappearance of fatherlands, no more than he or she aspires to their dissolution into a 'universal slavery'. He or she proclaims something entirely different, which Jaurès summarises in the following terms: 'Down with the egoism and antagonism of fatherlands! Down with chauvinist prejudice and blind hatred! Down with fratricidal wars! Down with oppressive and destructive fatherlands!' (1915: 454–5).

As one will have understood, the fatherland is therefore not Jaurès's final word. But it is an indispensable lever to which those who recognise a common belonging testify by revealing the sense of their unity and the continuity they incarnate: namely, the sense of a self-overcoming [*autodépassement*], understood as the achievement of justice. This is what transforms the notion of fatherland according to a higher idea. Once it supposes greater equality and greater justice, this supreme realisation of collective individuation imposes a movement according to which the fatherland is no longer recognised in the force that it manifests but, rather, in the justice that it bears.[2] Thus, with its pacifist vocation, internationalism presupposes a transformation from within, the very modification of the sense of belonging, what Jaurès calls the 'call for the new fatherland' (1915: 458). If there truly is something instinctive in attachment – Freud would say compulsory – that predisposes it to all sorts of manipulations, including the most exclusive and the most murderous, the power of this transformation lies in giving it a spiritual dimension that valorises the justice that unites over the force that divides, friendship and fraternity over unbridled competition and rivalry, the federation of powers over the war that opposes them. One henceforth understands that patriotism is conditional. It implies a double duty that Jaurès describes as indivisible, a double duty the indivisibility of which alone permits one 'to save' the notion of the fatherland from the aggressive excesses that demand violence as a tribute to its wellbeing: on the one hand 'to keep the peace [. . .] by any means'; on the other hand 'to safeguard the independence of all nations' by any means (1915: 458), which means, in the final analysis, to oppose war. There is 'fatherland' and 'fatherland' because, in the spirit of Jaurès (and this is what constitutes the whole singularity of his analysis), one will not make the proletariat accept just any conflict, just any war, in the name of the fatherland's wellbeing and because it will always be necessary to mistrust the men and women who speak in the name of the fatherland (or its current avatars, like 'national identity') in order to appropriate it. They never count the deaths necessary to serve their interests as they glorify their sacrifice. Because it has lost nothing of its actuality, moreover, the expression that Jaurès invents to describe them will remain. They are, he says, 'fatherland peddlers [*maquignons de la patrie*]' (1915: 460).

Thus, his tone becomes more threatening at the end of the chapter he devotes to the necessary, if not vital, link that associates patriotism and internationalism. Governments should be warned of what awaits them if they venture into a useless war, he writes four years before Europe, ignoring his prognosis, wreaks bloody havoc:

> The people have only one means of defence; the proletariat have only one resource: to indicate that 'it will not march' in these ventures or, rather, that it will march against all the criminal machinators, that it will break – if it can – the forces of war, that it will rise to uproot the fatherland from the fatherland peddlers! (1915: 460)

And he adds a little further on:

> if hawkish governments on the prowl are obstinate [. . .], then, yes, it will be the right and the duty of the worker class, it will be its right and its duty, through a simultaneous and concerted effort on the part of its militants in the countries exposed to the horrible catastrophe, to rise, to call desperately for revolutionary force, to break these delirious, plundering and murderous governments and to throw the language of peace and the

language of justice to the storm for the safeguard and honour of fatherlands, for the safeguard and honour of humanity. (1915: 461)

Reading these lines, one understands why, between 1910 and 1914, Jaurès could appear to be a 'dangerous man' in the eyes of all who nourished the rise in international tensions with their rancour and thirst for revenge, or all those who impatiently subscribed to the war that this rise announced. One also understands how he could be the object of unequalled hatred and defamation, concretised in multiple calls for murder, beginning with those from Charles Péguy himself, from whom I borrow this warning from 1913: 'The moment war is declared, the first thing we will do is execute Jaurès by firing squad. We will not leave this traitor behind us so that he can stab us in the back' (cited in Becker 1988: 11). For Jaurès never believed that the war was defensive and consequently legitimate and necessary. One after the other, he denounced every diplomatic step that contributed to making war inevitable and the increasing bellicosity that accompanied them. All the manoeuvres that prepared the way were, indeed, far more related to what L'Armée nouvelle ceaselessly refused as an acceptable motive: commercial and colonial rivalries, politics of secret alliances like the one instigated by Raymond Poincaré that reinforced the ties between France and Russia. And, if the war should unfortunately happen, from 1910 on Jaurès knew that it would not be brief; he knew the destructive violence that would result and the lives it would break would make it 'the worst holocaust since the Thirty Years' War' (cited in Duclert 2013: 71). As one rereads the numerous articles he publishes between the assassination of Archduke Franz Ferdinand of Austria in Sarajevo and the declaration of war, they appear as a series about a forthcoming catastrophe that is desperate, with the passing months, to save the peace in time. Thus, he writes on 5 July 1914 in *La Dépêche de Toulouse* [*The Toulouse Dispatch*]:

> Who can picture without horror what a universal war would be when we already see the sinister effects of partial wars? Under the excitations of pride, in the drunkenness of hatreds, murders and retaliations, in the despondency and enervation of all orders of charges that weigh upon it, European civilisation suffers I know not what fermentation of violence. [. . .] Everywhere brutal thoughts are fermenting. Everywhere barbaric instincts are developing. (Jaurès 2009: 880)

II. Dying for the Fatherland

If one thing becomes apparent upon reading Jaurès's texts, it is the ambiguity of 'patriotism', that is to say, the deceitful, calculated and interested character of invocations of the fatherland once it constitutes the privileged weapon of hawkish politicians for justifying their bellicosity and precipitating populations into the abyss. And it is true that war accommodates the truth with difficulty. One might even say that its first victory, the victory that in the summer of 1914, for instance, followed Jaurès's assassination by a few hours, is always that of an instituted and skilfully orchestrated lie over a debated truth. Jaurès's death had no other meaning. Its goal was to suspend the debate in order to let all the rhetorical artifices necessary for war deploy, the smokescreen of words and mechanical formulas that, repeated at will, were to forbid all discussion. Yet, among these words and these formulas, none would be more evident than those that made sacrifice for the 'wellbeing' of the fatherland a sacred duty.

69

'Dying for the fatherland'! Once Romain Rolland makes the decision to oppose the war in September 1914, denouncing it as 'the ruin of European civilisation', that is to say, the triumph of that nameless barbarity that Jaurès already foresaw, he knows that no objection to his 'call for peace' is more dreadful than the consensual dogma and the would-be universal injunction of a 'yes, but . . . !' and a 'you must . . . !': '*Yes*, it is just to desire peace, *but* the fatherland is in danger and therefore *you must* (we must collectively) sacrifice yourself (ourselves) for its wellbeing. We have nothing more sacred, indeed, than this demand'. This sacrifice, the legitimacy of which no one should be authorised to contest, is the arc that brings voices into unison – the voices guiding morality, masters of opinion, religious or laic leaders, artists and scholars – in order to create the union that henceforth *must* be taken for 'sacred'. These are the voices that Rolland attacks; first a playwright, writing a dozen plays published by Péguy that, little known today, relate the great episodes of the French Revolution, Rolland suddenly became famous in the years preceding the war upon publishing ten volumes of a humanist and generous *roman-fleuve* between France and German: *Jean-Christophe*. And he reproaches these voices precisely for having found nothing better to offer a whole generation than the idealisation of a sacrifice that hides its name, that does not say what it is. This is the point on which his critique of the war concentrates! It implies that we must free ourselves from these 'screen-words' – fatherland, sacrifice, sacred duty, etc. – that dress up violence in order to render it consensual and acceptable by masking its reality. His critique presupposes that we invent and defend another word that, toward and against all the authorities opposing it, bares *its* intolerable truth: the death of millions of singular beings. The hypocrisy of invoking 'sacrifice', its ritornello and litany is that they are never, in the final analysis, anything other than a means of disguising the monstrous, absurd, scandalous and, in more than one way, criminal erasure of an entire generation promised to another future, a means of justifying this erasure and, finally, a means of imposing upon mourning the only framework that suits this heroisation of death: the 'pride' of having had a son who 'fell on the field of honour'.

> Let us be bold and proclaim the truth to the elders of these young men, to their moral guides, to their religious and secular leaders, to the Churches, the great thinkers, the leaders of socialism; these living riches, these treasures of heroism you held in your hands; for what are you squandering them? What ideal have you held up to the devotion of these youths so eager to sacrifice themselves? Their mutual slaughter! A European war! A sacrilegious conflict which shows a maddened Europe ascending its funeral pyre, and, like Hercules, destroying itself with its own hands! (Rolland 1916: 40–1)

Rolland therefore does not refuse *sacrifice* in itself; he does not condemn the idea in itself. One can sacrifice oneself for another; one can give one's life to science, to one's art, etc. And nothing forbids finding that admirable. At the risk of being taken for a traitor, like Jaurès in 1913, the author of *Jean-Christophe* refuses something entirely different, namely, the declared object of sacrifice and the reasons advanced for it: the very reasons that contribute to making the necessity of sacrifice an object of belief. One *must* believe in sacrifice in times of war, in other words, and everything is done, and all means are implemented, including the most liberticidal, for this to be so. Sacrifice must be an object of faith. But it becomes one only on the condition that *that for which* one sacrifices oneself justifies the absolute necessity of it. The cause itself must therefore be *sacred*. One does not sacrifice

oneself *for nothing*, unless one shows that – this is everything at
stake in the debates before and, more so still, during the war
that turn upon the notion of the fatherland – that for which this
sacrifice is demanded is in fact *nothing*: a phantom, an illusion,
a figment of the imagination or, worse still, the object of a
manipulation. And unless one shows that, to this end, nothing
requires it. Unless one maintains and proves, then, that the
reason for the call to sacrifice is *factitious* and *fabricated* and, for
example, that it is illusory and deceptive to define the fatherland
as a great family (with everything this definition presupposes
and imposes concerning inheritances, debts and duties), because
it is a class invention that only serves the interests of the bourgeoisie. To give one's life is a *duty* – this is orthodoxy – for the
wellbeing of and *love* for the fatherland. But what becomes of
sacrifice if what we call 'fatherland' is nothing more than the
invention of 'a minority of privileged' who, profiting from the
laws made for their benefit alone, exploit 'a majority of pariahs',
outcasts over whom the minority has given itself a *right of life and
death*, as Gustave Hervé held before the war in a book ironically
titled *My Country, Right or Wrong* [*Leur Patrie*] (1921: 24)? What
becomes of sacrifice if the war is nothing other than the exercise
of this iniquitous right? In times of war, they say, it is imperative
to testify to an unconditional love for the fatherland that never
takes into account the bloodshed that serves it, that even glori-
fies this bloodshed, and one would fill entire libraries with the
texts, speeches, poems, novels and essays that restate this in every
tone, in every language. But if, with its 'cult of earth and the
dead' declaimed by Maurice Barrès for pages on end, this love
is nothing other than the object of a dogma, the act of faith of a
religion common to political and religious authorities, then all
of this comes from deception, if not an increasing criminality,

that Hervé already described in these terms before the war. Public consciousness is

> poisoned by [. . .] the religion of the fatherland. This religion, which children learn at school and the bourgeois periodicals sustain in old age, teaches the stupidity that all the French [les Français] form one big family, [. . .] that they have interests in common, that they have a common heritage of glory to defend, that one must always be ready to die for the honour of the flag and other nonsense [. . .]. (Hervé 1901: 57)

These positions, as we have seen, are not those that Jaurès held on the eve of the war and still less those of Péguy. Once war was declared, Hervé himself abandons them, becoming in turn the most accomplished and most uncompromising war thurifer. And nothing could have indicated, on the eve of the war, that these would be Rolland's positions. They nevertheless imposed themselves upon the author of *Jean-Christophe* in the first months of the conflict with a courage that cannot be minimised. For, if it is one thing to debate the fatherland upstream, when the war is still a figment of the imagination or a calculation of the diplomatic imagination, it is another to confront the question when the experience of war has become day after day, as Freud will say in the same epoch, an experience of proliferating death, a death *en masse*, the number of which exceeds all our powers of representation.

'The fatherland'! It is an understatement to say that, during four years of war, Rolland will have ceaselessly debunked the 'idol' of the fatherland. It constitutes, in his eyes, the node of all lies: not only because, in its name, one generation (that of fathers) believe it legitimate and necessary to demand the sacrifice of another (that of sons), but also because, in so doing, it perverts the most natural feelings. The idol of sacrifice does violence, even in mourning, to the attachment that binds generations together and to the fact that they mutually and successively protect each other. The *fatherland* is the 'idol' that turns the *protection* of fathers against death into the *exposure* of their sons to sacrifice. This is why the invocation of the fatherland in times of war, as a double consent to death (the death of others and the death of loved ones), produces an incomprehensible rupture in the blood and spiritual relation of care and help that binds generations to each other. Rolland often alludes to this in his essays, in particular in the essay that he publishes in December of 1914 under the title of 'The Idols'. His analysis of the notion should be retained. What is an idol? First and foremost a 'phantom' of the mind (Rolland 1916: 118) distinguished by its power to capture negative passions: the passion for enslavement and for murder. This is how one passes from ideal to idol. And let there be no mistake! This passage happens each time the object of an idealisation and, to that extent, of a love (like justice, for instance, liberty or truth) comes to crystallise something entirely different, namely, the passion for domination, enslavement and murder or any of the other equally negative and destructive passions that Rolland calls 'the evil instincts' (1916: 109). So, nothing forbids attachment to one's own country; nothing forbids one from dreaming of it or feeling nostalgic when one's country is far away or being debased. But war needs more; it needs this love to be murderous and even doubly murderous. Not only because it gives a licence to kill but also (this is the radicality of Rolland's thought) because it turns fathers (this is the very essence of sacrifice) into the murderers of their sons!

The best way to oppose, then, is to do justice to the singularity of each death and all mourning beyond abstract considerations, to revivify through the imagination the singularities that death destroys *en masse*. Such is the power of literature. Nowhere does Rolland utilise literature with greater force than in *Clérambault*. Written during the war and published in 1920 in a country *in mourning*, the novel is incredibly audacious. One must picture what it meant to publish such a book at the time, a book that literally turns the notion of fatherland (the fatherland, the land of the fathers) against itself with a word of intrigue in its eloquent subtitle: *Story of an Independent Mind During the War*.[3] Rolland tells the story of a man – a writer and poet in his free time, a committed international pacifist – whom the war, from its first days in August 1914, makes the most enflamed patriot, never short on bellicose words or rhymes to vilify Germany and exalt revenge. Clérambault has two children, a son and a daughter, and his son leaves for war with infectious enthusiasm. During one of his leaves, he already returns changed, nearly mute, a stranger to the jingoistic unison, hurt that no one around him except his sister understands that life in the trenches and enemy fire are, far from a shared exaltation, foremost a nightmare. Above all, however, the inevitable occurs. Like millions of others, he dies. And it is then that slowly, after the first shock has passed, the fogs of his father's patriotic blindness dissipate. He perceives what he refused to see until then: the monstrosity of the imposed sacrifice, the emptiness of the arguments that justify it. He picks up his pen again, alone against everyone, abandoned by his friends who do not share his doubts, the distance he takes from war propaganda or, finally, his uncompromising condemnation of patriotic lies. What he then writes, with increasing anger, is extremely virulent. Let us listen to it at length. It is a letter he addresses to all the 'fathers' of Europe after his conversion *against* the war, he who for a time had been acclaimed for supporting it.

This reversal, which is also an emancipation of mourning from the frameworks imposed by war, occurs as a public confession in the form of a self-accusation: painful acknowledgements that bear a musical phrase – David's grief as he cries over his son Absalom – for an epigraph.

> *I had a son whom I loved, and sent to his death. You Fathers of mourning Europe, millions of fathers, widowed of your sons, enemies or friends, I do not speak for myself only, but for you who are stained with their blood even as I am. You all speak by the voice of one of you, – my unhappy voice full of sorrow and repentance.*
>
> *My son died, for yours, by yours – How can I tell? – like yours. I laid the blame on the enemy, and on the war, as you must also have done, but I see now that the chief criminal, the one whom I accuse, is myself. Yes, I am guilty; and that means you, and all of us. You must listen while I tell you what you know well enough, but do not want to hear. [. . .]*
>
> *I was never one of those who compounded with the passions of jealous nationalities. I loved men, and their future brotherhood was a joy to me. Why then did I do nothing against the impending danger, against the fever that brooded within us, against the false peace which made ready to kill with a smile on its lips? [. . .]*
>
> *We will say nothing of those who still believe in the old idol; grim, envious, blood be-spattered as she is – the barbarous fatherland. These kill, sacrificing themselves and others, but at least they know what they do. But what of those who have ceased to believe (like me, alas! and you)? Their sons are sacrificed to a lie, for if you assert what you doubt, it is a falsehood, and they offer up their own children to prove this lie to themselves; and now that our beloved have died for it, far from confessing it, we hide our heads still deeper not to see what we have done. After our sons will come others, all the others, offered up for our* untruth. (Rolland 1920a: 111–13, translation modified)

Several motifs here should hold our attention. The most important is obviously the motif of the fatherland repeatedly denounced as a lie – a lie that, following the example of so many others, is prepared and constructed for a long time when it finds its origin already in that 'false peace' that furnished its arms before the war and, five years later (in 1919), would commit the same errors, launch into the same ventures, prepare the same dangers on the occasion of the Treaty of Versailles. The essential thing for the author of *Clérambault* (who speaks through the voice of his hero) is to make those who unconditionally support the war understand how a 'patriotic lie' to which they unthinkingly subscribe operates the reversal of *protection* into sacrificial *exposure* and to show them how its *deception* works. Everything rests upon interlacing love and hatred, that is to say, upon the central and terrible idea that wants 'love of the fatherland' to demand 'hatred of the enemy'. The second text this angry man publishes against the war puts it more explicitly still. Entitled, 'To Her Whom We Have Loved', he does not hesitate to describe Europe's unrest as the self-betrayal or even the self-destruction of the notion of fatherland. The latter, indeed, could have signalled uniting, gathering. Its voice, then, would have wished to be one of 'fraternal love', capable of exceeding, of transcending, of being understood or heard beyond borders. Instead, it leads only to hatred and consented murder. It claims to defend freedom and leads only to slavery, to bring happiness and devastates all joy, to promise life while it is nothing, he concludes, but a '*yoke of death*' (Rolland 1920a: 117). For it to cease to be a murderous idol, it would have needed as its horizon the universal fraternity that Jaurès so deeply desired.

Only '[t]he whole Earth [*Terre*] is the mother of us all', Clérambault writes (Rolland 1920a: 58, translation modified). And one will note here the paradigm shift between 'mother-fatherland-of-fathers', authoritarian and bloodthirsty, and the other universal mother that, because she knows no borders, also finds herself immediately freed from the weight of deaths and the law of blood. As propaganda and war rhetoric capriciously abuse 'family ties', which for everyone amounts to finding themselves taken hostage in the clutches of sacrifice, one must dream of another family, he tells us, and one must work toward its construction if one desires peace. Other ties demand to be knotted. Because the first thing to recognise is that this 'family' does not reside where one would like to make us believe it does, and once and for all it has nothing to do with the military-industrial limits that bellicose patriotism, the very patriotism that ceaselessly plays with all the genetic and generational metaphors, wishes to impose upon it. The true fatherland is elsewhere, 'here and there', as much on the enemy's side as on 'ours'. It is discovered as soon as one begins to recognise that, *on both sides of the border*, there are people in poverty, workers (this is family!) who, far from rising against each other, would have every interest in gathering together, for they have no need (and, in reality, no desire) to serve the rivalries that tear asunder those who nevertheless intend to exploit them.

But nothing is more difficult to eradicate from consciousness in wartimes than the prejudices that war maintains. For war is not only the product of a fermentation of violence that broods for years before exploding; it is at least as much an ideology that sticks to your skin [*colle à la peau*]. This is why the fatherland is ultimately like old rags,[4] which Rolland illustrates magisterially in terms that are not far from recalling Freud's analyses in the same era in *Reflections on War and Death* and the analyses he will later develop concerning the death drive. This is no doubt the most difficult truth to understand. It amounts to saying that, in the final analysis, the exaltation of the fatherland – not to say its excitation, forbidding none of the sexual connotations this suggests – must be thought in its relation to this drive.

> Sick with disgust, he saw first what he was loath to believe; how this greasy fleece had stuck to his flesh. He could sniff the musty odour of the primitive beast, the savage instincts of war, of murder, the lust for blood like living meat torn by his jaws. The elemental force which asks death for life. Far down in the depths of human nature is this slaughter-house in the ditch, never filled up but covered with the veil of a false civilisation, over which hangs a faint whiff from the butcher's shop [. . .] This filthy odour finally sobered Clérambault; with horror he tore off the skin of the beast whose prey he had been.
>
> Ah, how thick it was – warm, silky, and beautiful, and at the same time stinking and bloody, made of the lowest instincts, and the highest illusions. To love, give ourselves to all, be a sacrifice for all, be but one body and one soul, our fatherland the sole life! [. . .] What then is this Fatherland, this living thing to which a man sacrifices not only his life, all lives, but also his conscience, all consciences? What is this blind love, whose other Janus face with gouged eyes is a blind hate? (Rolland 1920a: 57, translation modified)

The fatherland 'sticks to your skin' because it solicits buried instincts, the most obscure passions: that call for blood that sleeps in everyone. But it does not do so spontaneously, *naturally*. It is helped, brought about, stimulated one might say by the factory of hatred, the most powerful motor of which remains the diffusion, week after week, of the venomous information that the historian Marc Bloch will magisterially analyse after the war in the name of 'false news'. I will address this question at length in the following chapter, but the murderous character of the fatherland's murderous ideology or idolatry cannot be interrogated here without doing it initial justice. For the death instinct to wake, indeed, it is necessary for the enemy to be made worthy of hate and thus for it to appear 'monstrous', 'brutal', 'bestial', 'barbaric'. It is necessary for the 'ideological State apparatuses' along with the State's repressive apparatuses, beginning with censorship, to be placed in the service of the imperial and exclusive construction and diffusion of an 'enemy culture'. And, therefore, it is necessary to raise an army of functionaries in the service of this 'culture' – intellectuals, scholars, artists, journalists, all those symbolic fathers, those cantors of the 'fatherland', mastersingers of love – in order to work toward the construction of this new *superego*. They then become the incarnation of the fatherland, the object of a glory that seeks to be incontestable. Rolland and Clérambault reserve their harshest words for them. They both denounce, one through the voice of the other, the absurdity of the logic that makes war unanimous: a demanded consensus, the argumentation for which rests upon deductions that are not only groundless but, moreover, murderous. This logic is the following: it wants love for the fatherland *to imply*, imperatively, hatred of others who are themselves defenders of their own fatherlands. Its principle is that love is gauged, love is engaged, love proves itself only in the manifestation of hatred. Rolland forcefully recalls this in *Above the Battle*, the book in which he gathers the articles he wrote against the war from 1915 on.[5]

> It would seem, then, that love of our fatherland can flourish only through the hatred of other fatherlands and the massacre of those who sacrifice themselves in the defence of them. There is in this theory a ferocious absurdity, a Neronian dilettantism which repels me to the very depths of my being. No! Love of my fatherland does not demand that I shall hate and slay those

noble and faithful souls who also love theirs, but rather that I should honour them and seek to unite with them for our common good. (1916: 47, translation modified)

It is thus important not to mistake the enemy. War does indeed confront us with a hostile power, but it is not the force that, dragged into the conflict, peoples think they can designate. If one does not want to pay for all the deceptive words of war, one must recognise the veritable enemy elsewhere. This enemy is at once *interior* and *exterior*, and this is what makes the enemy infinitely more dreadful. Where is it? Who is it? It is not the soldier crouching in the trenches up ahead, covered in mud and vermin. As Rolland writes, in the desire to have finished with the heroic reasons for war and return the latter to its least admissible motives, the enemy can be none other than 'the monster of a hundred heads, the monster named Imperialism, the will to pride and domination, which seeks to absorb all, or subdue all, or break all, and will suffer no greatness except itself' (1916: 50). The turn is decisive here, and we will study all of its consequences in the chapters that follow: the enemy (and one would be tempted to say that, a century later, nothing has changed) is whoever cultivates hatred, whoever maintains it, whoever has an interest in seeing it develop and perpetuate. Whence the strategy that Rolland will adopt from the beginning to the end of the war: to call upon 'independent minds', wherever they are, to change the face of the enemy, to demand an *other* politics that knows how to designate it as such and the institutions charged with implementing it. This is what the Churches and Socialist Party should have done! As is known, this is not how things went. For the moral and spiritual authorities will have been, from the beginning, contaminated by the fever of hatred, by the nationalist furore that will have made them join the enemy camp.

One henceforth understands why, in the last resort, this opposition to the lies of war – and we now know that everything that contributes to hatred situates us at the heart of the deception – rests upon a moral idealism and upon the belief in the efficacy of its 'power' to oppose war. 'Ye know not your moral power, O ye of little faith!', writes Rolland at the end of the article that lends its name to *Above the Battle* (1916: 53). But in question is a risky power [*pouvoir*] that, in times of war, goes against the grain of opinion and collides with forces [*puissances*] that have every interest in breaking it. This is why it must first be the object of a *belief* that leaps into the unknown. This belief supposes the restoration of the confidence in our *moral* capacity to oppose war by resisting its lies. This is what is important precisely when all the signs incite thoughts to the contrary: to rediscover lost faith in the duty 'to build higher and stronger, dominating the injustice and hatred of nations, the walls of that city wherein the souls of the whole world may assemble' (1916: 54). One must believe, because the abdication of this power would be 'humanity's dishonour'. Thus, it is not surprising that the essay concludes on the experience of *shame* (the shame that war thurifers do not know): 'it is *shameful* to see [the elite] serving the passion of a puerile, monstrous policy of race' (1916: 53).

III. Economy of Patriotic Love

Among so many others, finally, there remains one last voice to evoke, no less radical than those of Jaurès and Rolland: the voice of Alain. It is significant, indeed, that the first chapter of *Mars ou la guerre jugée*, one of the great books of philosophy inspired by the 1914–1918 war, should be dedicated to raising doubts about 'love for the fatherland' as the first motivation for war and that the first chapter should interrogate the sense of allegedly consensual sacrifices to this love. What drives men and women to agree, most often passively, to expose their lives and die *en masse*? No question is more imposing, and it should rightfully open every reflection on war, of which it constitutes the most mysterious part. Alain's strength lies in responding to this question by accenting the 'interests' of war in a sense of the term that is not so much political as rigorously economic. If 'love for the fatherland'[6] effectively lay at the origin of this motivation, Alain explains, it would hold sway over every market calculation, and no profit should be made – thanks to war – on the back of the fatherland. While every conflict has its profiteers, love for the fatherland, which they at times proclaim in support, should be powerful enough to convert their profit into a generous offering deposited on the altar of this same fatherland. It is an understatement to say that this is not at all the case, and it would rather seem, as Alain underscores with grinding irony, that 'citizens give their lives more willingly than their money' (1930: 26). Thus, it is not certain that this 'love for the fatherland', presented as a sacred duty, is 'strong enough of itself to bear the great strain put upon it by a war' (1930: 25), which drives men to agree to kill each other. If such is the case, moreover, it is because other passions are at work in war: passions to which one must do justice at the risk of missing what Freud analyses from 1915 on as *the truth of every war*, the indissociable cause and effect of its essentially murderous character, namely, the complete upheaval of our attitude before death.[7] Which passions are in

83

question? Numerous, no doubt, are the passions that take part in the genesis of conflicts, in their development and sometimes also in what compromises peace before it has ever been signed, but for Alain, as for Rolland, no passion is more powerful than hatred, which so many forces work together to maintain. Whence the question that imposes itself: what if 'love for the fatherland' was but the virtuous mask of a motivation otherwise more powerful, namely, the 'hatred of the other'? What if war always presupposed the complex production and construction in time and space of this 'enemy culture' that I just evoked in reading *Clérambault*? What if, finally, we were never to escape this ideological artifice, this great political machinery of hatred?

Notes

1 G. G. Coulton presents *Democracy and Military Service* (1916) as an 'abbreviated translation' of Juarès's *L'Armée nouvelle* (1915), but a large part of the work is, in fact, a loose summary. All translations of *L'Armée nouvelle* are therefore our own. For the same reason, we retain references only to the original work. – Translators

2 We have a confused feeling of this today, we who well know that, whatever the arguments put forth, France's incapacity – from the heights of the place it claims to occupy in Europe – to play its part in welcoming refugees, that is to say, to incarnate the idea of justice and fraternity that the principle of welcoming bears in itself, does not contribute to its greatness!

3 *Clérambault: Histoire d'une conscience libre pendant la guerre* (1920a). A more literal translation of the subtitle would be: 'story of a free consciousness/conscience during the war'. – Translators

4 Forgoing recourse to more natural expressions like 'get stuck in your head' or 'get under your skin', we have translated the French idiom *coller à la peau* literally as 'stick to your skin' because Crépon's reference to 'old rags', which in turn picks up Rolland's description of the fatherland as a 'greasy fleece [that] had stuck to his flesh', would be unintelligible otherwise. – Translators

5 See Part II, Chapter 2, 'Of Hatred'.

6 Crépon's formulation here refers to the title of the first chapter of Alain's *Mars*, 'L'amour de la patrie' (1960: 551), which the English translators reduce to 'Patriotism'. – Translators

7 See Freud, *Reflections on War and Death* (1918).

2

Of Hatred

I. Enemy Culture

Violence, beginning with the violence that characterises wars, always surprises those who, a few weeks before its irruption, wanted to hold onto all the reasons for reassuring themselves, believing violence to be *impossible* despite all the annunciatory signs that it was coming: the rise in internal and international tensions, the threatening declarations on all sides, the alarming articles published in the press. Before the flood of violence's destructions becomes evident, it always seems that the *reasons* for preventing and stopping it will hold sway over madness; it always seems, in other words, that speech remains *possible* and that a solution will present itself in the end because, they say, no good is more precious than *understanding* [l'entente], *civil and international peace*, and no memory more traumatising than the memory of past wars. This is why the surprise is double. On the one hand, war itself, in which no one or almost no one wanted to believe, is a shock [*saisissement*]. On the other hand, as the immediate effect of the first victims, the first destructions and – with them – the first suspicions of abuse and crimes, the voices of peace – those who wanted *to believe* war impossible – from one day to the next are snuffed out as rapidly as a candle flame, along with the ideals that maintained the flame, whether cultural, moral or political. For, henceforth, warmongering 'reason' – but also literature and science – then places itself *in the service of violence*, rare being the voices that still find the courage to oppose the general rage, that is to say, the 'enemy culture' and the construction of hatred that are its most efficacious and imperial instruments.

Hatred must first be understood according to its essence: a rage for destruction, a radical will to annihilate. It reduces neither to a conflict of opinions nor to a political opposition. It is neither reasonable nor rational, regardless of the arguments and pretexts it advances. Hatred is a passion – and the classical philosophers have always described it as such. It is a passion that introduces a murderous madness [*déraison*] into politics. Yet, it is not natural or spontaneous. It cannot be explained by a hypothetical, conflictive essence of the relation that would precipitate some against others. Even if all the signs – always more orchestrated than one thinks – indicate otherwise, and whatever the murderous drives that make it possible, hatred is always a construction. This is the first thesis that this chapter will uphold: hatred is the spring that political forces need so as to wage both their internal and their external wars. For every war presupposes that an enemy is targeted insofar as it must be annihilated. Yet, as we have seen, perceiving the enemy as such never goes without saying. Once again, there is no 'natural' enemy. The enemy always presupposes a culture that 'cultivates' its designation and its perception as the enemy, a culture that develops this perception long in advance, gives birth to it, raises it, develops and maintains it, a culture that does not draw back from any means, any verbal outrage, any caricatured image, any lie, any false news to achieve this perception. This culture is inseparable from a history of information-diffusion techniques that were transformed into instruments of propaganda as soon as they appeared: the press, radio, television and, finally, the internet, which transforms the very nature of this culture by its formidable withdrawal from State control. I will call it *enemy culture*.

Hatred is this culture's instrument. Like all passions, it has interests. It is a passion with an interest in reinforcing and consolidating the perception of the designated and targeted enemy as what must be destroyed. Nevertheless, hatred never reduces to calculation, even if it includes many calculations. One must immediately add, as its second distinctive trait, that the forces freed on this occasion, the pleasure in or desire for murder, the desire for vengeance and the death drive always end up becoming uncontrollable. In the final analysis, hatred always escapes all control; it exceeds the limits within which those responsible for unleashing its manifestation thought they could maintain it. This excess, this immoderation, this contagion is what makes a sorcerer's apprentice of anyone who risks calling upon hatred to make use of it. Not in vain do we speak of hatred in terms of unleashing, overflowing or explosion. If there may well be motifs meant to explain hatred, to organise its discourses and images, its rhetoric and the montages that produce it, one must at the same time recognise that what is provoked always escapes reason and overflows all calculation. This is why the enemy – and this point is crucial – never reduces to its rational construction. The production of the enemy, which makes it the object of an incalculable and infinitely explosive phantasm, always ends up exceeding every motive of this order.

Indeed, there comes a time – and the time always comes – when hatred has taken hold so strongly on the fertile ground of enemy culture that it seems impossible to tear it away, to turn back, to staunch the overflowing, to escape the spiral of violence that it ineluctably engenders. Everything then happens as if it were impossible for those who have abandoned themselves to hatred to do what reason would nevertheless order: to distance oneself, to moderate, to put a stop to the murderous rages. Such is the responsibility of hatemongers. The passion they unleash on all sides deprives them of all distance, and it knows no moderation. It refuses mediations, beginning with those of language. It gives speech and dialogue no chance to heal hatred, to cancel it or even to attenuate it: hatred knows no attenuation. This is why it is a trial [*épreuve*]. It is a trial for all the men and women who wish to resist its grasp, to keep an independent mind,[1] to care for the truth and, above all else, to protect everyone from violence. Let there be no mistake indeed! Violence is the node of the question. Hatred seeks violence, demands it, desires it more or less explicitly and knowingly; it wants nothing else; it cannot escape the invasive obsession with violence.

This is the reason why this trial is also a trial for politics. Fortunately, politics cannot tolerate destructive hatred escaping its control permanently. Politics cannot allow hatred to rise beyond its need when, to wage this or that war, it caves in to the temptation; it cannot allow hatred to rise beyond its use, at its own risk and peril, in very determined circumstances and in a very targeted way. Hatred, in this sense, presents a challenge not only for those who wish to oppose it because they are conscious of its ravages, like Romain Rolland in the autumn of 1914, but also for those who unleashed it and no longer know how to stop it and, finally and above all, for those who inherit a political situation and a moral climate or a human context that, one should say, hatred profoundly gangrened long ago, as we will see in the following chapters in encounters with, each in turn, the figures of Gandhi, Martin Luther King, Jr and Nelson Mandela. For conquering hatred, countering it, exceeding it consists first of all in suspending these violences and reversing the course of a history that they dominate. To conquer hatred is thus to distil in hearts and minds, and to impose upon institutions, a determined form of 'non-violence' by finding the resources necessary to escape the concatenations of destruction. The whole question of this book, once again, lies in knowing where to find the political, moral or spiritual resources for this interruption, this exit ramp, this very reversal of mutual destruction into common construction.

A word on violence, which was addressed at length at the beginning of these reflections, must still be said.[2] There will always be two ways to think violence. The first supposes that violence has virtues; it justifies violence through the *sought-after goal* that it presents as beneficial: a life-saving justice, an indispensable revenge, the restoration of an order, the payment of a debt, a necessary revolution. Yet, to obtain this flattering perspective, those who proclaim violence must compromise with the truth of the pursued goal and its consequences, which means arranging a perception and a selective interpretation of it. This is why, under the auspices of hatred, all justification of violence at the same time renounces the truth and its benefits. This is what Romain Rolland ceaselessly recalls for the hounds of hatred, as well as for the heinous cohorts that − convinced that they are motivated by a just anger − the hounds aggressively urge to take to the streets: the hatred of the other − with the insults, outrages and calls for murder that hatred entails − and the refusal or denial of truth always go hand in hand. The resources that permit one to overcome this trial first presuppose that the masks fall, that the lies be denounced and that the conditions be re-established for a shared word, animated by the care and courage for this same truth. Inversely, the heinous idolatry not only of the 'Fatherland' and 'Identity'[3] but also of a strange 'Justice', a strange 'Freedom' and even a dubious 'Peace'[4] – which must be written here in quotation marks and with capital letters to indicate that it is not a question of ideas but, rather, their 'murderous idols' – is distinguished in that it must always accommodate a repeated lie concerning the effects of the violence that it authorises; it must always mask itself, veil itself, minimise what is destroyed in the name of these notions. Yet, what is destroyed is always a discontinuous addition of singularities: $1 + 1 + 1$, etc., and not this or that indeterminate group in its extension, a 'mass', a 'class', a 'race' – any of these 'alterities' that the heinous discourses and acts target. Once one says, consequently, that one's own lies make hatred blind, it ignores first and foremost these singularities $(1 + 1 + 1$, etc.), can no longer see them, no longer wants to see them. This murderous idolatry does not know, does not want to know, that what it destroys each time is singular.

This blindness is the essence of violence's contagiousness in times of war. To give way to hatred is always to lie to oneself – and to others at the same time – and to blind oneself. Even when exercised upon a particular individual it knows and can name, hatred in truth wants to know nothing of what constitutes the absolute, irreplaceable, unsubstitutable singularity of whomever it condemns. It wants to know nothing of their vulnerability and still less of the responsibility for attention, care and help that their vulnerability demands. I have named this eclipse 'murderous consent'; if many forms of such a consent exist without any need for hatred to be manifest (all the passive forms, those that stem from negligence, indifference or forgetfulness), hatred nonetheless remains one of its most powerful motors when war breaks out and this consent becomes active, participatory, and requires unanimity.

This is why there is a second way to think violence, the principle of which consists in placing the accent first and foremost upon what it destroys. Not what it destroys in general or in particular! Not a determined group (an order, institutions, a system, a group, a 'class', a 'people' or an 'ethnicity') – in which case this other way of thinking would only reverse the first and remain just as global, blind and reductive – but rather what violence destroys each time singularly: the discontinuous addition of singularities, $1 + 1 + 1$, etc.! Whence what distinguishes this way of thinking: it attaches to the unicity of every human relation. Relaunching from the fabric of every human relation, which makes every singular existence a world solely unto itself, it recalls that violence destroys these relations foremost when it deprives children of their parents, parents of their children, friends of their friends; it recalls that there will always be some intellectual or military deception pretending to think violence without retracing it to the misery of all the mourning and broken lives. This thought opposes a microanalysis or, one might say, a microphysics of violence to the steamroller of hatred. It *refuses* to ignore, it *refuses* to hide (because that is how the lie always begins), it *refuses* to forget to see and to recall each instant what violence destroys for each and every one.

Because it makes a rule of understanding violence in the multiplicity of its effects, irreducible to all generality, this thought of violence thus calls for testimonies and stories that, rendering rights to the singular, at times take the form of fiction, as we saw in the preceding chapter while briefly following the path of *Clérambault*. These testimonies and stories make those who take this rule for their principle the inventive witnesses of truth.

Their invention is at once the invention of a way of talking and a way of acting other than those that precipitate into violence, an *other* action that makes possible an *other* language: other words than those that come spontaneously to mind, whenever a question of the calculations and murderous accommodations in politics, to describe and think violence *otherwise*. But whence this *alterity*? What is its 'resource'? We already know that it is difficult to name and identify it.

II. A Moral Tribunal

Let us begin, once again in 1914, by resuming our reading of Romain Rolland, which was left suspended at the end of the previous chapter. Reading his correspondence, especially with Stefan Zweig, along with the set of articles he publishes in the *Journal de Genève* beginning in the autumn of 1914, it indeed seems that, of his contemporaries, no writer's heart or mind was more profoundly marked by hatred's victory. A little later, when he compiles his texts denouncing the war, he even hesitated between two titles – *Au-dessus de la haine* [*Above Hatred*], then *Contre la haine* [*Against Hatred*] – and ended up retaining neither, giving his collection of articles the title by which we know it: *Au-dessus de la mêlée* [*Above the Battle*]. The resistance to hatred connoted by the preposition 'against' and the will to overcome hatred recalled in the preposition 'above' should be understood in their triple dimension: refusing the negative passions that war provokes and solicits, at the same time as those passions nourish it; the 'courage for truth' implied in such a refusal; and, finally, gestures of help, support and mutual aid, if not love, meant to clear the dangerous path of an alternative to the mechanical workings of hostile sentiments. Indeed, as we know, hatred in 1914 was first of all hatred of the 'adversary', and not only political but also spiritual and moral forces of belligerent countries seemed to conspire for its development and maintenance: the motor of this invading and contagious 'enemy culture', without which the *sacred* demand of 'sacrifice' imposed upon an entire generation could not have captivated consciousnesses. To confirm this point, it suffices to reread the most ardent declarations and the most caricatured judgements that surged from the pens of the most advanced, the most astute, the most cultivated, the most universally honoured minds from both sides. From September 1914 on, Rolland ceaselessly denounced them, emphasising their rhetorical artifices, deploring the radical capitulation of the men and women that the war managed to place in its service, railing against the volte-face that consisted in burning overnight the convictions, ideals and admirations defended just the night before, becoming alarmed, finally, by the flood of lies that had nourished hatred from the beginning – all components of this 'murderous consent' that constitutes the truth of every war. As one can easily imagine, his denunciations were also the *target* of a generalised and public hostility to which there were few exceptions. Thus hatred, the trial of which had to be overcome, was not only the hatred directed against the enemy, which he refused to share, but also the hatred to which he had exposed himself in making it publicly known. He would recall this in the profession of faith that concludes the introduction he wrote in September 1915 to his collection of articles:

> One single word will I add. For a year I have been rich in enemies. Let me say this to them: they can hate me, but they will not teach me to hate. I have no concern with them.

My business is to say what I believe to be fair and humane. Whether this pleases or irritates is not my business. I know that words once uttered make their way of themselves. Hopefully I sow them in the bloody soil. The harvest will come. (Rolland 1916: 18)

Yet, in a Europe that no longer knew any other logic than that which immures everyone in the bellicose rhetoric of its camp, to hold oneself 'above hatred' was also to affirm a third thing: not only opposition or courage to expose oneself, then, but also an alternative or another *exit* ramp, namely, the wager that the artifices of this rhetoric and the lies it involved were not *inevitable*, because there is always a way to think and act *otherwise*, as so many men and women attempt to do still today in warzones where violence rages. If *Above the Battle* bears a dimension common to both morality and politics, it pertains not only to the refusal of hatred but also at least as much to what it opposes to hatred in the most concrete way possible: another discourse and another action. The first thing that must be said and that one must certainly learn to hear anew, a century later, the first appeal that Rolland addresses to the European peoples to resist hatred, consists in reminding them that hatred is not a 'natural' datum of the relation between peoples and that it is wrong to believe – as they attempt to do today at the other end of Europe, after having done so twenty years ago in the Balkans – and murderous to imagine, even in the Middle East, that hatred would have ancestral and pluri-secular grounds that would make it a historical inevitability. No, one had to tell the European peoples in 1914, beginning with the Germans, British and French, that their supposed and respective hatred was above all *constructed* by an army of ideologues who, engaged in hawkishness and armed with the most powerful rhetorical instruments, would not recoil from any lie or phantasm to serve the war interests. And one still had to add that, if it were so dangerous to say so, it is because this construction was, moreover, sustained by a veritable confiscation of speech: the governmental censorship relayed by opinions, both the censorship and opinions depriving free spirits of all means for opposing hatred and the violences that it legitimates with a counterword.

This is what Rolland will first of all and ceaselessly emphasise in his articles, his *Journal* and his correspondence with Zweig! The first victory of war is always this sort of confiscation! It imposes, on both sides of the frontline, two discourses opposed in their respective presentation of the enemy as an object of necessary hatred, two logics that nevertheless amount to the same through their method, their automaton thinking and their strategic calculations, both foreigners to any horror with regard to the violence for which they call – thus in principle hostile to the least 'independence of mind', as if each were always but the mirror of the other. The following speech, then, had very little chance of being heard:

> There was no reason for war between the Western nations; French, English, and German, we are all brothers and do not hate one another. The war-preaching press is envenomed by a minority, a minority vitally interested in maintaining these hatreds; but our peoples, I know, ask for peace and liberty and that alone. (Rolland 1916: 49)

Between what the German and French said about each other, there was therefore no difference once they were caught in the uniform nets of their heinous rhetoric without critical distance, without examining the facts and without analysing the discourses. But there was no possible debate either, no space for a contradictory distribution of speech that clears the possibility for an objective judgement. The first effect of hatred was to introduce confusion and obscurity into minds such that one no longer knew what was true and what false, or rather truth itself, the objectivity of reported facts, the reality of denounced violations was no longer an object of scrutiny. Who will say that things have changed a century later? Rolland would experience the difficulty of seeing things clearly throughout the letters that, from the beginning of the war, he exchanged with his friend and admirer Stefan Zweig. Their correspondence was not at all easy, not only because it had to circumvent censorship, but also because, if from their first contact they agreed to situate themselves 'above hatred', they still had to resist the partial presentation and interpretation of the facts imposed by the newspapers – on both sides of the border – to which they had access. Indeed, it was first in the French press and in the declarations of French public figures that Zweig, who believed what he read in the German newspapers, discovered hatred and believed he had to denounce it. Because they spread extravagant noise concerning the barbarity of German soldiers, the Parisian newspapers – and they alone – were at fault for having distilled those ferments of hatred that poisoned French hearts, while the German newspapers, he was convinced, managed to retain their 'dignity' (Rolland and Zweig 2014a: 79).[5] Try as Rolland might to prove the contrary by explaining to Zweig that the display of enemy newspapers in the press of warring peoples was a disinformation tactic incapable of objectivity and impossible to take at face value; try as he might to explain that the articles cited were first chosen for their outrageous character, then systematically truncated, cut and deformed to disseminate with maximum effect; it was no use. Zweig could not find the resolve to suspect his country's press of a guilty partiality. The invasion of Belgium, the destruction of the library at Louvain (among so many others) and the destruction of the cathedral at Reims were the particularly sensitive points, and we will have occasion to return to these because no set of facts will have poisoned minds more in the first weeks of the war. There again, Zweig wanted to believe what was said on these issues in the German press. 'Reims was calumny', he wrote (Rolland and Zweig 2014a: 108). With respect to Belgium, passing over the destructions in silence, he contented himself with recalling that, until then, the Germans – unlike the French – never mocked Belgians! To which Rolland responded that he could not let the accusation of 'calumny' pass, demanding from his friend, with great irritation, a little more discernment:

> How can you, with your critical spirit, accept lone testimonies from only one side [. . .]? I gathered testimonies from all over [. . .] If you were in Switzerland, and if you had knowledge of the exact facts, you would cry tears of regret for having approved or accepted without protest, through too much confidence in those shaping opinion in Germany, horrific acts that nothing in the world will ever excuse. I assure you, my friend, German intellectuals are betrayed by their leaders. They do not know the truth. And later, they will be judged as accomplices, although this is not the case. (2014a: 111–12)

The polemic continued for a long time. In a later letter, Zweig returns to the offensive, attempting to persuade Rolland that the Germans in no case could have opened fire on the cathedral at Reims '"*out of pure malice*"', as they were unjustly reproached for doing, but only 'out of military necessity', because the cathedral was used 'for shelter', 'as cover for troops' (2014a: 116). If the cathedral had been bombarded, the French were to blame since, under pressure from the German army, they had refused to retreat; for, in truth, no people '*cared as much as the Germans for preserving artistic and cultural monuments*' (2014a: 117). The proof was the importance accorded to the history of art in Germany, which was much greater than in France! Above all else, Zweig attempted to protest, with the most vigorous energy, against the prosecution of the German people for being cruel and for having nothing but scorn for '*cultural values*' (2014a: 117). This denial is not only captivating for the naïve complacency, if not the Machiavellianism, that motivates it. While Zweig appeared before the war as a great cosmopolitan consciousness, this denial testifies to the persistent grip of a sentiment of irreducible belonging that the war reanimated, an almost instinctive solidarity with 'German culture' attested to by the elements of comparison between France and Germany that Zweig cannot stop himself from slipping into his argument – as if (this is the naïveté!) a country of such 'great culture' could not be guilty of the crimes for which it was reproached! Above all, however, this denial puts the infernal machine that manufactures hatred into perspective. Try as Zweig might to resist, proclaiming throughout his letters that he will not cave in to its contagion, he takes no distance from the discourses that nourish hatred when they come from the German press, which cannot find words strong enough to justify the army's acts of violence in Belgium. Nothing, then, is easy in these bonds of friendship struggling against the murderous unrest of consciences. From one end to the other, Zweig's letters are inhabited by a tension between, on the one hand, the generous and humanist convictions that, shared with the author of *Jean-Christophe*, carefully preserve the chances for a future peace and, on the other hand, the national (not to say chauvinistic) idiosyncrasy that hinders the impartiality of a critical judgement. The force of that attachment described by Jaurès in *L'Armée nouvelle*, once again, appears between the lines.

The affair goes further. Not without irritation, Rolland responds once again. In the letters that followed, two elements should be retained. The first is a recognition that the acts of violence were not the privilege of either camp; there were always enough convincing facts that either side could advance to incite hatred, if not even to make hatred an irrepressible feeling. Consequently, if one wanted to escape the cyclones of hatred, one had to free oneself from every form of 'unilateral confidence' and suspend the credit that, at times even unwittingly, one was tempted to give spontaneously to the opinion of those with whom one recognised a common belonging:

> My friend, I repeat, I accuse no one, I accuse only the war and I lament all the unfortunate people that are its distraught victims – those who do wrong, as well as those who suffer it. But you yourself must manage to escape your unilateral confidence. The tragedy of the current situation is that there is, on both sides and in both camps, enough to justify the worst mutual reproaches as well as the enthusiasm that each people feels for its cause. (2014a: 123)

The second element to isolate in Rolland's responses to Zweig is his premonitory conviction that the end of the war would not put an end to the work of hatred, whatever camp ended up victorious, and one must not wait for its end, consequently, to try by all means to save not only the 'European spirit' but also – greater still – the 'universal spirit' (2014a: 123), on the condition, however, of avoiding the empty declarations that, once again, engage no one and hold only for the time during which they are formulated. Such wellbeing, indeed, presupposed that one begin to save oneself by escaping the grip of fatherlands. To proclaim great humanist principles was one thing; another was *to act on oneself* to ensure that those principles do not remain purely theoretical, their memory a pious wish, and thus to ensure that no partisan attachment, no criminal complacency, no blindness and deafness could hobble the construction of future peace in advance.

Thus, the first means for opposing the perpetual maintenance of hatred had to consist in restoring rights to a speech freed from the 'prejudices of all fatherlands [*patries*] and all parties [*partis*]' (2014a: 124), however profoundly anchored in the hearts of the warring countries, by inventing an unprecedented public space, a high court, a tribunal of consciences capable of recrediting the 'independence of mind' that the rages of hatred had caused it to lose. Throughout the whole war and in the years that followed, this would be Rolland's great task; he ceaselessly demanded its constitution and functioning throughout considerable corre-spondence exchanged with everyone that not only Europe but also the United States and India could count among its pacifist writers and thinkers.[6] If an assembly of this order was to see the light of day, it must – without further ado – be formed of free individuals, individuals sufficiently *resolved* to let themselves 'be circumscribed by a fatherland' (2014a: 124) no longer, so that, with infallible and constantly vigilant attention, they could bring an impartial judgement to the violations and crimes, without distinction and whatever their origin. None of this went without saying, as Zweig's clumsy tergiversations and timorous hedging showed, which essentially centred on *his* solitude, *his* suffering, *his* need to hide, to keep *his* feelings quiet while waiting for the war to end. Not to mention that the murderous games of politics had led to exactly inverse positions. Everyone had been commanded to subscribe to diplomatic calculations, those secret alliances that had precipitated Europe into the abyss. To escape this abyss, it was therefore imperative to restore credit to a force radically heterogenous to their criminal interests – an *other* force that one needed to find the means to rethink.

This other force no doubt translates into the courage and intransigence that, without concession or delay, the author of *Above the Battle* showed in his articles and letters. But how should one describe and name this force? What power must one convoke? Nothing less, as we have seen, than 'humanity's moral and spiritual' power! To be sure, but what can one see in this power today other than the dated formulation of an obsolete spiritualism and moralism? In 1914, however, the expression was hardly anything to smile about. Dramatic circumstances called for it. However deeply it lay buried beneath the debris of humanism, only a power of this order could transcend divisions of class, race and nation ever since the political force meant to incarnate this transcendence – the Socialist International in which Jaurès had placed so much hope – had been dispersed, divided, compromised and discredited when everyone rallied around the bellicose propaganda of their own country. The universal fraternity inspiring so many dreams had not resisted the first impacts of war.

This is the conversion that Rolland so deeply desired! If one wanted to overcome the trial of hatred,[7] the first step was to disavow politics! He had to reiterate this to Zweig in 1915 in terms that, as we will later see, were in reality no way definitive:[8]

> in a general way, I can say that for several months I have completely left the political terrain in order to establish myself on the purely human terrain. I feel too clearly that *not one single* politics is innocent; all politics have their hands more or less dirtied from crime. (Rolland and Zweig 2014a: 197)

Yet, because the voice invoking 'the holy cause of humanity' (2014a: 197) clamoured in the desert in 1914, the moral power that it convoked could be nothing but the object of a renewed *belief*, a *new faith*. He demanded a sidestep, if not a dangerous leap, that challenged all prudent resignation and all delay by wagering upon the extremely untimely possibility of making it happen, of creating it piece by piece, by gathering energies everywhere open to establishing this step in a unified voice on which one must count in order to prepare peace. And the serious issue was no longer having the ability to take this step, losing confidence in the human ability – beginning with the men and women of science and culture who were so quick to rally to violence's cause – to gather their forces so as to institute this salutary power. If one should choose to keep quiet, by contrast, and expand this withdrawal into a '*universal* silence' (2014a: 143), like the silence for which Rolland reproached Zweig (who always in principle refused to recognise and condemn the acts of violence committed by the German army), this would be a moral disaster, however the events turn out. And one could be sure of one thing: all reconciliation would become impossible, and there would be no just peace.

> I only say that if, for whatever reason, the best wait for peace to return in order to speak, it will then be too late. [. . .] All reconciliation will have become impossible: for, whoever the victor, the peace will have been unjust. It will have been unjust if, between now and then, all the just keep silent. (2014a: 151)

The conclusion is irrevocable. Supposing one surrendered to the idea that the task was impossible, supposing one caved in to discouragement, renounced the hope for a common *counter-word* by thinking that all discourse and all action, by essence partisan and therefore partial, was from the beginning tributary to community interests with which they remained in solidarity, then – as the author of *Above the Battle* does not hesitate to affirm – there would be nothing left but to take note, once and for all, of humanity's dishonour!

> Let this invisible tribunal be seen at last, let us venture to constitute it. Ye know not your moral power, O ye of little faith! If there be a risk, will you not take it for the honour of humanity? What is the value of life when you have saved it at the price of all that is worth living for? (Rolland 1916: 53)

And he continues a bit further on:

> neither family, friend, nor fatherland [*patrie*], nor aught that we love has power over the spirit [*l'esprit*]. The spirit is the light. It is our duty to lift it above tempests, and thrust aside the clouds which threaten to obscure it; to build higher and stronger, dominating the injustice and hatred of nations, the walls of that city wherein the souls of the whole world may assemble. (1916: 54)

Nevertheless, this moral power did not fall from the sky. It had its own resources, which belonged to each culture of the warring nations that, far from attesting to separation and immurement in an identity foreign to the others, constituted and manifested on the contrary their common patrimony: the patrimony, precisely, of humanity. The 'will to peace' – of which the intellectual warmongers had to be reminded – had precursors whose example urgently needed to be reappropriated![9] When the 'moral force' was lacking in Europe, which no longer had ears for anything but the heroism of the sacrifices demanded on both sides, it was up to each nation to draw this 'moral force' from its language and its culture because, open to the rest of the world, they were a testament to a sharing more profound and solid than the logic of conflicts, and because they attested to a circulation among peoples thanks to the uninterrupted dialogue of arts and letters that made the ruptures produced by hatred incomprehensible. The call for a tribunal of consciences was thus accompanied by a plea for literature, the vocation of which was to traverse borders by breaking circles of affiliation. If one wished to resist identifying Germany with Prussian militarism or Russia with the despotism of the tsars, one had to recall the voice of writers and reiterate what was owed to them. Against all globalising perceptions of nations, inseparably heinous and caricatured, one needed the courage to speak, *from elsewhere*, of the debt that had been incurred, in France and everywhere else in Europe, in the encounter with German and Russian culture and vice versa. During the war, in fact, Rolland would ceaselessly multiply appeals, open letters and addresses to writers,[10] and at the same time he could not find words harsh enough to denounce those who – so numerous – had placed their pen in the service of violence and hatred.

III. The Idealisation of Culture

Calling upon the legacy of universal literature to oppose the heinous construction of images of the enemy! However powerful this symbolic resource might be, it nevertheless constitutes only an indirect recourse against hatred; although raised against the representations and characterisations that nourished hatred, it did not yet oppose hatred with the two essential weapons needed to counter it: on the one hand, a rigorous establishment and examination of the facts that would restore to truth its rights;

on the other hand, the gestures of help and care, those tangible signs of humanity that would most concretely prove that it was possible *to do* exactly the opposite of what hatred seemed to prescribe as an inevitability. We have just seen that, in the first months of the war, the polemics and controversies associated with this establishment and examination were concentrated in two sets of facts, along with their ineluctable cortège of denials and unwarranted justifications: the acts of violence committed by the German troops in Belgium with, among others, the destruction of the library at Louvain and the cathedral at Reims.

These acts are not only at the heart of the tense correspondence that Rolland and Zweig exchange in the autumn and winter of 1914. They are also the object of the first article Rolland publishes in the *Journal de Genève* on 2 September 1914: a letter addressed to Gerhart Hauptmann, the famous German novelist and Nobel Laureate in Literature, in response to the German writer's support for the invasion of Belgium – support that denounced the Belgians and sought to justify the first destructions in the name of war and its means. For Rolland, such an intellectual endorsement from a writer *heir* to the whole cultural *patrimony* of Europe originates in a double betrayal: the betrayal of *culture* and the betrayal of *spirit*. Supposing that the deaths of men left him indifferent and even if he found the war justified, Hauptmann should have been indignant about the war's effects, on the one hand, by manifesting his commitment to keeping safe the works of arts constitutive of a common heritage shared by all cultivated Europeans and, on the other hand, by testifying to the independence of mind that obliged writers to resist the collective fury. Culture and spirit, thus *idealised*, should have incited him to protest against the martial madness of 'Prussian militants', understanding that this madness contradicted the

Germany that Rolland continued to admire: the Germany of Goethe and Beethoven. In the name of the 'great' German culture, he should have understood that he could remain in solidarity with the destruction of artworks only by betraying the universal scope of that culture:

> And not content to fling yourselves on living Belgium, you wage war on the dead, on the glories of past ages. You bombard Malines, you burn Rubens, and Louvain is now no more than a heap of ashes – Louvain with its treasures of art and of science, the sacred town! What are you, then, Hauptmann, and by what name do you want us to call you now, since you repudiate the title of barbarians? Are you the grandsons of Goethe or of Attila? Are you making war on enemies or on the human spirit? Kill men if you like, but respect masterpieces. They are the patrimony of the human race. You, like all the rest of us, are its depositories; in pillaging it, as you do, you show yourselves unworthy of our great heritage, unworthy to take your place in that little European army which is civilisation's guard of honour. (Rolland 1916: 21)

A terrible declaration, the untimely character of which must be stressed. From the beginning, Rolland took a stance against the commonplace that was forced upon the bellicose discourses on Germany and the Germans from August 1914 on. 'I am not [. . .] one of those Frenchmen who regard Germany as a nation of barbarians' (1916: 19), he writes at the beginning of his letter. When war was declared, contrary to most of his contemporaries, he refused to renounce and burn what he had adored the night before: the culture of the German language – its writers, musicians and philosophers. He would have thereby betrayed himself, moreover, since the author of *Jean-Christophe* had no other objective in his novel – the hero of which, one must recall, is German – than to construct 'bridges' and a 'dialogue' between two cultures by bringing to light and collapsing the prejudices that the two peoples continued to hold against each other after the war of 1870. Next, one will note that the author of *Above the Battle* forbade himself from passing judgement on the Germans as such: *peoples*, understood as a collective and homogenous subject, should never be held *responsible* for destructions but, rather, a military and political elite that finds its interest in ordering them, dragging the population into a murderous madness that it decides and programmes in full awareness. Finally, one will retain the fact that, in his analysis of the destructions wrought by the war, the destruction of cultural works first caught Rolland's attention. What he deplores about war, which was then only just beginning, was not yet the horror of the trenches, the sacrificed generations, but rather a *crime* against *spirit* and *culture* understood as the guarantors of humanity – and the destruction of the library at Louvain symbolised this crime. This is what blind hatred made possible. In attacking works, even more so than eliminating lives, it committed a crime against the humanity *idealised* and *incarnated* in its cultural patrimony. Rolland, moreover, would explain himself in a second text, written a few weeks later, in September 1914, after the bombardment of the cathedral at Reims, joining in the immense wave of emotions that it caused.[11] Wondering why, '[a]mong the many crimes of this infamous war', he had to choose to 'protest the crimes against things and not against men, the destruction of works and not of lives' (1916: 23), he invoked the function of artworks as the *common arch* that brought peoples together. Even if artworks remained, each one singularly, the particular expression of a determined people's 'spiritual life' and 'the tree of the race' (1916: 25), writes the author of *Jean-Christophe*, it was necessary to recall that they constituted, at the same time, what this people offered to humanity, which made it a common patrimony. To destroy artworks was thus to attack precisely what transcends affiliations; it was to erase what should have been kept safe, rather, as a *testament* to unity and the human spirit. It is no coincidence if, eulogising the cathedral at Reims, Rolland presented it as a 'people' unto itself, to be sure, but also and more generally as 'the harmonious response made by the human race to the riddle of the world':

> A piece of architecture like Rheims is much more than one life; it is a people – whose centuries vibrate like a symphony in this organ of stone. It is their memories of joy, of glory, and of grief; their meditations, ironies, dreams. It is the tree of the race, whose roots plunge to the profoundest depths of its soil, and whose branches stretch with a sublime *èlan* [*sic*] towards the sky. It is still more: its beauty which soars above the struggles of nations is the harmonious response made by the human race to the riddle of the world – this light of the spirit more necessary to souls than that of the sun. (1916: 24–5)

Henceforth, one understands why Rolland attacked writers first of all; he deplored the fact that no 'German' voice was raised with his own after the destruction at Louvain and regretted that the establishment of that 'international of spirit', the vocation of which would have been to protest against the destructions of war, thus seemed impossible. This is because, in reality, 'spirit' gives intellectuals a double responsibility. Perhaps spirit is even defined, ever since the Dreyfus affair, by the double commitment that the latter exemplified: to maintain its independence and to search for the truth. Whence *the trial* [mise à l'épreuve] that war constituted for those same intellectuals! It tested [*éprouvait*] *their* capacity for resistance to the pressures of opinion and the political, moral and religious forces manipulating opinion, thereby verifying their aptitude to maintain the *care for truth* through and against all the seductions of organised violence and fanatic consent to it. This is why writers *ought* not be duped by what the newspapers and those controlling its contents imposed upon them. Writers *ought* to know the source of the news they received, how to identify that notorious 'false news of war' as such[12] and, by that very fact, how to take on the task of diversifying the source of their information. Finally, founded upon the 'search for truth' capable of protecting itself from imposing passions, writers *ought* to investigate contradictory debates for every question linked to the conflict. Such was the writer's first and most imperious duty! And yet, Rolland observed the very opposite: the capitulation of minds, the renunciation of truth, the abdication of culture. His comment in the notorious article titled 'Above the Battle', dated 15 September 1914 and published in the *Journal de Genève* on 22 September, was henceforth irrevocable: 'the unanimity for war' would relate to nothing less than an 'epidemic of homicidal fury'.

> None has resisted it; no high thought has succeeded in keeping out of the reach of this scourge. [. . . A]ll the forces of the spirit, of reason, of faith, of poetry, and of science, all have placed themselves at the disposal of the armies in every state. There is not one amongst the leaders of thought in each country who does not proclaim with conviction that the cause of his people is the cause of God, the cause of liberty and of human progress. (1916: 43)

IV. A Helping Action

Nevertheless, re-establishing truth is not enough. For it is also important to show the belligerents a face other than hatred.

If Rolland's commitment during the war had another exemplary dimension, it was that he was well aware of this necessary displacement. One not only had to fight against heinous representations with the weapons of critique; one also had to act, on the same scale, in order to transform the determined situations that contributed to maintaining or reanimating those representations. Such is the meaning of the action Rolland carried out at the heart of the International Prisoners of War Agency in Geneva, which he vibrantly praised in the essay titled '*Inter arma caritas*'. No longer discourses that deconstructed its mechanisms and inner workings, no longer truth in opposition to lies, indeed, this agency's action opposed to hatred very concrete gestures of support that, in the present case, only sought to collect the necessary information about the warring nations in order to reassure families, whenever possible, about the fate of those who had disappeared, to re-establish contact with prisoners, to receive and deliver letters that enabled reconnecting the interrupted thread of life. Where war eclipses all responsibility for the attention, care and help demanded everywhere and for everyone by the vulnerability – that of the prisoners and their families – and mortality of the other, the Agency restored a minimal meaning to the 'solidarity', if not the 'goodness', that everything about the conflict contributed to breaking. Thus, both vulnerability and mortality occupy a central place in Rolland's correspondence with Zweig. They return like the leitmotiv of a mutual exhortation, beginning and reinforcing the bonds of friendship: 'Do something for the wounded, for the prisoners, for all the victims of this absurd war!' On both sides of the frontline, the two friends would ceaselessly encourage each other, as if it were their responsibility to oppose the partisan representations of war in order to do justice to what transcends the friend-enemy division that constitutes the incommensurable, anonymous and mute destitution of warring peoples:

> Wherever there is war, we must – I have already written this – in my opinion keep quiet, but the wounded, the sick, the prisoners – that is no longer war; that is only misery, the endless, tragic, human misery for the poet to defend. I await word from you about the wounded, about the sick, because if we cannot help others, those that must kill and be killed, if we cannot hold the monstrosity of the deed back a brief hour, then we should nevertheless assist the victims and pursue the helpless with love. [. . .] Years from now, when we think back on this war, you will ask yourself: what did I accomplish back then? And if you make only *one* sick soldier in enemy territory feel a shred of goodness, you can say of yourself: I was not entirely useless during that time! (Rolland and Zweig 2014a: 79–80)

Once again, it was a question of re-establishing the truth as objectively as possible, even as false rumours circulated and nourished both a 'culture of fear' and an 'enemy culture'. Against the suspicions of generalised barbarity and cruelty, it was a question of showing – not only by collecting and transmitting this information but also by delivering letters and packages – that gestures of humanity remained *possible* despite all the violence of war, thereby preserving the little bit of confidence in the future necessary to make each shred of saved or restored humanity the antidote for hatred.[13] Such is the symbolic force that Rolland recognised in the Agency's actions. Wherever war consecrated negative passions' grip on politics, the encouragement and promotion of these gestures of humanity – gestures of peace that came to the aid of prisoners as well as all victims of war, whether military or, above all, civilian – painstakingly outlined the place to address a minimal *moral* injunction to politics. For, if it is true that singular initiatives and energies were most often at stake, like those of Dr Ferrière, who sought to draw up 'a list of the missing', 'to inspire confidence in their anxious friends', 'to discover the place of internment' and, finally, 'to re-establish communications between relations and friends' (Rolland 1916: 89), these initiatives and energies had to be undertaken within the framework of the institutions that those animating them strove to impose upon warring governments as legitimate interlocutors.

Step by step, peace works no differently in the trial of hatred. Everything that contradicts and opposes its cries, the barking newspapers and the background vociferations that Louis Guilloux would describe so well in *Sang noir* [*Black Blood*], all those words, gestures and acts of humanity earn a chance. From the autumn of 1914 on, four years before the armistice was signed, the long delays for which no one could have been foreseen, Rolland showed in advance his care for the conditions that would have to prepare a 'just peace' during the war. This peace, as he already foresaw, could not be achieved without reforming 'public European opinion' in its entirety. Yet, the more one allowed the venom of hatred to spread, the more this reformation would be compromised from the outset, and the less the conquerors and the conquered – blinded by accumulated resentments – could agree upon its conditions. The conquerors, once again, would make peace a revenge that they would take for justice, and the conquered would live it as a humiliation. This is why, as Rolland writes to Frederik van Eeden on 12 January 1915, no task was more urgent than gathering, by the 'intimate and permanent bonds' that give them a 'united strength' (Rolland 1916: 137–8, translation modified), the voices throughout Europe who knew it was necessary to avoid minimising the disastrous traces that a heinous rhetoric deposited in consciousnesses, the murderous ferment of future catastrophes. Dreading the possibility that the factory of hatred had already produced something *irreparable*, he called upon the warring nations to preserve what could still be preserved for the future. On 17 November 1914, Rolland responded with these few words to those who accused him of treason; they must be heard as a warning on the threshold of a century that will have had hardly any ears for hearing it:

> You will have to re-establish supportable and humane relations: so set to work in such a manner as not to make them impossible! Do not break down all the bridges, since it will ever be necessary to cross the river. Do not destroy the future. A good open, clean wound will heal; but do not poison it. Let us be on our guard against hatred. If we prepare for war in peace according to the wisdom of nations, we should also prepare for peace in war. (1916: 105)

Notes

1 As the next chapter makes clear, this formulation – *l'indépendance de l'espirit* – refers to Rolland. In French, *esprit* means both 'mind' and 'spirit'. Consistent with available translations of Rolland's work, we translate *esprit* as 'spirit' when Rolland describes a cultural identification threatened by the destruction of war, as 'mind' when he describes the mental effects of warmongering and hawkish propaganda. This division, of course, is not always clear in the French. – Translators

2 See Part I, 'The Experience of Violence'.

3 See Part II, Chapter 4, 'The "Snares of Identity"'.

4 See Part II, Chapter 3, 'Non-violence and Revolution', p. 118 ff.

5 As Zweig announces to Rolland and, in turn, the editor to readers of the French edition of the *Correspondance* (Rolland and Zweig 2014a: 77 and 24), Zweig wrote to Rolland in German during the war because letters were subject to censorship by Austrian authorities. While we give pagination for the French edition here and below, we have translated Zweig's letters directly from Zweig's German in *Von Welt zu Welt* (Rolland and Zweig 2014b). – Translators

6 See Part II, Chapter 3, 'Non-violence and Revolution', p. 118 ff.

7 This is the step that would lead the author of *Above the Battle* to take an interest in Gandhi's work and thought after the war, dedicating an essay to him and maintaining regular correspondence with him. See Part II, Chapter 3, p. 118 ff.

8 See Part II, Chapter 3, p. 129 ff.

9 It is from this perspective that, in 1919, Rolland would publish another collection, entitled *Les Précurseurs*, which he would later add to the articles comprising *Above the Battle* in a single volume entitled *L'Esprit libre* [*The Free Spirit* or *Mind*].

10 Cf. Rolland, *Above the Battle*: 'You, my German friends – for those of you who were my friends in the past remain my friends in spite of fanatical demands from both sides that we should break off all relations – know how much I love the Germany of the past, and all that I owe to it. Not less than you, yourselves, I am the son of Beethoven, of Leibniz, and of Goethe. But what do I owe to the Germany of today, or what does Europe owe to it?' (1916: 58).

11 Romain Rolland, *Les Allemands destructeurs* (1915). I thank Jean-Yves Le Corre for having pulled this precious volume for me from his library.

12 Marc Bloch, 'Reflections of a Historian on the False News of War' (2013). See also the historian's 'Souvenirs de guerre' – as well as his photographs – in Bloch, *L'Histoire, la guerre, la resistance* (2006).

13 'This renewal of intercourse between a prisoner and his family is not the only beneficial result of our organization [the International Prisoners of War Agency]. Its peaceful work, its impartial knowledge of the actual facts in the belligerent countries, contribute to modify the hatred which wild stories have exasperated, and to reveal what remains of humanity in the most envenomed enemy' (Rolland 1916: 84).

3

Non-violence and Revolution

If I am going to maintain, as I did in Part I, the necessity of opposing violence and hatred, articulated together, with a principle of non-violence, then two objections immediately present themselves: complacency and weakness. The first, already mentioned, consists in maintaining that, by refusing all violence, one necessarily plays into the hands of those with whom one refuses to engage in armed combat, which amounts to the same thing as accepting violence, condoning it or putting up with it. On this account, even indifference or neutrality would be impossible. Like it or not, it would be naïve to think one could escape violence. Violence would be the very substance of history; it would merge with the real, forcing everyone to choose the attitude to adopt in the face of violences, whether they adapt to them, accept and at the same time endure them or decide to oppose and aim to suppress them, even at the cost of violence itself. As far as the objection of weakness is concerned, it complements the former objection. Here, the argument rests on the idea that, in the face of intrinsically violent systems of oppression (totalitarian systems, authoritarian regimes, colonial imperialism, State racism), the non-violence that refrains from bearing arms would remain ineffective and would have no chance of reversing the course of history. Resistance to oppression would thus require that some concessions be made to violence, unless one takes refuge in silent opposition like a *belle âme* or a good conscience refusing to dirty its hands. It is an understatement to say that these objections haunted twentieth-century literature and philosophy. In the name of a promised freedom and justice, they authorised all the commitments to and support for the most bloodthirsty political hawkishness and the most murderous revolutions.

Both objections nevertheless come up against a major counterword and a major counterexample that return recurrently in the controversies provoked by the support for such a form of terror, such terrorist action, in the name of revolution and under the pretext that it needs such terror or terrorist action to progress. Aiming at overthrowing the British domination in India, Gandhi's thought and non-violent action embody this alternative. They imposed their force of conviction upon every continent throughout the last century. On the first battlegrounds for Gandhi's thought and action in South Africa, Gandhi was a source of major inspiration for Nelson Mandela and the other leaders of the African National Congress (ANC). In the United States, Martin Luther King, Jr adhered to Gandhi's principles when organising the struggle for civil rights. Finally, in Europe, Romain Rolland himself introduced Gandhi's thought in the years following the so-uncertain and so-menacing return to peace at the end of the First World War. What an astonishing relation that will link these two men together! Their tense correspondence and their meeting, neither free from misunderstandings, are exemplary in more than one manner. They bear witness foremost to the recent attention paid to India by European intellectuals, who are attuned as much to its spiritual traditions as to its political fight to attain independence. The long story of their support for the struggles of decolonisation begins. Yet, because the author of *Above the Battle* began to turn his gaze toward the Soviet Union at the end of the 1920s, this story is equally indicative of the tension already highlighted between non-violence and revolution. In this light, these tensions speak to us today. This is thus the prism though which I will study their relationship in the pages that follow.

I. The Meeting with Gandhi

Peace! It is an understatement to say that none of the conditions for peace will have satisfied Rolland, who ceaselessly denounced the Treaty of Versailles. In 1934, when he assembles what he calls his 'wartime writings', he unflinchingly puts forth a panoramic statement in the foreword: 'Peace will not ease the mind. The harshest fights remained to be waged' (Rolland 1935: ix). The man who confesses to having entered politics in August 1914 became twenty years later the 'voice of peace', if not the very incarnation of European pacifism, as evidenced by the important correspondence he tirelessly maintains with men and women all around the world whose commitment to peace associates them with various pacifist movements alarmed by the risk of a new war.

But the texts from the autumn and winter of 1914 are not only marked by the 'entry into politics'. As was seen in the preceding chapter, the trial of hatred that these texts confront in more than one way simultaneously gives them the dimension of moral resistance. Bolstered by an undeniable 'courage for truth', they recall on each page the need for writers who managed to preserve the 'independence of the mind' to address a 'moral injunction', driven by the hope for a just peace, to rulers blinded by the interests of war. A wasted effort, for Europe – during the fifteen years that separate the armistice of 11 November 1918 and Hitler's rise to power on 30 January 1933 – proved no less hateful than it was in 1914, to say nothing of the fifteen years that would follow. For Rolland, however, two major events occurred in the meantime that radically transformed the theoretical and practical facts of the problem: on the one hand, the October Revolution and the arrival of the Soviet Union on the international scene as the fatherland of the Revolution; on the other hand, the non-violent revolution started by Gandhi in South Africa and continued in India against the colonial domination of the British Empire. On the one hand, then, the Bolshevik Revolution seems to open new horizons despite the bloody events that accompany it (the civil war, the first manifestations of terror) in the name of political imperatives that hardly shy away from casualties; on the other, 'non-violence' draws the force of its conviction and its political effects from a spirituality derived from elsewhere, foreign to Western compromises. These two sources of inspiration doubtlessly create the singularity of Rolland, who tries to unite them in a collection of articles under the suggestive title *Par la révolution la paix* (*Peace Through Revolution*) (1937). Yet, to what degree were they compatible?[1] Can these two requirements be upheld together simultaneously, or must one ineluctably supersede the other, at the risk of resignation or the betrayal of convictions that this entails?

The meeting between Rolland and Gandhi was not straightforward. It first took time to fall into place; before the two men were finally able to meet in Switzerland in December 1931, Gandhi had pushed back his voyage to Europe several times, sometimes for health reasons, at other times for political reasons relating to the situation in India, to his imprisonment, to young protestors. It was also complicated on an intellectual level – and it is not certain that their meeting dissipated the misunderstanding. Despite a few reservations with regard to his nationalism and traditionalism, with immense admiration for the work he had accomplished in South Africa between 1883 and 1914 and the battle he had led in India since then, in 1924 Rolland took the initiative of sending Gandhi the monograph he had devoted to him. Once again, hatred constituted the guiding thread; the white population's xenophobia toward Asiatic immigrants, institutionalised racism and systematic persecutions described the trial of hatred ('they were burdened with overwhelming taxes and subjected to the most "humiliating" police ordinances and outrages of all sorts, ranging from the looting and destruction of shops and property to lynching, all under the cover of "white" civilisation' [Rolland 1948: 9]). Rolland recalls that – often imprisoned for having peacefully organised the non-participation of Indians in public service, condemned to forced labour, beaten by furious crowds – Gandhi himself experienced this hatred. Nothing, however, caused him to fold and, after a struggle that lasted nearly twenty years, he managed to establish his non-violent movement throughout the entire country. On the eve of the First World War, this non-violent movement had extended from Transvaal to Natal, punctuated by interminable strikes, inflamed meetings and a long march. The ending is well known: the British government was finally forced to concede.

By taking an interest in Gandhi's work, therefore, Rolland intended to bring Europe and its violence to trial once again, this time in their colonial dimension. What imperial governments made those they dominated endure, the way they exploited them and enlisted them in war without – despite all their promises – granting them the slightest independence in return, resembled what the European nations had inflicted upon each other during the four years of conflict: a succession of endless murders that occurred for no reason other than the material interests they served. The battles waged by Gandhi in this sense constituted a supplementary revelation of the criminal waywardness of European civilisation. And one can imagine that the author of *Above the Battle* was not unhappy to have found the following phrase from Gandhi's pen, which Rolland could undoubtedly have countersigned:

> The last war has shown as nothing else has the Satanic nature of the civilisation that dominates Europe today. Every canon of public morality has been broken by the victors in the name of virtue. No lie has been considered too foul to be uttered. The motive behind every crime is not religious or spiritual, but grossly material. (Rolland 1948: 37)

The strategy of Rolland's monograph thus becomes clear. Since, far from Europe, the exploited and maltreated non-European populations – in whom Rolland, a contemporary of the constitution of colonial empires, had shown little interest until then – were also subjected to a trial of hatred, all the more violent and murderous once they claimed their emancipation, what served as a lesson was, first of all, Gandhi's response, namely, the oppositional strength represented by non-violence, the wager that the strength of the soul, freed from fear and raised against the will of the mainstream, could 'defy the whole might of an unjust empire and lay the foundation for that empire's fall' (Rolland 1948: 49). Since no force had so far succeeded in preventing either the European wars or, less still, the overwhelming triumph of the moneyed powers that profited from them, one could not exclude the potential need to invent another form of opposition or the possibility that the religion of non-violence might offer an example if one recalls that, as Gandhi wrote, it applies to everyone in common and that the soul it wins over could defy 'the physical combination of a whole world' (Rolland 1948: 50).

Yet, can India serve as an example to cure Europe of its violence? Will one find the solution to the European problem by turning one's eyes and thoughts away from criminal Europe? In other words, can the non-violence that demonstrated its efficacy elsewhere constitute the privileged path of 'European pacifism', since it was so profoundly suffused with Hindu spirituality? When Rolland wrote his book, he still knew little about India and his guesswork was frequent. His enthusiasm was nevertheless proportionate to his expectations! He hoped Gandhi could play the role of spiritual guide for 'European pacifism', a role that he was undoubtedly not ready to assume entirely. Moreover, it is not trivial that the first controversy that put the two men at odds with each other concerned Gandhi's engagement in the First World War and his justification of it.[2] Did the non-violence advocated by Gandhi imply a radical pacifism and the absolute refusal of all war? In an anxious letter dated 16 April 1928, which carried to the extremes the writer's responsibility toward future generations, a letter once again encouraging him to come to Europe, Rolland called upon Gandhi to clarify his position on this point. I must cite it at length, for the beginnings of a doubt already appear, which the subsequent exchanges would confirm. The question arose in the following terms: faced with the rise of new perils that would give hatred the face of fascism, xeno-phobia and anti-Semitism, would it still be possible to consider as the most appropriate measure – not only political but also moral – the self-sacrifice demanded by the refusal of violence, or was it already necessary to look *elsewhere* for new and more effective weapons to face the coming catastrophes?

[I]t is indispensable that you should give an absolutely clear, precise and definitive formulation to the listening world of your doctrine, your faith, on the matter of war and non-acceptance.

We are both of us fairly old and of suspect health; we may disappear any day. It is important that we should leave a precise testament to the youth of the world which it can use as a rule of conduct, for it will have a terrible burden to bear in the coming half-century. I see fearful trials building up in front of them. It no longer seems to me a matter of doubt that there is in preparation an era of destruction, an age of global wars beside which all those of the past will seem only children's games, of chemical warfare which will annihilate whole populations. What moral armour are we offering to those who will have to face up to the monster which we shall not live to see? What immediate answer to the riddle of the murderous Sphinx, who will not wait? What marching orders? [. . .]

The young men of Europe are aware of the trials awaiting them. They don't want to be duped about the imminence of the danger, which too many 'pacifists' are trying not to see and to put out of their minds. They want to look it clearly in the face, and they ask: 'To what extent is it reasonable, to what extent is it human, not to accept? Must the sacrifice be total, absolute, without exception, without any consideration either for ourselves or for the things which surround us and depend on us? And in all honesty to ourselves, can we be sure that this total sacrifice will diminish the sum total of future human sufferings – or does it not risk handing over man's destiny to a barbarity without counterweight?' (Rolland and Gandhi 1976: 112–13)

This letter went unanswered, and Gandhi postponed his trip to Europe for two more years. In the meantime, his arrest and imprisonment had raised a vast protest movement in Europe. This is why, in the letters he continued to address to Gandhi, Rolland reaffirmed his conviction concerning Gandhi's moral exemplarity for *all of humanity*, even though, Rolland wrote to him, violence around the world was 'on the point of bursting the last barriers restraining it' (Rolland and Gandhi 1976: 147). However, the task for the Europeans was becoming more acute. The author of *Above the Battle* was now certain: there was no possible hope of escaping a new war without the prospect of completely renovating the social order within the framework of a new organisation of labour that would put an end to the capitalist system of domination and exploitation. The question was thus whether non-violence and 'love' would be powerful enough to accomplish the Revolution that such a renovation implied, so that this Revolution could counter what Rolland called, once again, the 'blind forces of hatred' (Rolland and Gandhi 1976: 148), or whether the individuals who proclaimed non-violence (the non-resistants) were already too isolated and too unorganised militarily to impose such a reversal. The objection was classic. It was the one Max Scheler had opposed a few years earlier to what he called 'heroic pacifism' in *The Idea of Peace and Pacifism* (1927). How, then, should the promised revolution be envisioned? Could the major movement in India communicate, in one way or another, with Europe? Here again, Rolland's questions went unanswered, as if the fate of Europe, with the looming wars, was not Gandhi's concern.

And then, on 6 December 1931, the meeting finally took place. And Rolland offered Gandhi on the first day (which was for the latter a 'silence day') a long exposé on the moral and social state of continental Europe and the perspectives opened by the proletarian revolution. The author of *Jean-Christophe* gives a precise account of it in his journal, dated 31 December 1931. What did Rolland discuss with his distinguished guest? First, democracies handed over to the power of money, and then the vital necessity no longer only of opposing war, in its own right, but also of blocking the route toward monstrous capitalism, described as 'a cancer gnawing at the West and America, and seeking to eat away the rest of the world' (Rolland and Gandhi 1976: 168), by drawing support from what seemed to him to constitute the only effective force of non-resistance, the only one likely to stand against the alliance of fascism and capitalism: the workers' proletariat. Then Rolland came to the question that, though presented as a simple tactical problem, had considerable scope in another way. This question will serve as the guiding thread of this chapter, but it is on the horizon of most of the chapters comprising this book. What are the means to attain a just and necessary order that would be, in the same stroke, free from all ferment of violence?

> By what means can it be achieved, non-violent or violent? The best means will be the one that actually obtains the just order; so is non-violence capable of it? Yes, if applied in the absolute and uncompromising spirit represented by you (Gandhi) in India. But you would not be able to apply it if there were not to be found in India an environment ready to receive it, that of a religious people used to Ahimsa for centuries. In Europe there is nothing like this. (Rolland and Gandhi 1976: 169)

Violence or non-violence? The question deserved to be posed, but in fact Rolland already had the answer. For what happened after the exchange – and one must imagine Gandhi in profile, seated in the large swivel office chair, legs crossed beneath him, wrapped in his burnous, attentive and collected, immersed without a word because of his 'silence day', facing his loquacious and demonstrative interlocutor – was a vibrant plea in favour of the USSR and the means the new power needed to implement to defend itself against 'imperial aggressions'. The phrases that follow in the story, indeed, leave no doubt about his choice. The author of *Above the Battle* calls for the 'self-sacrifice' of the Western proletarian masses, which is to say, their renunciation of non-violence by accepting all means, including the most murderous, necessary for the revolution to reach its goals (Rolland and Gandhi 1976: 170).

At the end of a monologue that had lasted nearly an hour and a half, in the shape of murderous consent, the conclusion delivered by the great voice of European pacifism to the apostle of non-violence was without appeal – and the lesson it claims to give, terrible. It justified violence as a historical necessity, provided that the movement of history (the advent of a just and necessary order) imposed it and *not the hatred* of those upon whom violence was exercised. Since the Soviet Union embodied this hope, none of the judgements condemning the murder legalised and imposed by war could legitimately assess the violences imposed by the revolution.

A page was thus opened that was not soon to turn, and whose signatories – poets, writers, philosophers who would yield to the justification of murder for similar reasons – were far from being limited. Many will be Rolland's companions in the years that follow. In a few sentences (addressed to such an interlocutor!), Rolland gave violence its due. Here, in veiled terms, fifteen years after the texts that had denounced the war, he declared himself ready to recognise that, for exclusively political reasons, certain forms of violence were necessary *as long as they occurred without hatred*, which is to say, as long as nothing subjective, idiosyncratic or even pathological were done on its account and that the reasons justifying it were purely objective. Violence became the object of a rational calculation and ceased to be the object of a principled refusal! Ultimately, a strict delineation of morality and politics began to form, as if any invocation of a moral ideal and its interior force erected against history was wasted effort in the urgency of necessary combats. Listen one last time to the story Rolland tells of his 'political lesson'. Rarely will anyone have so clearly idealised Soviet justice, minimised repression, beatified Lenin's action. Words are never harmless, and those Rolland uses to address Gandhi show glimmers of a new fascination with the powers of this unusual State violence: 'crush' and 'destroy' recalcitrant 'creatures'.

> [A]ction must be as efficient and as prompt as possible. If obstacles are placed in the way, human or otherwise, they must be crushed, without pits and without anger. I want to show Gandhi the moral neutrality which characterises Soviet justice: it is never, in principle, meant to be vengeance, but aims to destroy creatures harmful to the community. If such a person ceases to be dangerous, whatever his crime, justice does not take vengeance on him or kill him; it is content to render him harmless and, if possible, it gives him the means of making himself useful. Lenin had no personal hatred, and he had a passionate desire for the good of humanity. He served humanity by the means he considered most effective and energetic. (Rolland and Gandhi 1976: 171)

Gandhi was hardly mistaken, and the next day when he returned to the long monologue from the day before, of which he had forgotten nothing, it was to oppose his host with two

127

'beliefs': his profound conviction concerning the universal application of the principle of non-violence and his certitude that the 'faith' placed by Rolland in the historic mission of the Soviet Union was uncertain and relative (1976: 180). On the one hand, he emphasised, non-violence – the demands of which, as he will recall a few days later, are radical – remained for him the object of an unshakeable *faith*, and its scope was not limited to a determined cultural, spiritual or religious sphere. This is why, in his eyes, only such a principle could 'save Europe', which otherwise would run headlong toward perdition (it is December 1931, fifteen months before Hitler takes power), if only a man, who had not yet appeared, knew how to incarnate it (1976: 180). At stake, he specified, was an inner conviction that defied the laws of history and the order of the world and for which it had no force other than a *moral force*. On the other hand, the hopes and the 'faith' – for it is indeed, here as well, a question of belief – that some, like Rolland, placed in the USSR had no guarantee, to Gandhi's mind, other than the relative and contestable success procured by the use of force and violence. The system born of revolution, explains Gandhi with a rare lucidity, remains for him an enigma, the object of mistrust and worry, for it is held up only by its original, constitutive violence, from which it has not managed to escape and, as a result, has no example to offer the rest of the world other than that of intolerance and terror. This is why it represents a 'challenge to non-violence' (1976: 180).[3]

The two men did not go much further. When they saw each other that evening, Rolland had the feeling that 'Gandhi's way is so clearly marked out before him' (1976: 192), so distinct from his own, that they had very little to discuss together: 'But what do we have to say to each other? – beyond what we did say on the first day, taking his hands in mine, looking at each other

face to face and smiling, while he laughs his jerky little laugh'
(1976: 193).

II. Peace Through Revolution

The USSR: a 'challenge to non-violence'! It is an understatement to say that Rolland was one of the first to take up this
challenge. For, as radical as it seems, the position he defends
in his interviews with Gandhi results from a long process and
a few ruptures. If he indeed welcomed the October Revolution from the beginning, he was also the first to denounce its
commandeerings (the confiscation of freedoms, the enslavement
of thought, the bloody repressions, the first manifestations of
terror) and all the forms of consent for which these facts could
call. Two principles then seemed indissociable for him to orient
his judgement and to determine the limits of his commitment
and the backing he was ready to contribute to the revolution:
the principled refusal of all violence and the unwavering attachment to what he had strongly defended during the First World
War, to the point of drafting in spring 1919 a 'Declaration on
the Independence of the Mind' in the form of a manifesto. Thus,
he wrote to Pierre Jean Jouve in May 1917:

> We are told that sooner or later we will come to a violent revo-
> lution. For my part, I respond: 'never'. All violence repulses
> me, that of the revolutionaries as much as that of capitalist and
> military imperialisms. These are all imperialisms (*imperare* – the
> squashing of freedom). If the world cannot do without violence,
> my role, at least in the world, is not to come to terms with it but
> to represent another and contrary principle, which would serve
> as a counterweight. (Jouve 1920: 152)

And it must be said that, for at least ten years, in a context marked by antifascist struggles, his thought effectively attempted to inscribe such a counterweight in the debates, and the willingness to give this counterweight peaceful 'weapons', to associate it with a major 'moral idea' capable of supporting it, brought him to Gandhi. His desire to reconcile the two forms of revolutionary action – the one taken by the October Revolution, the other by the non-resistance or non-violence embodied by Gandhi, reaffirmed in the prologue to *Quinze ans de combat* [*Fifteen Years of Struggle*] – will have had no other meaning. The principled refusal of violence thus appears, for many years still, as the guarantor and *sine qua non* of a 'moral freedom' that preserves the independence of the mind by keeping away from all political parties, refusing to submit blindly to their bloody slogans, to their murderous demand for an unconditional support of the means as much as the ends, in short, to their imperative demand for unyielding support. For, if it was one thing to recognise the historical necessity of the revolution by remaining attentive to the hopes it represented and choosing a side accordingly, it was another thing to sacrifice this independence by renouncing, from fear of appearing reactionary, all judgement and, if need be, condemnation of authoritarian excesses and murderous deviations. From this perspective, it is not trivial that, responding to a letter from Guilbeaux inviting him to side with the Bolsheviks not long after the October Revolution, Rolland unhesitatingly clarified that, although Bolshevism had accomplished 'a necessary work in the material domain', the revolution remained in his eyes '*insufficient in the domain of the mind*', since it trampled on the 'moral freedom' that 'gave life its only value' (Rolland 1992: 33).

Why talk about 'moral freedom' here? Because if it was true that thinkers, artists, scholars have during all these years 'added an incalculable quantity of envenomed hate to the plague which devours the flesh and the spirit of Europe', as the 'Declaration of the Independence of the Mind' – signed by a large number of European writers at Rolland's initiative – recalls, if it was true that 'in the arsenal of their knowledge, their memory, their imagination, they have sought reasons for hatred, reasons old and new, reasons historical, scientific, logical, and poetical' (Rolland 1920b: 209), then the least one could expect from a revolution intended to open a new era was that it would be not only a *material revolution* that would reverse the order of dominations, but also a *moral and spiritual* revolution that would liberate the people from violence and free them from hatred. One hoped for an upheaval, a reversal of consciousness that would not reproduce on the internal scene *another war* that, by using the same procedures, would be guilty of the same exactions and the same violations in the same enslavement. Indeed, in 1919 Rolland observed that the 'mind' had emerged damaged by war and that thought had fallen, compromised by 'unworthy alliances' and 'veiled slaveries', and nothing was more urgent than exiting this state, at the price of a change of hearts and minds (1920b: 209). Thus, the pacifist, radically non-violent ambition of his Declaration was considerable, and he thought that the only means of escaping a future war, if that was still possible, was to stay the course:

Mind is no one's servitor. It is we who are the servitors of mind. We have no other master. We exist to bear its light, to defend its light, to rally round it all the strayed sheep of mankind. Our role, our duty, is to be a centre of stability, to point out the pole star, amid the whirlwind of passions in the night. Among these passions of pride and mutual destruction, we make no choice; we reject them all. Truth only do we honour; truth that is free, frontierless, limitless; truth that knows nought of the prejudices of race or caste. Not that we lack interest in humanity. For humanity we work, but for humanity as a whole. We know nothing of peoples. We know the People, unique and universal; the People which suffers, which struggles, which falls and rises to its feet once more, and which continues to advance along the rough road drenched with its sweat and its blood; the People, all men, all alike our brothers. In order that they may, like ourselves, realise this brotherhood, we raise above their blind struggles the Ark of the Covenant – Mind which is free, one and manifold, eternal. (Rolland 1920b: 209)

One can easily understand why Rolland might have dreamt, like so many others, that the October Revolution would carry the hope of this 'universal people', but one also understands why, in fact, nothing was more difficult to grant than the international of spirit proclaimed by the 'Declaration' and the increasingly rigid framework of proletarian internationalism. Most surprising is the belatedness with which he rallied to this idea, since there were no longer any doubts about the nature of the Soviet regime. Throughout the 1920s, by contrast, all of his efforts consisted in maintaining the often tenuous thread distinguishing the vocation of the 'Declaration' that still stood 'above the battle and parties' and the multiple attempts at politically recuperating his commitment, which his correspondence tirelessly makes evident. As he wrote to Jean-Richard Bloch on 30 January 1920, he had no illusion about how, no less than any other regime, the Soviet regime hindered – if not constrained or repressed – the 'search for truth': 'Clemenceau oppresses it, Lenin oppresses it, every State founded on majoritarian supremacy oppresses it, and [. . .] on minority dictatorship, even more. Social struggle is one thing; the battles of the mind are another' (Rolland and Bloch 2019: 72).

This is why, despite much pressure, he will have initially refused, in the name of a 'vital need for freedom', to offer the slightest backing to what seemed to him to ridicule the most elementary recognition – all the forms of violence characterising what he did not hesitate to call 'communist dictatorship': State reason, militarism, police dictatorship. As he wrote to Henri Barbusse, with whom he was at odds due to a difficult controversy, free thought – which means, if we believe the 'Declaration', *thought free from hatred* – took no orders: not from Paris, not from Rome, not from Moscow.

Yet, if it is true that there was less and less doubt about the violence constituting the Soviet regime, it was no longer possible to ignore the fascist threats weighing upon Europe either. Should one then refrain from condemning the fascists without also associating the Soviets with them, as an uncompromising and independent mind would have demanded? Or, by giving due to the urgency of the struggles against fascism and the calculation of the forces they involved, should one reaffirm – *over and against all reservations* – an unconditional faith in the USSR so as to strengthen the antifascist side? Did the strategy of the radical opposition to European fascisms demand silence regarding the crimes of which the Soviet regime was guilty? In the late 1920s, each time Rolland was asked to take a stand against fascism, he found himself in this dilemma. He resisted at first . . . and then finally conceded. Asked by Barbusse to sign, along with Einstein, a 'call to free thinkers' to assemble a committee 'intended to fight against the wave of barbarous fascism', he at first expressed reservations about the text, regretting that the condemnation was unilateral. If one wanted to denounce attacks against freedom, one should do so without exception and without concession to any form of dictatorship whatsoever!

'I am against fascism and I am against dictatorial bolshevism. I tolerate no equivocation on this point', he wrote to Barbusse on 10 February 1927 (Rolland 1992: 45). Rolland insisted all the more since he pushed the parallel between the forms of violence shared by Bolshevism and fascism rather far, going as far as to consider (and write in a later letter) that the cult of violence practised by the former, at bottom, engendered the latter in turn. Nevertheless, the call appeared, signed with his name, without the reservations and amendments he suggested. He explained himself in a letter to Stefan Zweig dated 19 March of that same year. One must recall this letter, since it explains the machinations in which, almost in spite of himself, the author of *Above the Battle* now found himself caught: the machinations that constituted, for him and a few others, the new configuration (ideological and political, estranged from any morality) of *the test of violence*:

> In truth, I had protested against the narrow protest, which I wanted to extend to condemn all Terrors, all violence, and the text was published with my additions abusively truncated. But the need to speak out against fascism and in support of the victims of this black abject terror is so urgent that I cannot back away from the responsibility. And all the less since such a role implies danger. – You are good, you and Romain, for saying that the communists are harming the just cause and that it would be better for honest, reasonable and moderate people to support this cause! I think so, too. But where and when have we seen honest, reasonable and moderate people take the initiative of dangerous action against armed violence? And since they will always be silent, we are forced to ally ourselves (for a time, for a specific goal) with the only ones who dare to act and to speak. (Rolland and Zweig 2014a: 651–2)

In fact, the die had been cast for some time, and Rolland heeded less and less the critiques, protests, cries and alarming tales that reached him, like those of Panaït Istrati, who, returning from a long trip to the USSR, had just published an implacable indictment that Rolland would not accept: *Vers l'autre flame. Après seize mois dans l'URSS* [*Toward Another Flame: After Sixteen Months in the USSR*]. His choices were made. Beyond the biographical considerations linked to Marie Koudacheva's appearance in his life (she would become his second spouse in 1934), a major factor henceforth intervened in his choice increasingly to parenthesise – that is, to refrain from expressing publicly and for a long time – all moral considerations and to recognise a certain 'legitimacy' to the State violence that continued to increase as Stalin extended his hold over all State apparatuses: history, the laws of history. This is the decisive turn! Having until then placed himself in a privileged way upon the plane of morality, its strength and the *faith* that makes it possible, Rolland began to invoke, like so many others after him, the meaning and necessity of history. One letter attempting to account for this contradiction is particularly indicative in this sense. It was addressed to Armin Wegner on 15 January 1930. Then focused on writing his last major novel, *The Enchanted Soul*, Rolland adopts in that letter what he calls his 'cosmic point of view': the conjunction in himself and in all consciousness of two Selves (the Self of an individual and that of everyone), two in one, the difficult – if not impossible – harmony of which would constitute the problem posed to every life (Rolland 1967: 290). The first comes from one's own knowledge and culture, which have their own laws; it is indissociable from the creative impetus proper to each life. The second is that which identifies this singular Self, jealous of its singularity, with the movement of history that

Rolland compares alternately to a marching army and to an ocean with its 'ebbs and flows and waves'. The Self thus searches for harmony, haunted by the fear of missing out, of remaining on the sidelines of history or in withdrawal, of suffering collective life rather than understanding and participating in it. It must be in unison at all costs. But nothing goes without saying, for most often the agreement between these two Selves constitutes a trial [*épreuve*], should neither of the two be ready to sacrifice itself to the other. However, such a sacrifice always ends up happening. This is what Rolland confesses, at the risk of betraying his initial commitments. Faced with rising perils, there would be less and less room for the 'Self of an individual' that he had nevertheless so relentlessly defended in the figure of Clérambault.[4] He would get carried away in the 'Self of everyone' – the very Self of which he had nevertheless learned to remain wary, convinced since the summer of 1914 that it implied abdicating 'the independence of mind' that was nevertheless vital to preserve.

> I know and see clearly that, in the immense tide of present days, it [the Russian Revolution] is the powerful first line of a marching wave on the attack. It is brutal, and it destroys in its path beings I like and ideas and values I venerate. But it is the very march of the Cosmos, of the eternal Self – which will break it after having used it to reach the next stage. (Rolland 1967: 290)

But there was more. This 'march of the Cosmos' imposed a new requirement: putting its ideas and convictions to the test of what, in the introduction to *Par la révolution la paix*, Rolland calls the 'incessant movement of reality's march' (Rolland 1937: 7). The risk, he wrote, was (and still is) remaining prisoner to an 'ideology maladapted to reality', which no longer held (which no longer holds) except by the 'force of the inertia inherent in the dead weight of the past that the mind drags behind it, or of the ruse in not seeing what would compel it to a new effort to extricate itself' (1937: 8).[5] And the risk was also refusing to admit that the words used to think the real, the formulations and the slogans that had been made into combat weapons, had been recovered and overused by the forces most hostile to one's own convictions, rendering them useless, even turning them against themselves. It was one thing, in 1914, to lash out at the ideology of the fatherland by calling for a 'just peace'; it was another thing, in the 1930s, to oppose the forces that had contributed to making this very same peace a 'pirated' peace, the 'false peace of industrial and military imperialisms' that were also 'lying and pestilent'. These formidable and, indeed, powerfully armed forces made necessary something other than past words: another commitment and another action that would take the measure of what was brewing. For heralded henceforth (Rolland had a premonitory certainty) was a cataclysm of such magnitude that any denunciation of it would have no meaning and no effect unless it was inscribed in the framework of a collective movement sustained by the only power in his eyes capable of opposing it: the Soviet Union. This is the meaning of all the declarations he proliferates over the course of the year in 1932 in view of the World Congress Against War and Fascism in Amsterdam and barely a year after the meeting with Gandhi. So, on 1 May: 'War is coming. War is coming from all sides. It threatens all populations. It may break out tomorrow' (1937: 29). And on 10 June: 'We are living under the sword of suspended war. This is the state of peace that the provocative treaties of 1919 gave us' (1937: 31).

Confronted with such threats, who could believe that 'non-violence', the 'independence of the mind' and above all

the choice of holding oneself 'above the battle' still constituted effective weapons? Who could believe that, by sticking
to one's words and one's individual intellectual positions, one
would not be duped by warmongers again? These words had
their legitimacy, but they remained marked by the seal of an
ambiguous individualism, a wilful isolation that fragmented the
forces necessary to fight against the war that the alliance between
fascism and capitalism was preparing, to the point (here is the
most terrible part) of not disturbing 'domination – secret or
dispersed – by the big capital of industries and banks interested
in the slaughter', of accommodating these industries and banks,
if not even, in the final analysis, of serving them.

> Could we have foreseen (one must always foresee) that they
> would come to pillage us even when entrenched in our 'in-
> dependence of the mind', in 'peace', in 'universalism', even in
> 'non-violence' and, shamefully distorted, turn the phantoms of
> our grand words against us?
>   But this is precisely because we no longer need grand words.
> The first task is to dethrone them so that they fall into rank.
> The measure of an idea is taken with the yardstick of action.
> (Rolland 1937: 9)

It is thus not surprising that, all through the years preceding the
Second World War, texts attesting to an almost unconditional
support for the USSR followed one after another despite all the
warning signs – as if all 'moral' scruples had to be discarded in
the name of the political urgency called for by the only law of
history that made any sense: the law that described the struggle
between the 'European reaction' and the progressive revolution,
for which the Soviet regime alone was on par to inspire hope.
Which amounts to saying that it was no longer possible to remain

'above' the battle, foreign to any fatherland. On the contrary, one urgently had to descend 'into the battle' so as to take part in the 'fight organised against all the oppressive forces of the past to construct a new world, the Union of Soviet Socialist Republics of human Labour' (Rolland 1937: 15). To throw oneself 'into the battle' could have no other vocation than bringing to light and defending the universal dimension of the path traced by this new 'international Fatherland'. The loop is thus closed for the man, even before meeting Gandhi, who had written in the 1930s:

> I in no way accept a Europe that, without a second thought, refuses to accept the USSR. For, whatever its errors (errors easily explicable in an immense country, surrounded by enemies, undermined by betrayals), [. . .] the USSR still remains the indispensable barrier against the European Reaction, the necessary counterpoint to the fascism that, in all its forms, infiltrates the veins of the West. (Rolland 1935: 98)

The cost was considerable: nothing less than the first (or the last) *renunciation of truth*. Everything negative that would be said of the USSR – the critiques, the testimonies that would soon flow ceaselessly – would be systematically suspected of participating in an international conspiracy in which the united forces of 'capitalist interest', 'bloodied fascism' and all the 'clerical hypocrisies' allegedly agreed to weave their web of lies day after day. Rolland had already set the tone in a 1930 article titled 'In the Defence of the USSR'.[6] Later still, he who had appealed fifteen years earlier to public debate and various witness testimonies would repeat his refusal to judge a 'great country' like the Soviet Union on the faith of 'gossip from tourists or foreign employees' (Rolland 1992: 63) who did not even speak the Russian language!

The trip he took to Moscow from June to July 1935, on the occasion of which he kept a substantial journal, did not change his perspective. Like many others, he saw nothing (or preferred to see nothing), plugging his ears so as to hear nothing of the *heinous campaigns* that, nevertheless, were already setting the 'people' against whomever those in power chose to present as their enemies, closing his eyes to the terror that managed to instil itself. Hatred had returned, however, as powerful in the East as it was in the West, with the same methods of intimidation, disinformation, defamation in a crucible of all murderous consents that would ceaselessly divide European consciousness henceforth. This chapter opened with the story of a meeting: Gandhi and Rolland in December 1931. The chapter can conclude with another, symmetrical meeting: Rolland and Stalin in the Kremlin in June 1935.

The author of *Par la révolution la paix*, a work published that same year, gave a precise account of the meeting in his journal. Shining through was an immense admiration (and undoubtedly also a naïveté) on the part of the man who, welcomed with due ceremony, presented himself to Stalin – in whom Rolland sees the 'herald of new humanism' (Rolland 1992: 133) – as both an old friend and a fellow traveller of the USSR and as a witness from the West. Arriving with a few questions prepared, particularly about the Soviet penal system, the first trials, the law concerning the punishment of children aged over twelve, to say nothing of the USSR's military alliances, Rolland leaves satisfied with highly diplomatic answers from Stalin, who assures him that – among other efforts – they 'reduce death penalty cases to a minimum'. In Stalin, over the course of the interview, Rolland believes he can distinguish the following character traits: 'a perfect, an absolute simplicity, loyalty, veracity', traits of a man who 'does not impose his opinion', a man who is 'always ready to revise his judgement', and – finally – a man who always leaves 'the door open to experience and, if need be, to its rectification' (1992: 133).

What follows is terrible. Soon after, it was no longer possible for the author of *Par la révolution la paix* to ignore what he had refused to admit until then, nor to deny that the hope and faith placed in the revolution had long since been betrayed. Powerless, Rolland saw the last of his illusions fall one after the other. He nevertheless forbade himself to denounce the Moscow Trials publicly; at the request of the French Communist Party, of which he had become a quasi-hostage, he reaffirmed his loyal support for the Soviet youth, its trials [*épreuves*], abnegation and struggles, until January 1937. His correspondence, in turn, testifies to his credulity vis-à-vis the official propaganda,[7] while Lenin's companions, people he knew and met in Moscow in Gorky's entourage, gradually disappeared one after the other. The letters that Rolland wrote to the leader of the Kremlin pleading on behalf of some of them (like Bukharin) evidently went unanswered; having withdrawn to Vézelay, he painfully began to understand the role he had been made to play. However, he would have to wait until the summer of 1939 and the German-Soviet Pact, 'this magisterial villainy', as he wrote in his journal, for the rupture to be definitive.

The victory over hatred, the independence of the mind, the refusal of all forms of murderous consent, the courage for truth! Reading the texts spanning the quarter of a century that separates the outbreak of the First World War and the German-Soviet Pact, it appears that these four moral exigencies are indissociable – and that they were the condition of a political commitment that the ruses and vicissitudes of history would not

141

risk gravely disavowing *a posteriori*. Today, because they were reunited, the essays comprising *Above the Battle* have not lost any of the original strength of their interpellation. We certainly have not finished with the trial of hatred, which will ceaselessly invent new targets. We are in it! Murderous consents, as we know, remain an irreducible dimension of our belonging to the world. We live with [*Nous vivons avec*].[8] The forces mobilised to enslave the mind on both sides of the cultural, linguistic, religious, ethnic, ideological borders that divide the world are the first and most formidable support for the violence that remains the vitrine of these divisions. This why, for everyone everywhere, truth always demands so much courage. When Gandhi and Rolland met, both were convinced of the necessity and the efficacy of a new moral and spiritual force to resist murderous consent and preserve the independence of the mind in the courage for truth. No political demand and no historical urgency should be able to force them to silence their voices, which is to say, to compromise on their principle.

Crowned with courage from his earlier commitments in favour of peace, when Rolland abandoned his principled refusal of violence in the 1930s by coming to terms with the facts, when he calculated which part of truth to silence so as not to harm the USSR, when his speeches depended on the political organs that solicited and supervised them, we no longer heard this voice. But how can we deny that the destructive forces threatening Europe with a new conflagration were powerful, organised and complicit enough to produce what would retrospectively seem like blindness or folly? Surely, it is always dangerous to renounce morality in order to venture into politics while entirely ignorant of the facts. Because Politics, with a capital P, practises this cult of secrecy, whose essence [*propre*] is to dissimulate its constitutive violence, and because it has considerable means to maintain this secrecy, whoever commits to it runs the risk of being misinformed or underinformed and thus of contributing a formidable, if not criminal, approval of the worst of what his or her conscience reproaches. Stalin became a master in this practice, and Rolland was duped by it, like so many others after him.

Notes

1 Announcing this last book in a note to *Quinze ans de combat*, Rolland indeed specifies: 'For material reasons, I had to remove from this essay collection a whole suite of discussions on pacifism, disarmament, and the necessary alliance – in the fight against war and fascism – between the non-violent and uncompromising Gandhians, conscientious objectors, and partisans of the Revolution. Since I attribute a major importance to these questions at the present moment, and since one of my tasks has been to work on the rapprochement between these two forms of revolutionary action, I will publish this group of articles [*Par la révolution la paix*] as a separate pamphlet via Éditions Sociales Internationales' (Rolland 1935: vii).

2 Letter from Rolland to Gandhi on 7 March 1928: 'for a man of great courage and absolute faith like yourself, who uncompromisingly condemns human bloodshed and national warfare, to take part in such activities – and out of choice, without being forced –, in that case, nothing in the world can make either admit or even understand it. [. . .] And what grieves me is that an example like yours may and certainly will be exploited by our political masters as an acquiescence, as consent to the most loathsome of their crimes, which is the enlistment to help in their wars of sordid interest, of the wretched human masses of Asia and Africa, which they exploit and use as cannon and machine-gun fodder, as a substance less precious than European flesh' (Rolland and Gandhi 1976: 100–2).

3 Ten years later, in *Darkness at Noon* (1940), Koestler dramatises this same challenge very explicitly in an interview between Rubashov and his investigator. And it is this same challenge that Maurice Merleau-Ponty will reinvestigate in *Humanism and Terror* (1947) in terms that will call for a response from Albert Camus in *The Rebel* (1951). All these debates and philosophical discussions will have in common the fact that they replay the

confrontation between the exigencies of the Revolution (the justification of violence and terror) and the principle of non-violence, embodied by Gandhi – between a politics freed from morality and the transcendence of an ethical principle 'imposed' upon politics.

4 See Part II, Chapter 1, 'The Fatherland, a Murderous Idol?', p. 75 ff.

5 See also, in this same work, the letter to Reginald Reynolds, secretary general of Britain's No War Movement: 'It is high time to leave sterile ideology. In the world of action, the question does not arise between absolute non-violence and absolute violence but, rather, between more or less violence exercised on facts and people. [. . .] One must boldly defy the necessities of action and the consequences of decisions made. If one wants to struggle against war effectively, it is altogether insufficient that an elite group of minds refuse war individually' (Rolland 1937: 88–9).

6 Rolland's essay 'Pour la défense de l'URSS' in *Quinze ans de combat* (1935: 99–100).

7 See in particular the letter Rolland wrote to 'X' on 12 September 1936: 'What else could be done if the crimes were proven (and even confessed)? Pardon the criminals? That happened twice, and twice they had broken their promise and recommenced. One cannot reproach Soviet justice for having proceeded hastily. The investigation had continued for two years (since the assassination of Kirov). And other terrorist attacks had happened during the investigation. Last year, when I was in Moscow, I learned from various quarters that Stalin had narrowly escaped an assassination attempt in the Kremlin itself. Is a revolutionary government – even more than another – not bound to defend itself inflexibly?' (Rolland 1992: 319–20). See also the letter to Liliane Fearn: 'I have no reason to doubt the justice of the condemnations against Kamenev and Zinoviev, characters long despised, twice renegades and traitors to their word. And I do not see how one can reject as fabricated or falsified the statements made by the accused publicly and in the presence of foreign witnesses' (Rolland 1992: 331).

8 Not as audible in English as in French, and thus an initially awkward sentence in English, is Crépon's direct reference to *Vivre avec*, the title of his book translated into English by its subtitle: *The Thought of Death and the Memory of War*. – Translators

4

The 'Snares of Identity'

And the problem of living as a Negro was cold and hard. What was it that made the hate of whites for blacks so steady, seemingly so woven into the texture of things? What kind of life was possible under that hate? How had this hate come to be?
Richard Wright (1991: 164)

Part I of this book recalled the degree to which the question of identity, its ideology, its instrumentalisation for political ends, the reductive identifications to which it gives rise are a source of uninterrupted violence. Does this mean that any claim to 'identity' made by a minority – be it linguistic, religious, cultural, ethnic or otherwise – is illegitimate? Those who so contend are rarely disinterested, whether they do so for the benefit of a dominant power, for the conservation of an empire or its ruins or in the name of an abstract universal that hardly masks the particularity it defends: a determined system of values, a 'civilisation' that wants to make its own 'principles' recognised as universal in order better to ensure its domination. Should we therefore renounce the universal and give all particularity its due? There is nothing abstract about this question concerning the relation between figures of the universal and the diversity of 'cultures'. The question, which the following alternative summarises, arises with an urgency that ceaselessly reminds us of the conflicts that bloody the planet in the name of a supposedly threatened 'identity'. On the one hand, there have been (and still are) instances where the universal or, rather, that which is given as universal presents itself in the form of a political, military or economic domination that denies 'cultures' the right to oppose, to question or perhaps to destabilise the domination in the name of their disturbing particularity. This domination thus takes the form of a mission that masks its hegemonic interests as a defence: of reason against obscurantism, of freedom against oppression, of civilisation against 'savagery', of law against its violation, of good against evil. Everyone knows that here, from the crucible of these hierarchical oppositions, colonial empires drew for more than a century (and in different forms perhaps continue to draw today) the most powerful arguments to justify their politics of conquest and the multiple crimes, exploitations, segregations, humiliations, etc. that characterise those politics. This same crucible nourishes the most recurrent forms of that forgetful resignation and guilty complacency that have been (and most often still are) the ordinary form of our relationship to the violences of a conquering 'universal'.

Yet, on the other hand, it is not without brutality that, reactively, those who have claimed in the past and continue to claim today to adhere to a given 'culture', unilaterally assuming for themselves the right to speak in 'its' name, have thought it their duty to protect that culture not only against such an ambiguous – perhaps colonial – figure of the universal, but also against the very idea that something like a 'universality' could transcend the division of appearances by opening onto forms of solidarity and loyalty other than those limited to the narrow and exclusive links of a 'cultural community'. And we know that violence then manifests itself twice over: internally and externally. Internally, violence presents itself as the constraint of an allegiance, the imperative obligation – under penalty of 'ex-communication', if not elimination – to bend to the rules of the community, to its rites, to its mores, but also to bend at least as much to the exclusivity entailed by belonging, to the discrimination, that is, to the forms of hostility and resentment, to the instinct of revenge with which the belonging is forcibly inherited. Everything thus happens as if these manifestations must be recognised and accepted at all costs as a necessary component of this identity in order to *comfort* it in its particularity, to give it in a way the comfort of hatred and violence. And it is true that there are innumerable conflict zones in which those who have assumed for themselves the right to decide the form this allegiance should take encourage terror through extortion.

Hence the way violence manifests itself externally! To prove one's belonging, one must espouse invectives, insults and, more generally, all the forms of murderous consent that guarantee it, such as the justification of terrorism, which are supposed to express one's solidarity and fidelity by stifling any feeling of horror under the pleasure of revenge. Such radicalism is found in all the forms taken by the designation of the enemy that, from crude and stereotypical characterisation to multiple forms of rejections and including the most destructive, accompany *its* identification. Like the contagion of violence recalls far from combat zones, every conflict offers an example of this point in the way it is exported through its globalised images of mutilated bodies, abandoned corpses and bombed cities.

I call this alternative the double snare of identity. In the first case, the snare is similar to the risk of complacency toward the violences of a 'dominant state' that presents itself as if it should be 'universally' accepted because, as they say in all modes, its order is immutable and has on its side the weight of history and tradition, when not justified by still more obscure reasons on a theological or metaphysical register. This snare pertains to what La Boétie called 'voluntary servitude' and concerns both those who passively suffer the crushing weight of this subjugation and those on the other side who accommodate themselves to it, all while condemning it with mere lip service. Thus, as so many scenes exemplify, this domination often translates into the denial of their own identity for those very people for whom *being what they are* exposes them to violence; furthermore, the memory and traces of humiliation and servitude, the heritage of fear transmitted from generation to generation, often condemn them to the shame of being themselves if not, more destructively still, to *self-hatred*. In the second case, motivated by an inextinguishable resentment and a need for vengeance or obsessional revenge, *hatred of the other* constitutes the snare. This hatred prevails and builds up, step by step, in its individual and collective dimension as a 'new', exclusive and imperative pedestal for identity. As if everything thus had to reduce to that terrible adage evoked in Part I: 'Tell me who you *hate*, and I will tell you who you *are* and if you *are* who you *ought* to be'!

I. Self-Hatred

It is thus apparent that, on both sides, there is room only for hatred. This is why hatred constitutes the first trial for anyone who tries to escape its double spiral, refusing both to accept a violent state of affairs, with what such complacency implies concerning the denial of 'identity', and to contest that violent state of affairs by a reactive and equally negative violence. Thus, the history of the twentieth century is not only marked by the multiplication of political leaders, groups and party heads, religious authorities and other ideologues who make a 'particular identity' and its ideological and political instrumentalisation, with all the phantasms of belonging that accompany it, a pretext for terror; it also includes men and women who will have attempted to escape this double snare. And among those who, faced with a situation of this kind, tried to make *another* voice heard and tried to propose another action on the basis of an expanded and renewed vision of identity, there is no one more important than Martin Luther King, Jr, who engaged in an interminable battle – a struggle that, as the events of the past few years from Ferguson to Baltimore recall, is far from over – not only to guarantee African Americans the civil rights owed to them, but also to change their conditions of existence and give them the self-esteem and confidence in their 'identity' of which segregation robbed them.

Dealing with non-violence's double challenge of hatred and violence, at least one reason must be invoked to justify the choice to highlight the disastrous situation of African Americans as a privileged example, among so many others, of this double snare of identity. So far, analyses have primarily brought to light the *hatred of the other*. With the 'double snare of identity', a supplementary dimension emerges: *self-hatred*. Yet, to read the testimonies and stories that evoke the segregation of African Americans in the United States, all recall the extent to which – articulated and intertwined with hatred of the other – self-hatred constitutes the crux of the problem. Dwelling upon such a major oeuvre of African American literature, it even appears that hatred, in its double and in reality triple dimension, constitutes the most recurrent, if not obsessional, motif.

To give an overview before coming to the thought of Martin Luther King, Jr, I will linger for a moment on a novel that brings this motif to light with particular acuity: Richard Wright's *Black Boy*. It is, as is well known, an autobiographical story that recounts a young black boy's childhood in the South, between Memphis and Jackson, during the First World War and in the 1920s. Presented as a Bildungsroman [*roman de formation*], it recounts at the same time the discovery of a vocation: writing, tried and true as a conduit for freedom. But from what must one be freed to find freedom? What weighed on existence? In reality, nothing other than the obsessive and paralysing grip of hatred. 'Education' [*La formation*] has no other object. Indeed, *Black Boy* recounts step by step, through the eyes of a child, the genesis of the progressive perception and the definitive consciousness of white hostility through a recurring experience: racist acts of violence, repeated insults, tolerated affronts, unpunished blows and arbitrary executions – the right over life and death, psychical and physical, to which hatred lays claim. The child initially understands nothing about segregation, until the day when it finally imposes itself upon him as an element constitutive of his individual and collective identity such that, at the end of the day, 'being black' means nothing other than inevitable exposure – transmitted from generation to generation as an inevitability – to repeated violences of a heinous racism:

> A dread of white people now came to live permanently in my feelings and imagination. [. . .] I had grown able to respond emotionally to every hint, whisper, word, inflection, news, gossip, and rumor regarding conflicts between the races. Nothing challenged the totality of my personality so much as

this pressure of hate and threat that stemmed from the invisible whites. (Wright 1991: 73)

At stake is an affective taking-root, an incorporation of hatred, as a primordial emotion. If hatred constitutes a trial for whoever submits to it, it is, indeed, because hatred is not limited only to its punctual manifestations. The permanent threat that these manifestations will unpredictably irrupt, which a look or one word too many suffices to trigger on the corner of any street or in any public space, and the anxious anticipation of the humiliations and blows to come make hatred a growing – if not invasive – part of the child's existence. Wright can thus speak of the tumour in the imagination that reminds him at each moment that hatred had become *his* culture, *his* faith and even *his* religion. Once autobiography, written in the first person, presents itself as the genetic story of an affective and intellectual experience, this is the heart – the essence – of the learning process it restores! And this is not all. For the author of *Black Boy* also describes the way hatred begets hatred, and what grows within him is not only the perception of the violences suffered, understood as a major element of his psychic and collective individuation, but also his own hatred with regard to white people, who, in turn, end up assigning him his place in society. Such is the essence of segregation: on both sides of the border it establishes and relentlessly preserves, segregation wants each to hate the other. This is its pleasure [*jouissance*], the foundation of its cruelty! Whites want to be hated by blacks, probably want *nothing* else, and there is *nothing*, in any case, that testifies more to the success of their discriminatory brutality than this mechanistic contagion. Everything is orchestrated (the humiliating signs placed in storefronts, the caricatures and other disgraceful characterisations, the blows delivered on the slightest pretext, the lynchings, all the usual manifestations of quotidian racism from the most ordinary to the most murderous) so that each is inevitably returned to his or her hatred of the other. As if hatred defined for each the racially determined place he or she is assigned in the world, as if society should have no edifice (is it otherwise today?) other than the joint, articulated factory of fear and hatred.

> We were now large enough for the white boys to fear us and both of us, the white boys and the black boys, began to play our traditional racial roles as though we had been born to them, as though it was in our blood, as though we were being guided by instinct. All the frightful descriptions we had heard about each other, all the violent expressions of hate and hostility that had seeped into us from our surroundings, came now to the surface to guide our actions. (1991: 83)

Such is the double immurement of hatred within the spiral proper to it. And yet, this is not hatred's last word, since the consequences that give it a third dimension, also included in Wright's story, must still be measured. Segregation, indeed, not only separates whites and blacks geographically in cities, on public transportation and in public spaces; it also, in the most tangible way, deprives the latter of the conditions of existence that enable (or at least should enable) the former to invent their own singularity: the security given by an education, available work that is not confined to subaltern jobs at the limits of subsistence, and decent lodging. In short, anything that can allow one to imagine for oneself – and to give oneself – a future. It is no coincidence that *Black Boy* is also a great book on the hunger that, along with the manifestations of racism, ultimately constitutes the most frequent of the experiences it makes known.

Nor is it a coincidence that these two experiences, hunger and racism, join as the most insurmountable obstacles that Wright's protagonist has to face to take on his vocation as a writer. The first time he ventures to formulate his desire, the adolescent hears in response: 'You'll never be a writer [. . .]. Who on earth put such ideas into your nigger head?' (1991: 147).

Everyone knows the most famous dream, the dream King risked confessing on 28 August 1963 in front of 250,000 people during the March on Washington. It agrees with the dream that constitutes the cornerstone of *Black Boy*. The dream to which Wright testifies is forbidden, incongruous and displaced; the mere formulation of the dream constitutes a counterword, the invention of a singularity opposed to confinement in programmatic violence, a dream whose confiscation ultimately reveals the very essence of segregation:

> I was becoming aware of the thing that the Jim Crow laws had been drafted and passed to keep out of my consciousness; I was acting on impulses that southern senators in the nation's capital had striven to keep out of Negro life; I was beginning to dream the dreams that the state had said were wrong, that the schools had said were taboo. (1991: 169)

This impression of confinement and powerlessness, the acute feeling of being unable to escape the place that the laws of segregation seem to have fixed for present and future generations once and for all, is the muffled reason – the most secret motive [*motif*] – for the *self-hatred* I recalled at the outset. This impression undoubtedly concretises the victory of racism over free spirits and its ultimate degree of destruction: the destruction of *self-esteem* and *self-confidence*. It thus constitutes the primary motive of Wright's follow-up to *Black Boy*, which describes his arrival in Chicago: *American Hunger*.[1] There, significantly, we find from the outset the painful – if not the desperate – analysis of the implacable mechanisms that render the dream impossible. They are the *raison d'être* of the racial hatred that can achieve its goal of convincing black people that they are naturally destined to occupy a position inferior to white people only by pushing black people to hate themselves. 'Hated by whites', writes the man who, fleeing the South, thought to have found a world free from racism in Chicago, 'and being an organic part of the culture that hated them, the black man grew in turn to hate in himself that which others hated in him' (1991: 266). Such is the confusion of feelings, of emotions, the inextricable knot in which struggle those whom the weight of segregation no longer permits to look reality in the face. The doors are so closed to them that any of their dreams would instantly shatter. Kept separate from the lives of white people, bolstered by humiliation and servitude, all resistance and opposition held in check, every experience seems to confirm or to countersign the negative judgements that white people heap upon African Americans, as if African Americans were responsible for them first of all, and to legitimise the consequences white people draw from them.

> Slowly I began to forge in the depths of my mind a mechanism that repressed all the dreams and desires that the Chicago streets, the newspapers, the movies were evoking in me. I was going through a second childhood; a new sense of the limit of the possible was being born in me. What could I dream of that had the barest possibility of coming true? I could think of nothing. And, slowly, it was upon exactly that nothingness that my mind began to dwell, that constant sense of wanting without having, of being hated without reason. (1991: 267)

This intimate self-destruction, understood as the most implacable and immediate effect of hatred, is also the theme of another major work of African American literature: James Baldwin's novel *Another Country*, which opens with the slow descent into hell of a young black man, Rufus Scott, who is driven by the racial barriers of segregation to end his own life. Inhabited by an explosive violence he ceaselessly wields against those who love him, he ends up turning the system's violence against himself. The narration then concentrates on his sister Ida and her impossible mourning. Of all the scenes one could invoke, I retain one as particularly emblematic, since it recurs in both the literary representation and the cinematographic[2] staging of segregation. Ida's partner is white, and he decides after many years to present his black girlfriend to his family, unsure how to let his mother know in advance, to prepare her, that his girlfriend is a woman of colour. He dramatically anticipates her violent reaction, her sorrow (!), her feeling of humiliation (!) and what will certainly result from the confrontation with the rest of his family (his sister and brother-in-law, his brother, his father, etc.): 'the resulting miasma of piety and malice and suspicion and fear. [. . .] [T]he ditchwater-dull, infantile dirty stories, and the insane talk about politics' (Baldwin 1998b: 614). But this is not what is most surprising. Most surprising is the mad rage to which this 'official presentation' scheme brings Ida at the idea that her boyfriend could use her 'to educate' his family. Her anger turns the self-hatred that swept away her brother into a sovereign disdain for the racism of middle-class white people [*petits Blancs*]:

> I don't give a damn if there's any hope for them or not. But I know that I am not about to be bugged by any more white jokers who still can't figure out whether I'm human or not. If

they don't know, baby, sad on them, and I hope they drop dead slowly, in great pain. (Baldwin 1998b: 615)

In a whole series of written and oral public engagements throughout the 1960s, the era of the civil rights struggle, Baldwin ceaselessly returned to this theme, recalling the degree to which the entire segregated education system in the South had been designed to preserve this self-scorn, that is to say, not only to keep African Americans under control, but also to prevent them from becoming or feeling equal. More generally, this is the way the country told itself fables about its own history, fantasised about its past, constructed a double myth about the arrival of white people and the exploitation of black people and imposed this myth through the school that contributed to it.[3] The result for African Americans was a by no means evident task and a major challenge: to begin freeing themselves from the place ascribed to them by a racist society, which required a complete reversal of everything that had formed their identity. It was a question, once and for all, of making black children and students raised in this system aware that this 'identity', founded on self-scorn, was the result of what Baldwin unhesitatingly called 'a criminal conspiracy to destroy [them]' in a lecture delivered to New York teachers in October 1963 (Baldwin 1998c: 685). Be stronger than this conspiracy, refuse to make peace with it! Education had no task more urgent. Measuring the path travelled by the new generation of students engaged in the struggle for civil rights, the author of *Another Country* confessed in another text that it took him years to undo his education: 'It took many years of vomiting up all the filth I'd been taught about myself, and half-believed, before I was able to walk on the earth as though I had a right to be here' (Baldwin 1998d: 636).

II. Against the Race War

Now back to the question of the double snare of identity, which, reading Wright and Baldwin, we never really left! It is an understatement to say that this snare confronted King in all his activity, from the Montgomery bus boycott starting in 1955 to his assassination in Memphis in 1968. During these thirteen years, this question of the double snare of identity took the double face: on the one hand, that of black men and women worn out by years of segregation, resigned to putting up with violences with the hope of remaining safe from its brutal and unforeseeable manifestation, condemned over the years to close themselves off and sink silently into a negative, self-destructive perception of their own identity; on the other hand, that of the extreme movements determined to affirm a newfound, exclusive and combative identity – the Black Muslims of Elijah Muhammad and, from 1964 on, the Muslim Mosque, Inc. of Malcolm X. While locked up in the Birmingham city jail in April 1963, in response to an open letter sent to him by eight Alabama religious leaders – all white – challenging his strategy of non-violence, King describes his own situation in the black community in the following way:

> You speak of our activity in Birmingham as extreme. At first I was rather disappointed that fellow clergymen would see my nonviolent efforts as those of an extremist. I began thinking about the fact that I stand in the middle of two opposing forces in the Negro community. One is a force of complacency, made up in part of Negroes who, as a result of long years of oppression, are so drained of self-respect and a sense of 'somebodiness' that they have adjusted to segregation; and in part of a few middle-class Negroes who, because of a degree of academic and economic security and because in some ways they profit

by segregation, have become insensitive to the problems of the masses. The other force is one of bitterness and hatred, and it comes perilously close to advocating violence. It is expressed in the various black nationalist groups that are springing up across the nation, the largest and best-known being Elijah Muhammad's Muslim movement. Nourished by the Negro's frustration over the continued existence of racial discrimination, this movement is made up of people who have lost faith in America, who have absolutely repudiated Christianity, and who have concluded that the white man is an incorrigible devil. (King 2000: 99–100)

This text must be read attentively, since this problem will have rarely been posed so clearly. And there are undoubtedly many struggles, beginning with those that accompanied the end of colonial empires, the stakes of which this formulation of the double snare would suffice to elucidate. King himself did not fail to make this rapprochement on many occasions, inscribing his action within the more general framework of colonised peoples' struggle to end oppression. But how can one escape the destructive alternative of passive self-hatred and destructive hatred of the other? Of what do people, black and white alike – differently, of course, but conjointly – need to be reminded in order to open a third way that is not *negative*? It first had to be emphasised that racism is not a matter of nature but, rather, of right; that it has no natural foundation but, rather, takes a juridical framework; and that, consequently, this framework before all else must be modified. The fight must devote itself to its suppression. It was a matter, in other words, of beginning by displacing the question in order to dispel all fantasies of an alleged 'natural inequality', while showing that the result-ant 'negative peace' – the lethal peace that the entire system of segregation was charged with maintaining, inscribing in morals, anchoring in consciousnesses – was first and foremost a denial of justice. African Americans would have no need to feel inferior (and white people to persuade themselves thereof) if the legal mechanisms (the institution of separation) that gave rise to this state of affairs could be dismantled. Resignation, submission, the feeling of inferiority – these constitutive elements of a profound depreciation and perhaps even, one might say, depression of identity, the components that Derrida described in another context as a 'trouble of identity' (1998: 14, translation modified) – all of this did not come from nowhere. The trouble, if there was any, resulted from a *construction* that had given itself the means of its objectives, namely a juridical framework to legitimise racial violence and the affective, emotional springs of its support: the factory of white hatred toward blacks.[4]

The first important transformation pertained to the credit that African Americans themselves were unable to accord their belittled identity and, by that very fact, to the sight they could individually and collectively set on themselves. Without the form of psychical and collective individuation that such a transformation implied (the transformation, for example, that was to be concretised by all the major marches that, in the image of Gandhi thirty years earlier, King would organise), one could not possibly push the threshold of tolerance back. It was even necessary to recognise, more radically still, that the two went hand in hand. African Americans would be able to achieve a radical overturning of their self-evaluation by opposing the multiple forms of humiliation and threats imposed upon them by segregation. By revealing the intolerable as intolerable, as that which one can no longer coherently tolerate, for example, by boycotting public transportation or by occupying restaurants, they would attain what King unhesitatingly announced as 'a new self-respect' or a new 'sense of dignity' (1991: 6).

If it is true that no 'I' can exist as a singularity if not joined to a 'we', if it is true that the feeling of belonging is a fundamental given [*donnée*] of life because we always live with others (not the other in general but a determined set of 'others'), if it is true that all 'living' is thus a 'living with' [*vivre avec*],[5] it had to be admitted that this 'we' is too necessary to existence to abandon its description, circumscription and evaluation to the hostile forces of racism and segregation. It was not so much a question of reappropriating a 'lost identity' as of winning the right to invent it anew by projecting it into a future other than the one prescribed by these forces: the immurement of destiny in the exclusive frameworks traced by the police, legal and administrative apparatuses of segregation.

The struggle, in this sense, did not pit one 'identity' against an 'other', one 'race' opposed to an 'other', blacks against whites. On this point, King radically opposed what, in the same era, the Black Muslims and Malcolm X claimed under the title of 'black nationalism'. To relate the fight for which he called to a 'race war' would have done nothing, he thought, but confirm the partition and reinforce the separation. One had to take place oneself on the terrain of justice and justice alone. These are the forces of injustice that it was important to combat. 'The tension in this city [Montgomery, Alabama] is not between white people and Negro people', he writes in the same article (King 1991: 8). By stating the following, which would prove to be crucial, he made injustice one of his major arguments for retaining the method of non-violence as the sole mode of effective action:

[the] attack is directed against forces of evil rather than against persons who are caught in those forces. It is evil we are seeking to defeat, not the persons victimized by evil. Those of us who

struggle against racial injustice must come to see that the basic
tension is not between races. (1991: 8)

This refusal to think action in terms of a race war substitutes
the thirst for vengeance with the call for justice. But how to
distinguish one from the other? How to avoid confusing the
latter and the former? How to avoid taking as a demand for
justice this other call, obscure and irrepressible, which seems to
have the infinite guarantee of the weight of history, of wounded
memory and of belittled identity: the call of the thirst for blood
and the gears of hatred?

III. The Complacency of Delays

This is when the principle of non-violence imposes itself. Let's
start again from the beginning! The question of the relation
between the particular and the universal served as my reference
point, and I argued that this question could not arise without
raising the problem of violence and non-violence at the heart of
their articulation. We still do not know how to think – assuming
it must be thought – the universal for which we aim, wait and
hope (assuming it needs to be). But we are already convinced
that it ought not impose itself as a domination exercised in the
name of what one could call, via a portmanteau that presents
itself as an aberration, a 'universal particular': for example, that
of a given civilisation or a determined religion giving itself for
the universally valid incarnation of the good. This amounts to
recognising concretely that there will be no universal that holds if
all are not equally granted, without condition of belonging, the
same *right* not to existence[6] but rather to the minimum forms of

161

vital security: education, housing and employment – everything regularly targeted by segregation. Thus, we can understand that, when this right is denied to a minority and when, day after day, the very opposite is confirmed, with constant brutality, by the pitiless maintenance of State racism, there is great temptation to resort to violence to put an end to their unpunished injustice. As is well known, such is the solution advocated in the same era by Malcolm X, as evidenced by his public interventions, starting with the implacable indictment he delivered in Cleveland on 3 April 1964 in a speech entitled 'The Ballot or the Bullet'. There, the Muslim leader, who would be assassinated a year later, holds the following: the ballot has *no effect* as long as the Democratic leaders elected by black voices lack the capacity to hold to their commitments. They held all the keys in their hands, all the power, a majority in the House of Representatives and the Senate, but nothing was done, nothing came, nothing changed. They benefited from these voices, but their promises had meaning only for those naïve enough to believe them. Wasted effort, indeed! They yielded nothing, 'gave' nothing to African Americans in return, whereas everything African Americans claimed was fully owed to them! Because the electoral system allied with a 'segregationist conspiracy' is locked on all sides, democracy appears to be a fool's game in which African Americans are the 'dupes' [*pigeons*]:

> The same government that you go abroad to fight for and die for is the government that is in a conspiracy to deprive you of your voting rights, deprive you of your economic opportunities, deprive you of decent housing, deprive you of decent education. You don't need to go to the employer alone, it is the government itself, the government of America, that is responsible for the oppression and exploitation and degradation of black

people in this country. And you should drop it in their lap. This government has failed the Negro. This so-called democracy has failed the Negro. And all these white liberals have definitely failed the Negro. (Malcolm X 1990a: 30–1)

And yet, America owed African Americans considerably for their labour (its wealth) and their enlistment in the army (part of its power). Slavery, war – all of this had created a debt of blood (always blood), payment for which should have been obvious. But the authorities found no way of repaying their debt other than resorting to violence, criminally, with their batons and their dogs. How, then, could one resist the temptation to oppose this violence by taking up arms if every appeal to the law, to rights, to justice was ineffective? Would refusing this alternative not condemn one to powerlessness? Despite what the pastors said, would one not play into the hands of this first violence, that of the 'Whites', by refraining from responding to it? How much longer would one have to wait and hope in vain for a change that had no chance of occurring peacefully because white people, who had the law and morality against them but force with them, wanted to hear nothing, nor to surrender anything. For Malcolm X, there was no more time for black people to wait, to compromise, to appeal to America's *moral conscience* or to transform white people's *mentality* in order to obtain what had always been owed to them. Morality, which was nothing but a fool's game or the mask of hypocrisy, had nothing to do with this history. On the contrary, it had to be noted that racial animosity, hatred and violence had not diminished since the beginning of the struggle for civil rights in 1954, and it was necessary to draw all the consequences, beginning with the first among them, which was to demand, loudly and clearly, the *political* existence of a 'black nationalism'. And if this affirmation necessitated a revolution, as he had already argued a year earlier (in 1963) in the name of the Black Muslims, then it was necessary to remember that a revolution, including the American Revolution, never happened *without bloodshed!*[7]

King was nevertheless the first to be aware of the impossibility of a further delay. It was unjust to demand that African Americans continue *to wait*, responded King in the letter that, from the Birmingham prison in which he found himself jailed in April 1963, he wrote to the eight religious authorities who had asked him about the issue. For every demand of this sort, regardless of whence it comes, in reality signifies the most active 'murderous consent'. To maintain that the time was not right, that obtaining rights and acquiring freedom required patience, was to compromise with segregationist violence by allowing them to continue indeterminately under the pretext that it would be preferable to close one's eyes rather than upset an established order, even if the established order were the most unjust and the most contrary to the convictions defended elsewhere and to the profession of faith one claimed to be ready to defend. Above all, it meant refusing to take measure of what was unbearable about the system for those who continued to experience it every day; it meant ignoring what the system inflicted upon the bodies and minds of those who continued to be its victims; it meant forgetting what the system destroyed, namely a relation to others and to the world, to the space and time that a minimum of self-confidence still makes *liveable*. We shall soon see how the 'active passivity' of this murderous gradualism should be analysed. Meanwhile, with the attention that it deserves, let us read the long protest in which King reminds these clergymen of this:

Perhaps it is easy for those who have never felt the stinging darts of segregation to say, 'Wait.' But when you have seen vicious mobs lynch your mothers and fathers at will and drown your sisters and brothers at whim; when you have seen hate-filled policemen curse, kick and even kill your black brothers and sisters; when you see the vast majority of your twenty million Negro brothers smothering in an airtight cage of poverty in the midst of an affluent society; when you suddenly find your tongue twisted and your speech stammering as you seek to explain to your six-year-old daughter why she can't go to the public amusement park that has just been advertised on television [. . .]; when you are harried by day and haunted by night by the fact that you are Negro, living constantly at tiptoe stance, never knowing what to expect next, and are plagued with inner fears and outer resentments; when you are forever fighting a degenerating sense of 'nobodiness' – then you will understand why we find it difficult to wait. There comes a time when the cup of endurance runs over, and men are no longer willing to be plunged into an abyss of despair. I hope, sirs, you can understand our legitimate and unavoidable impatience. (2000: 92–3)

This incessant demand for delay by those who profit from segregation, whether they encourage it or defend it by any means, nevertheless revealed still one more thing. It emphasised that freedom is never granted by the oppressor of his or her own free will; it must be demanded, fought for fiercely, by the oppressed. This implies the exertion of a relentless *pressure*, and it is important to determine the nature of this pressure and measure its efficacity. Once again, we are at a crossroads. For it is here, once again, that the radical temptation to rush into violence had to appear, and we know the extent to which throughout the entire twentieth century, in the era of the struggle for civil rights and still today, this temptation bore and continues to bear the

165

face of terror. At stake, still again, was a decision and a choice: the necessity of deciding between, on the one hand, the violent counter-affirmation of a particular identity that, through the use of vengeance, affirms both the right to resist the violence of white people with violence and the 'right to exist' (the 'black nationalism' of Malcolm X) and, on the other hand, the will to maintain this same pressure in a more universal framework that extricates it from the snare of identity. Which universality? In a moment, we will see that this was – and remains – the whole question.

Concerning the choice of violence, one should first measure the chances of its success. This is what King did first of all by highlighting, in a very pragmatic way, its long-term ineffectiveness. This choice undoubtedly gives the (in reality always suspicious) satisfaction of timely results, ephemeral victories, spectacular feats, but these do not change the nature of things at all. If violence happens to cause hostile forces to fold, it is always provisionally and very relatively. For the thirst for blood, as well as the instinct for revenge that animates such a commitment, deprives it of any *universal* scope. Such thirst and instinct essentially forbid this universal scope, since they seek no agreement, no understanding, no 'change' of heart, no profound modification of relations, no peace; rather, they seek only identification of the enemy, direct confrontation, armed opposition, all-out warfare. By *particularising* to the extreme the stakes of the struggle, in the more or less explicit and avowed name of a race war, they in reality do nothing other than foster hatred and violence in actual fact and in people's minds.

Yet, was it not an illusion – an alibi to avoid exposing oneself – to think of peace in this climate while denying oneself the means of war? No, undoubtedly, not if one were to admit that, far from ignoring it, the doctrine of non-violence and its everyday exercise had no other objective than to provide the most concrete and effective answer possible to this question. To understand the explosive possibilities of the doctrine of non-violence, one needed the means to analyse the fact that the underground participation of both sides in the system of violence and the forms of *consent* that, from the most passive to the most active, made the violence possible were infinitely more extensive – even more innocuous – than one suspected, and there were consequently means to act against violence and to destabilise the whole edifice by challenging this participation and this consent. This is why non-violence in no way resembles a gradualism, contrary to what the Christian image of the 'other cheek' might suggest.[8] It would be wrong to assume that this withdrawal was without risk. Just read *Why We Can't Wait*, the book King devoted almost exclusively to the 1963 Birmingham campaign in order to reveal how much this withdrawal translated into, above all else, the exposure of bodies to a repression that proved the authority's terror by the very fact that it manifested itself so brutally, by blows, arrests and imprisonments. This was the meaning of the public transportation boycott, the restaurant sit-ins and every form of action invented by civil rights activists. These protests openly showed that there was a way to lash out at violence without falling into its spiral. To do so, it was enough to block, in the most immediate sense of the term, with body and mind everything that resembled immediately or from a distance any consent whatsoever, from the most passive acquiescence to the most insidious compromise. For this alone is the price to be paid to undermine the construction of hatred from within.

That the temptation created in society by non-violence was conceived as the key necessary to lower the threshold of tolerance for both African Americans and moderate whites, that it was thought to be the most effective means for making both perceive the unjust laws for what they were – an intolerable violation of the most basic principles of justice – and thereby creating a vast movement of opinion that transcended all affiliations and no longer supported such violations: nothing attests more to this more than King's conviction that the passivity of those same moderate whites constituted the main obstacle to the transformation of the *negative peace* that accommodates injustice into a *constructive peace* that refuses it. Violence had no support, if not a pedestal, more powerful than their complacency, the murderousness of which King ceaselessly emphasised since, in the name of the immutable order it wants to preserve, this complacency closed its eyes to the brutality to which the activists of this *other peace* were subjected:

> First, I must confess that over the past few years I have been gravely disappointed with the white moderate. I have almost reached the regrettable conclusion that the Negro's great stumbling block in the stride toward freedom is not the White Citizens Counciler or the Ku Klux Klanner, but the white moderate, who is more devoted to 'order' than to justice; who prefers a negative peace which is the absence of tension to a positive peace which is the presence of justice; who constantly says: 'I agree with you in the goal you seek, but I can't agree with your methods of direct action'; who paternalistically believes he can set the timetable for another man's freedom; who lives by a mythical concept of time and who constantly advises the Negro to wait for a 'more convenient season.' (King 2000: 96–7)

IV. Redemptive Love

These two key concepts of 'negative peace' and 'positive peace' require a moment's pause. Two traits distinguish the former. On the one hand, from a legal point of view, it refuses to differentiate between just and unjust laws. For 'negative peace', the law *is* the law, albeit the law of segregation, and for this reason no civil disobedience is 'authorised' to free itself with respect to it, regardless of the principle of justice invoked to do so. On the other hand, by virtue of this rule, 'negative peace' in fact chooses to close its eyes to the police violence that suppresses whatever is thus perceived exclusively and unilaterally as a violation of the law, all consideration concerning the injustice of the repression notwithstanding. Better, 'negative peace' guarantees, encourages, if not demands these violences in the name of maintaining or restoring the order that it deems to be compromised. It thus espouses all possible tiers of murderous consent, from indifference and passive resignation to active participation, even the racist activism of the Ku Klux Klan hordes blinded by hatred and bloodthirsty. Two solutions thus offer themselves to combat 'negative peace'. The first chooses to show it for what it is, a covert war, and demands a response to it with instruments of war. The second wagers on substituting it with a *positive peace*, thus escaping the spiral of violence that ineluctably results from the first solution.

How to characterise this 'positive peace'? And why does it impose the method of non-violence? This touches upon the heart of King's thought. For the response to these questions cannot be understood without interrogating his moral and spiritual resources for describing positive peace as the horizon for his action and for justifying the choice of non-violence as the only effective and legitimate method for succeeding. Let us begin again with the opposition between just and unjust laws, pausing once more on the letter written from the Birmingham jail. How should we judge laws? What criteria does one have the right to advance in order to distinguish them? Is there a superior law, a law of laws, to which one could then appeal to take them to trial? The answer King brings to these questions is at once simple and abyssal. What separates a just law from an unjust law, and vice versa, pertains entirely to how they conjointly condition and affect two types of relations: on the one hand, those relations that everyone maintains with his or her self and that protect or lose self-esteem, a sense of dignity, confidence in one's 'right to exist'; on the other hand, those relations that foster or destroy the possibility of a 'universal brotherhood'. Put otherwise, there are laws that enable one to love oneself and to love others, just as there are laws that provoke and sustain hatred – hatred of oneself and hatred of others.

This is why the principle of non-violence is inseparable from a doctrine of love. The implementation of non-violence opposes hatred's intensification in the world, the infernal cycle of crime and retaliation, with the force of its belief in the projection and imposition of an improbable 'ethic of love' in the heart of the life shared as much with 'one's own' [siens] as with enemies. This is its wager and its difficulty! For the political efficacy of this ethic must still be proven against all the opposing voices that persist in believing in the 'virtues' of violence. Against all those who would like to free politics from morality, one must show that the *ethical* implementation of a commandment of love, which is at the same time an open exposure to the brutal reactions of the police and, as such, a political intervention, can wrest both sides from the mechanical gears of hatred and, by that very fact, overcome segregation. To avoid any abusive reduction, however, any caricatural simplification, it is necessary to agree on what 'love' means!

Reviewing the three Greek terms that the translation of the New Testament uses to name 'love' (*eros*, *philia* and *agape*), the leader of the struggle for civil rights, aware of the risks of confusion, specifies that what he has in mind is neither the first nor the second but the third. While the first two (*eros* and *philia*), which designate respectively 'a sort of aesthetic and romantic love' and 'an intimate affection between friends', remain *particular* and in this sense relative and interested, the third (*agape*) – which ought to be understood as a mutual 'understanding' and as a 'creative goodwill' dedicated to bringing people together or, again, as 'the love of God operating in the human heart' – *asserts* a universal scope (King 2010: 46).[9] Opposed to the divisions that hatred *demands*, this love *wants* the confirmation of an original feeling of co-belonging more essential than all divisions, racial or otherwise. Against all the ferments of violence gnawing at it, it attests to the 'love of God operating in the human heart'. One therefore grasps the question that immediately imposes itself and should not leave us. It pertains less to the manifestations of this love than to the circumscription and the extension of the co-belonging to which it is supposed to bear witness. Does assuming the 'love of God' not impose upon Blacks and Whites alike – upon all differences, all beliefs, all convictions together or suspended – the violence of a 'universal particular' (in this case Christianity) with which this chapter began? If it is a question of 'love thy neighbour', does this not from the beginning bend the law that makes it possible to distinguish between the just and unjust to a Christian semantic, too exclusively Christian (and thus particular) to designate with this name both the friend and the enemy?

Let us return to the letter written from the Birmingham jail. Among the reproaches addressed to King by the religious authorities, to whom he replied from his cell, was that of having left the city of Atlanta, where he ministered, to sow 'disorder' far from his home by worrying himself with the fates of men and women who did not attend his ministry. One must understand his answer to clarify the preceding. For to justify the span of his activity and presence from Montgomery to Birmingham, everywhere the struggle continues, King invokes the necessity of responding to an *imperative call*: the call demanding that sensitivity to injustice and the responsibility for which it calls not stop at the borders of a particular State and less still of a given city. If he has come to Birmingham, he tells them, it is because the city is among those in which, in the southern United States, segregation is the most ruthless, and the staggering record of police brutality can no longer be ignored: a city in which such a particular distress, caused by the pile of one injustice atop another and the memory of unpunished crimes, has reached is paroxysm. The question was not asked as to whether, under these extreme conditions, it was possible merely not to hear this call. For he was convinced that it would be an unbearable disavowal to resist the call. The murderous consent, which has always paved the way for segregation, could not be refused more explicitly!

> I am in Birmingham because injustice is here. Just as the prophets of the eighth century left their villages and carried their 'thus saith the Lord' far beyond the boundaries of their home towns, and just as the Apostle Paul left his village of Tarsus and carried the gospel of Jesus Christ to the far corners of the Greco-Roman world, so am I compelled to carry the gospel of freedom beyond my own home town. Like Paul, I must constantly respond to the Macedonian call for aid.

Moreover, I am cognizant of the interrelatedness of all communities and states. I cannot sit idly by in Atlanta and not be concerned about what happens in Birmingham. Injustice anywhere is a threat to justice everywhere. We are caught in an inescapable network of mutuality, tied in a single garment of destiny. Whatever affects one directly affects all indirectly. (King 2000: 86–7)

This is what comprises the ethic of love at the foundation of non-violence. It proceeds from a common responsibility: the attention, care and concern demanded by all those who suffer from injustice, whatever it may be, beginning undoubtedly with the violation of segregation in all its forms, but also extending more generally, as King will prove over the years, to all forms of injustice that strike society and are synonymous with exclusion. Opposed to any sentiment of vengeance, this other law seeks to impose non-violence: the law of a rediscovered 'brotherhood' that translates into the conversion of hearts and minds to its commitment. The tension it causes among white people is intended to be the 'necessary stimulant' so that the double force of fear and hatred, accumulated generation after generation, will eventually give way and, once 'the dark clouds of racial prejudice [. . .] and the deep fog of misunderstanding' dissipate, 'in some not too distant tomorrow the radiant stars of love and brotherhood will shine over our great nation with all their scintillating beauty' (King 2000: 112).

Founded on love and brotherhood, this law is at once an asset and a problem. First of all, one could neither suspect nor reject, in the name of a politics allegedly freed from dogmas, the moral and religious character of the resources that King mobilises to give a foundation to non-violence. If it is true that violence stems from a political calculation and belongs to the impure, if not contaminated, logic of its confrontations, then – to counter it – it is necessary to 'exit' politics. It is necessary (here is the asset) to impose on it a heterogenous principle that 'draws' it *outside of itself* and submits it to another logic: not the logic of *negative peace* defended by all these unjust orders, not the logic of those pacifications that support so many murderous consents, but rather the logic of a *positive peace* that finds its ultimate foundation in an 'eternal and natural law', which is also, King writes, the 'law of God' (2000: 94). The paradox, and this is the only irony in the letter, thus lies in the unwillingness evinced by the religious authorities when it comes to recognising, in the name of ethical principles they ought to share, the rights to a political action that refuses to delay indefinitely the time for finally working toward the advent of this *other peace*. Complacently haloed with their religious authority, the bishops and rabbis who signed the letter reproaching King are incapable of this! Where we would have expected them to express the voice of conscience, the example they have always set and continue to give – regardless of their religion and their ethical convictions – is much more (and remains) one of compromise with every order of negative peace.[10] But this peace that is not one, this peace that amounts to submitting to an unacceptable political order, this peace that paves the way for all wars – 'race wars' or 'religious wars' – to which it accommodates quite well, this peace is not the 'work of God'. The latter could only be the positive peace that recognises in 'universal brotherhood' the unique and credible horizon of morality and religion: the horizon from which morality and religion could attempt (this would be their promise!), not to alter politics, but to overturn it. Such is the vocation of non-violence, and such is *in fine* the meaning of the lesson addressed to the clergymen with a feeling of urgency! It associates the 'work of God' with the promises of democracy that, in its present state, still seems far from wanting to support them. Whence the ultimate horizon for non-violent revolution: not the vengeful restoration or reinvention of a destroyed identity but, rather, the refounding of democracy!

> I wish you had commended the Negro sit-inners and demonstrators of Birmingham for their sublime courage, their willingness to suffer and their amazing discipline in the midst of great provocation. One day the South will recognize its real heroes. [. . .] One day the South will know that when these disinherited children of God sat down at lunch counters, they were in reality standing up for what is best in the American dream and for the most sacred values in our Judaeo-Christian heritage, thereby bringing our nation back to those great wells of democracy which were dug deep by the founding fathers in their formulation of the Constitution and the Declaration of Independence. (King 2000: 110–11)

The American dream! We have arrived, at the end of this chapter, at King's most famous speech, studied today by every student in every class in the United States: 'I have a dream. . .'. Concluding with the revelation of the glory of the Lord, with the faith and hope that revelation inspires, this dream alone – in all its rhetorical power – would suffice to show the recourse, if not the 'remedy', that the invocation of 'the law of God' constitutes in the struggle against segregation. And one grasps how, in his letter written from the Birmingham jail, the apostle of non-violence – by invoking the message of the first Christians – never stopped turning the Gospel against the Southern clergymen and their complacency toward hatred and their white flock's contempt for black people.

And yet, this asset is also a problem. There are even two, closely related problems. The first pertains to the universal particular character of the law of God invoked; the second, to the question of democracy. The difficulty comes from the fact that the 'extremism of love', charged with restoring democracy to its place in accordance with its foundational texts, is a Gospel extremism: a Christian extremism explicitly asserted and expressed as such. The law of God that is at the same time the voice of conscience – the very law that allows one to separate just from unjust laws and thereby decide which laws are necessary to obey and which compel disobedience like a duty from a higher order – refers to a particular religion. And it refers to a particular religion as if its message were by definition *universal* and as if it went without saying that all origins, all histories, all beliefs together, *all* agree upon this *universality*. 'Love' and 'brotherhood' are thus inseparable from a particular system of values, and it is presupposed that the recognition of these values will be imposed on everyone. When King summons love and brotherhood, he always refers to the message of the Gospel and invokes the will of God. No way to escape them. They define his culture and give rhetorical power to the language he speaks, the language that the vast majority of those whom he addresses understand and share, regardless of whether he has won them to his cause or needs to convince them. This language is the pacifist weapon of non-violence. But what can be said about those to whom this message does not speak, or no longer speaks, and who thus do not care about the Christian message? What can be said of those for whom this *heritage* is suspected from the beginning of being borne, defended, imposed by a hegemonic culture with which they feel nothing, or no longer want to have anything, in common?

On the one hand, then, the reinvested and revisited (one almost wishes to say 're-weaponised'!) Christian law of love constitutes a lever of incomparable power to wage non-violent combat against segregation. But, on the other hand, this law integrates it into its own system of values. For democracy, consequently, it is a question of rethinking, in light of its founding texts, a *distortion* between its principle (the government of the people by the people, the equality of *all* citizens before the law, civil rights shared universally without racial or class distinction) and the universal particular values that ground and support it. If it is important to claim adherence to these Christian values to reveal the contradiction between the reality of the country gangrened by endemic racism, destructive economic, social and political segregation, and the grandeur of its founding principle, can democracy still impose itself as a common good and a political regime (which is at the same time a system of values) within which all – without religious distinction – would be able to recognise themselves and to which they could feel legitimately attached? This is what makes the 'law of love' invoked by King, as it was by Gandhi a few decades earlier and as it will be by Desmond Tutu[11] thirty years later, doubly problematic! First – and all the polemical force of the letter from the Birmingham prison provides the proof – it does not exclude hypocrisy. The 'law of love' is constantly betrayed, circumvented, rerouted by those who ought to impose it and defend its demands with a radical intransigence that suffers no accommodation to violence. Next, it does not escape the perhaps insurmountable obstacle, emphasised at the beginning of this chapter, of the universal particular. Is this to say that it is impossible to exit this initial alternative? Does this make non-violence a new aporia?

Notes

1 Wright's novel was conventionally published as two separate volumes – *Black Boy* and *American Hunger* – until Harper Perennial combined them in 1991 to produce the current, 'corrected' edition of *Black Boy*. In France, these two volumes frequently remain separate and the French translation of *American Hunger* bears the title *Une faim d'égalité* (*A Hunger for Equality*). Therefore, when Crépon refers to the 'follow-up to *Black Boy*', he is referring to what American readers would know as the second half of the corrected edition of *Black Boy*. – Translators

2 One thinks in particular of Stanley Kramer's film *Guess Who's Coming to Dinner*, with Sidney Poitier, Katharine Hepburn and Spencer Tracy.

3 In a particularly illuminating passage from an essay entitled 'The American Dream and the American Negro', James Baldwin summarises this lack of credible history in the following terms: 'It is a terrible thing for an entire people to surrender to the notion that one-ninth of its population is beneath them. Until the moment comes when we, the Americans, are able to accept the fact that my ancestors are both black and white, that on that continent we are trying to forge a new identity, that we need each other, that I am not a ward of America, I am not an object of missionary charity, I am one of the people who built the country – until this moment comes there is scarcely any hope for the American dream' (Baldwin 1998a: 718–19).

4 King recalls this framework in an essay published on 6 February 1957 in the Protestant journal *Christian Century* entitled 'Nonviolence and Racial Justice' (1991: 5–9). This is the judgement of the Supreme Court in *Plessy v. Ferguson*, which in 1896 institutionalised a new form of slavery by establishing that the doctrine 'separate but equal' now had the force of law throughout the country.

5 Crépon's book *The Thought of Death and the Memory of War* (2013) originally appeared in French under the title *Vivre avec. La pensée de la mort et la mémoire des guerres*. – Translators

6 See Part I, 'The Experience of Violence'.

7 'Look at the American Revolution of 1776. That revolution was for what? For land. Why did they want land? Independence. How was it carried out? Bloodshed. [. . .] So I cite these revolutions, brothers and sisters, to show you that you don't have a peaceful revolution. You don't have a turn-the-other-cheek revolution. There's no such thing as a nonviolent revolution' (Malcolm X 1990b: 7, 9).

8 This is what, among other things, Sylvie Laurent highlights in a magnificent biography of Martin Luther King, Jr by recalling that, from the beginning, actions practised in the name of non-violence were a 'companion with death' (Laurent 2015: 127).

9 'How can we be affectionate toward a person whose avowed aim is to crush our very being and place innumerable stumbling blocks in our path? How can we like a person who is threatening our children and bombing our homes? That is impossible. But Jesus recognized that *love* is greater than *like*. When Jesus bids us to love our enemies, he is speaking neither of *eros* nor *philia*; he is speaking of *agape*, understanding and creative, redemptive goodwill for all men' (King 2010: 46–7).

10 'In the midst of blatant injustices inflicted upon the Negro, I have watched white churchmen stand on the sideline and mouth pious irrelevancies and sanctimonious trivialities. In the midst of a mighty struggle to rid our nation of racial and economic injustice, I have heard many ministers say: "Those are social issues, with which the gospel has no real concern." And I have watched many churches commit themselves to a completely otherworldly religion which makes a strange, un-Biblical distinction between body and soul, between the sacred and the secular' (King 2000: 105).

11 See Part II, Chapter 5, 'Exiting Apartheid'.

5

Exiting Apartheid

I. On Imposed Hatred

There was every reason to think that this exit could not happen without a bloodbath. The apartheid regime itself seemed to imply it was the ineluctable horizon of its history. For decades, iniquitous laws had piled up to reinforce the domination of the Afrikaners by segregating the populations; the violences this domination justified had inscribed in its essence the spectre of a terrible end. The brutal repression of liberation movements, beginning with the African National Congress (ANC), the unpunished crimes, imprisonments, torture and assassinations not only demanded reparation: one day, when the wheel of history turns, they would have to be avenged. Such was the cost of segregation. Since it had no other objective, segregation had long since achieved its end, fulfilled its function, which was to render all conciliation, all understanding, all agreement impossible. As nothing was less imaginable for it than the peaceful reunion of the segregated communities into a common entity (a people, a nation) that would no longer differentiate, it had programmed from the beginning a bloody confrontation as its only possible outcome: an outcome from which it thus had to protect itself at all costs. The laws of segregation, like the law that confined the residence and activity of black people to determined settlement zones, had no other fantasy [*fantasme*] than this exit, which, in the minds of Afrikaners, could only lead to the bloody reversal of domination. Consequently, the regime of the National Party could not bend to any logic other than that of an interminable headlong rush into repression, an escalation of violence to which nothing could correspond except, should the balance of power unfortunately invert, the bad infinity of vengeance it ceaselessly dreaded.

At the end of the day, there had been no other response to this immurement in a murderous spiral than armed struggle, the one undertaken by the ANC in the early 1960s in the hopes of ultimately forcing the authorities not only to change the law but also, furthermore, to restore the spirit of the law so that it would no longer serve an exclusive racial minority and would now constitute a nation, which would recognise the same rights for all populations of South Africa. The hope thus consisted not in exercising a right to retaliate, which substitutes one domination for another, but rather in putting the law back on the right track by giving the country a new Constitution, which is to say, a foundational text effectively 'constitutive' of a reunited nation. Such reasoning amounted to reversing the roles of the outlaw and the defender of the law. Indeed, the functionaries of repression, the police and security forces, were no longer to be considered protectors of the laws; the protectors, rather, were those who actively aimed to substitute another law [*droit*] for the apartheid laws [*lois*] in conformity with an idea of the law that does not *ipso facto* amount to its perversion in an unjustifiable regime. In this way, agents of apartheid should be considered outlaws, while outlaws had to be recognised as defenders of a just law *to come*. However, by an aberration of history, the just are the ones who stood in judgement in the courts of the former.

As is well known, this was Nelson Mandela's defence strategy at the Rivonia Trial, which was held from October 1963 to May 1964, at the end of which he was sentenced to life imprisonment. Already in 1962 and 1963, during the Pretoria Trial, which would place him behind bars, the leader of the ANC made known the iniquity of the court preparing to judge him. Composed exclusively of white men, the court in its own right provided Mandela with living confirmation that, in this country of South Africa, equality before the law was an empty phrase and, as a result, the verdicts it would likely render to black men standing trial for their resistance against oppression at the hands of the white minority could only be a parody of justice. Proof lay in the collusion between the Judge President of this pseudo-tribunal and the officers of the political police. Mandela was accused of having incited a part of the population to demonstrate and strike in protest against the law that had established the Republic in the South African Union. The reason for this protest, however, was clear: it pertained to the fact that, once again, only white people were involved in the process. As a result, the newly established Republic was not only partisan and partial but truncated from the start. Returning to the political organisation that existed before the white man's arrival, the memory of which was transmitted from generation to generation, Mandela had no difficulty explaining to his judges what this confiscation ratified: for the tribes of South Africa, the deprivation of *their* freedom, which translated into a suppression of *their* political sovereignty. In these conditions, was it illegitimate to demand – as the first condition for re-establishing justice – that 'all people, irrespective of the national groups to which they may belong, and irrespective of the colour of their skins, all people whose home is South Africa and who believe in the principles of democracy and of equality of men, should be treated as Africans' (Mandela 2018: 21)? Yet, adopted in 1955 not only by the ANC but also the South African Indian Congress and the Coloured People's Congress, the Freedom Charter asked for nothing else, and its principles had inspired the latest strike. It first and foremost aimed, once again, to confront the South African government with its responsibilities, while the government itself only ever answered the ANC's campaigns with renewed terror. But the Freedom Charter also obliged those who adopted it to oppose the law designed by the nationalist government insofar as it was '*immoral*, unjust, and intolerable' (Mandela 2018: 21, emphasis added). By what means? Once the government refused all discussion and chose only repression, once the democracy that would have required black voices to be heard equally existed only on paper, use of the only language that power seemed to understand (and Mandela's defence resonated like a warning) could not be ruled out: the language of violence.

Politically inadmissible, *morally* unjust! It will be noted, before returning to this point at length, that moral and political considerations mixed together indissociably in the assessment of apartheid laws. However, there was still more to the ANC leader's defence. Mandela, lawyer that he was, recited to these judges all the vexatious measures, the trammels suffered in the exercise of his trade for over ten years, the restrictions imposed upon his freedom to reside and move about, the interdictions against his participation in any public meeting, the discrimination – encountered even within the court system – toward and against any idea of an impartial and equitable justice. He exposed how the power that they, the judges, represented had harassed him for years, denying him any trusting relationship with his friends, his wife, his children, forcing him into the hunted life of an outlaw. This life, he confessed to them, is not the life one chooses to lead in a 'civilised community' (2018: 24), but it reflected the true face of South African society, a society within which, for decades, 'the government was busy whipping up an atmosphere of hysteria'.[1] Finally, the ANC leader threw in the faces of his judges the *hatred* that this entire system consequently inspired in him.

> I hate the practice of race discrimination, and in my hatred I am sustained by the fact that the overwhelming majority of mankind hate it equally. I hate the systemic inculcation of children with colour prejudice and I am sustained in that hatred by the fact that the overwhelming majority of mankind, here and abroad, are with me in that. I hate the racial arrogance which decrees that the good things of life shall be retained as the exclusive right of a minority of the population, and which reduces the majority of the population to a position of subservience and inferiority, and maintains them as voteless chattels to work where they are told and behave as they are told by the ruling minority. [. . .] Nothing that this Court can do to me will change in any way that hatred in me, which can only be removed by the removal of [. . .] injustice and [. . .] inhumanity [. . .]. (Mandela 2018: 25)

Hatred! It has hardly left us since the opening pages of this book. And, until now, we have always found its negative connotations, rejecting its past and present instrumentalisations: the factory of hatred. Yet, can one deny that singular and collective situations exist in which it is irresistible and perhaps even necessary to hate? In other words, can one deny that words, discourses, practices, laws, institutions exist that are *objectively hateful*? Can one contest that, in the throes of legitimate anger, it is better to feel hatred and get carried away by its devastation than to remain indifferent, to submit passively, to accommodate or resign oneself? These questions are incontrovertible, and they call for two responses. The first is that, when Mandela exposes the hatred that racism and its manifestations inspire in him, he expresses the effect of a *prior* destruction. He responds to a provocation that has proved devastating for a long time. Something must have *already* been irremediably broken for this irrepressible hatred to be legitimate. This anteriority, which is an upheaval, is well known: *racial hatred*. Hence the second detail for which these questions call: this posterior hatred, reactive in essence, cannot have the same motives. It cannot be – and can never be – of the same nature or stand on the same ground. It cannot present itself, inversely, as black people's hatred for white people. This is the most decisive point! It indicates – and this will have to be remembered – that in no case does hatred constitute a political solution. It responds to racism but only so as better to exit it; it has sense only in this overcoming.

Two years later, sentenced to three years of forced labour for inciting rebellion and an additional two years for leaving the country without permission, when Mandela was taken from his cell to be judged again in the so-called Rivonia Trial, the allegations against him were more serious still. Accused of sabotage and revolutionary conspiracy, the imprisoned leader risked the death penalty. One of the charges against him was founding uMkhonto, the armed wing of the ANC, and therefore for being responsible for the violent actions attributed to this organisation. Thus, he had to begin his defence by explaining the place of violence in the ANC's strategy, a violence into which – he never stopped repeating this[2] – the ANC leaders were cornered and to which they ended up resolving themselves after having long rejected it. In their eyes, two reasons had justified breaking from the tradition of non-violence that, inspired by Gandhi, had long served as the principle of the ANC's struggle. The first related to the National Party's will to obstructionism. The oppression exercised by the regime was so irremediable [*sans issue*] that it had made this rupture inevitable. It had created in society an explosive ferment that needed to be channelled and organised because, if left to itself, it would have led to a proliferation of disorderly terrorist acts. The risk, as Mandela explained to his judges, was to allow 'an intensity of bitterness and hostility' to settle 'between the various races of this country which is not produced even by war' (2018: 28). The second reason pertained to the fact that, with avenues for legal opposition having been suppressed by the party in power, the white minority had left the black majority with no other means of expression. 'We did not want an interracial war', he had to add, 'and [we] tried to avoid it to the last minute' (2018: 29).[3]

Three traits thus characterised the recourse to violence, which must be remembered when analysing the conditions for exiting apartheid some thirty years later: the abandonment of the principle of non-violence was not presented as a historical necessity but, rather, as the effect of extreme political circumstances. Nor was it an ultimate solution, the last word; rather, it constituted a *provisional* means for bringing the adversary – the National Party of the Afrikaners – back onto the path of dialogue and negotiations. Finally, it was essentially defensive; the black population was justified [*en droit*] in feeling assaulted for decades, and not the reverse. And yet, the black population had not sought war, had not wanted to bear arms, had clung to their principle of non-violence as much as they could, year after year, despite all of the provocations. Nor was their past or present objective the reversal of domination, as they ceaselessly repeated their hostility to a race war. They only demanded, with a radical intransigence that could no longer accommodate the violences they were suffering, that their legitimate rights [*droits*] be recognised. Throughout the rest of his defence, Mandela would never stop reminding his judges that he intended to stand first of all on this legal ground [*du droit*]. Thus, his defence strategy did not deviate from the path taken two years earlier. After having provided a clear report on the devastating effects of the apartheid laws, the destitution that its laws propagated, the criminality, the feeling of inferiority, the broken relations, the violations of human dignity, he reminded his judges, like Martin Luther King, Jr, at the same time in the United States,[4] of the extent to which these rights – in default of which the law turned against itself – symptomatically reflect the Afrikaners' fear of democracy, that is, fear of a regime in which black people, the majority, would be able to demand and obtain living wages, to choose freely the place of their residence, in a word, to leave their ghettos:

> Above all, we want equal political rights, because without them our disabilities will be permanent. I know this sounds revolutionary to the whites in this country, because the majority of voters will be Africans. This makes the white man fear democracy.
>
> But this fear cannot be allowed to stand in the way of the only solution which will guarantee racial harmony and freedom for all. It is not true that the enfranchisement of all will result in racial domination. Political division based on colour is entirely artificial and, when it disappears, so will the domination of one colour group by another. [. . .]

> I have fought against white domination, and I have fought against black domination. I have cherished the ideal of a democratic and free society in which all persons live together in harmony and with equal opportunities. It is an ideal which I hope to live for and to achieve. But if needs be, it is an ideal for which I am prepared to die. (Mandela 2018: 41–2)

II. On the Apartheid Laws

However, the analysis must be pushed further. For the principled refusal of violence, long preserved before being provisionally abandoned, is in the eyes of the ANC leader indissociable from what constitutes the second motif of his defence: his fascination with the law. This would not escape the attention of Jacques Derrida, who, participating in a 1986 collected volume modestly titled *For Nelson Mandela*, would title his contribution 'The Laws of Reflection: Nelson Mandela, in Admiration'. Let's stop for a moment on this title and its double genitive![5] It conjugates two admirations: the admiration undoubtedly signalled by the philosopher's homage to the ANC militant, imprisoned for a quarter of a century at the time, but also the admiration that Mandela professes in his defence for the law itself, the law recognised and applied by democratic States, the quintessence of which he sees displayed by 'the Magna Carta, the Petition of Rights, and the Bill of Rights' (Mandela 2018: 37). The second admiration conditions the first. What fascinates Derrida about Mandela is, among other things, his admiring relation to the law. And what Mandela admires about the law is its force: that of a lever, initially non-violent, non-bloody, intended to turn 'against those who claim to be its guardians', against the supporters of apartheid (Derrida 2008: 66).

It would be a few more years (we are thus in 1986) before Derrida writes his major work on the law [*la loi et le droit*], 'Force of Law' (1994), which – taking a sustained reading of Walter Benjamin's 'Critique of Violence' as its guiding thread – returns to the distinction between two forms of violence that Benjamin proposes: the constitutive or foundational violence of law, and the violence that conserves law. In many respects, the text devoted to Mandela foreshadows this. It already highlights that a *coup de force* lies at the origin of every political regime, the bloodiest effects of which are erased over time. This first, constitutive violence is later called to cede its place to a second, conservative violence, which is held as the only legitimate violence and has no objective other than to preserve the previously founded law. What thus distinguishes the apartheid laws is that the initial coup was a 'bad *coup*' (Derrida 2008: 67, translation modified). Since the Constitution benefits only a particular minority that is never assured of its rights [*droit*], as we have seen while reading Mandela, what it founds cannot be sufficiently and durably founded without the madly murderous, vertiginous and zealous reproduction of a repetitive, founding violence. The Constitution fails to establish or to institute performatively what it claims to reflect, namely, the unity of a nation, for the only thing it is capable of thinking, the only thing it intends to defend and ceaselessly wants to strengthen at any cost and against all principles, is the exact opposite: not a real or symbolic union, but a radical separation. Such is the logic presiding over the repetitive escalation of the apartheid laws, which we must remember in order to know what we are talking about, as Mandela did *a posteriori* in his autobiography, *The Long Walk to Freedom*. Let's recall them, then! Among others, there was the 1953 Bantu Education Act, which sought to stamp teaching with the seal of apartheid.

That same year, there was also the Public Safety Act and, at the same time, the amendment to the criminal laws that launched the repression of protest movements [. . .] and still many others. With his own, unique force of conviction, Derrida describes this escalation, which has all the bad infinity of an insatiable vengeance:

> Here, the violence of origin must repeat itself indefinitely and imitate right in a legislative apparatus whose monstrosity fails to allay suspicion: a pathological proliferation of juridical prostheses (laws, acts, amendments) destined to legalize down to the smallest detail the most everyday effects of fundamental racism, of a state racism, the only and last state racism in the world. (Derrida 2008: 67)

This is how conditions vertiginously pile up, conditions which are not conditions of a living-together, or whatever name one gives to the union constitutive of the nation, but rather conditions of a hateful division. They graft on to each other to make an absolute separation, or the fantasy [*fantasme*] of separation, the only supposedly liveable form of coexistence.

Let's return to Mandela's defence, then! A second trait that distinguishes it recalls what was already encountered in the previous chapter while heeding King. Since the leader of the ANC, who is preparing to spend a good part of his life in prison, does not call for a 'race war', what does he demand? If no desire for revenge against whites on the part of blacks shows through in his indictment of his judges, what does he want? Really, nothing other than this: the Constitution *to reflect* otherwise, which is to say, finally *to create* that of which it claims 'to constitute' the mirror – the *nation* with all its members, *including the white minority*. This is the reason why it is at once necessary and just to abolish all the laws, amendments and decrees that, far from contributing to what Mandela wants, oppose it with the whole force of their constraint. From the depths of his prison, Mandela will have never renounced this ideal, which remained intact until the day of his liberation. As long as the apartheid regime lasted, there resulted a distinction between just and unjust laws, a distinction similar to the distinction that, on the other side of the ocean, the leader of the struggle for civil rights judged necessary to establish. A law is unjust and calls for disobedience the moment when – far from resting upon the will of the whole people, reflecting it or serving the fiction – it reveals itself to be in the service of particular interests without any other possible reason or interpretation. Conversely, any law is just if carried by the dream or the promise of a Constitution and a legal regime that transcends divisions, that overcomes them and sends them to the dustbin of history: what Mandela will call, nearly three decades later, the 'rainbow nation'.

So, returning to Derrida, one can better understand the 'laws of reflection' he puts forward. The reflection is distorted, perhaps *disjointed*,[6] as soon as the law is privatised and its principle particularised. The reflection is distorted all the more violently insofar as it therefore masks what it deforms, not showing what it nevertheless reflects, which is precisely the absence or lack of its reflection. For, at the end of the day, the criminal apartheid laws do not reflect and will have never reflected anything other than the will to defend the exclusive and in the same stroke murderous interests of a community that grants itself, that will have granted itself rights over everyone else. This is what the ANC protested against, first of all by drafting the Freedom Charter in 1955, and never stopped reminding the defender of the law. Nine years later, Mandela's defence is in unison. It makes the

191

invisible visible. Even better, it finally produces the conditions for a new visibility, bringing to light what nobody wanted to see, which is the opposition between iniquitous laws – the apartheid laws – and a justice to come, a promised justice, the justice guaranteed by a new Constitution but first stubbornly whispered by the voice of the spirit, conscience or heart already familiar to us since Rolland[7] and King[8] both appealed to it, too. And yet, as one knows all too well, nothing excites the spite-fulness of the most murderous powers [*pouvoirs*] more than the untouchable forces [*puissances*] of these resisting voices. Nothing more was needed for the repression to intensify; for more than a quarter century, it dragged the country into a horrifying spiral of violences.

III. Healing the Wounds of the Past

Mandela would have to wait nearly thirty years for this justice promised by a new Constitution. Meanwhile, the crimes, destructions and traumas had accumulated to such an extent that there was no guarantee that such a process would be possible and that civil war could still be avoided. In any case, one thing was certain: there would be still less guarantee that civil war could be avoided if nothing were done to 'heal' the wounds of the past. Even if the agents of repression – the leaders, thinkers and functionaries of apartheid – would have liked it, these wounds could not close without revealing the truth of the crimes and violations that had engendered them, since everything that rests in memory, everything one cannot forget and dares not utter, bears a ferment of violence. Besides, nothing is decreed less, nothing resists all command and all political decision more, than forgetting. A traumatised memory is a force susceptible to being exploited, even instrumentalised, but no external will can abolish it. In a country ravished by impossible mourning, one must know that forgetting cannot be general or universal. There is nothing unifying about it; there is nothing in it that can assemble or unite. If some had to choose (but never can) amnesia, it could not be shared by all. It would be essentially partial, separating those who would force themselves (or who would believe they could force themselves) to forget from those who would never forget, would never want to forget and never could forget anything.

This is why amnesia, assuming that the strange idea of decreeing and imposing it should occur to a government, is always a miscalculation incapable of always excluding the risk of falling back into the infernal cycle of vengeance and its reprisals when the convenient, illusory or comfortable forgetting that some desire necessarily does violence to others' refusal to forget, if not even to their obsessive fear [*hantise*] of seeing the past erased. Then what should be done with the trace of the past? How to prevent the living memory of violations, their trauma, their after-effects from compromising in advance every peaceful solution? How does one rebuild a unity that has never existed, because others wanted and rendered it impossible from the start? It suffices to read, as I just did, Mandela's defence to understand that, from the day when the end of apartheid was finally in sight, this question hardly left him. As is known, this question would need a double response, not only by adopting a new Constitution but also, more so, by establishing in November 1995 the Truth and Reconciliation Commission (TRC), which was tasked with collecting the testimonies of victims and the confessions of criminals, all parties combined, to care for the former and amnesty the latter on the condition of shedding full light on their past crimes, one by one.

Yet, once again and with still more brutality, did amnesty not purchase peace by erasing crimes, asking all those who had kept alive in themselves the trace of violences suffered to parenthesise them so as to relearn finally how 'to live together'? In the foreword he wrote for the final report of the TRC, over which he presided, the Anglican Archbishop Desmond Tutu – aware of the risk of confusion – clarifies what radically distinguished the proposed amnesty from amnesia. While the latter seems like erasing the past for the sake of settling accounts, the former cannot in principle be assigned a definite end. Since testimonies could only be collected and crimes amnestied *one by one*, it was effectively impossible for the truth to be given *at once* and *once and for all*. No more than the past could be erased, in other words, its truth could not be definitively instituted or established. Assuming the historian could make this claim, this was certainly not the case for this Commission. The process put in place was akin to neither an unveiling nor even a revelation but, rather, a laborious presentation that, step by step, would not end even with the completion of the Commission's work. Paragraphs 17 and 18 from the 'Foreword by Chairperson' should be read carefully:

> 17. The past, it has been said, is another country. The way its stories are told and the way they are heard change as the years go by. The spotlight gyrates, exposing old lies and illuminating new truths. As a fuller picture emerges, a new piece of the jigsaw puzzle of our past settles into place.

> 18. Inevitably, evidence and information about our past will continue to emerge, as indeed they must. The report of the

Commission will now take its place in the historical landscape
of which future generations will try to make sense – searching
for the clues that lead, endlessly, to a truth that will, in the very
nature of things, never be fully revealed. (Tutu 1998)

The principally endless process of bringing forth the truth:
such was the condition of its political efficacy. Tutu was aware – as
were, undoubtedly, the other members of the TRC and Mandela,
who put the TRC into place – that the past, refusing to 'lie
down quietly', retained an explosive charge that needed to be
constantly neutralised. It is significant that the metaphor used
to conceive the past should be a wound that runs the constant
risk of festering, which one must not only watch over to ensure
that it initially heals but also prevent from reopening. Levinas,
for his part, spoke of a 'tumour in the memory'[9] to evoke the
memory of the Shoah, to which – rightly – the Chairperson
of the TRC also makes reference in his foreword. When one
speaks of wounds of the past or a 'tumour in the memory',
indeed, one should guard against generalisations. These wounds
and tumours always have a double dimension. On the one hand,
they effectively refer to an entire community – cultural, religious,
linguistic, national, 'ethnic', 'racial' or otherwise – upon whom
these expressions bestow the status of victim in precise historical
and political circumstances. On the other hand, they designate
a discontinuous addition of singularities without an assignable
end. Indeed, each time, *singular beings* harbour the trace of past
violences in their own flesh or in the memory of loved ones –
a husband, a wife, grandparents, parents, brothers and sisters,
children, friends, comrades – who have suffered violences. This
is what should not be forgotten and what justified the decision
to focus amnesty upon the crimes of individuals, the violations

those crimes signified and the traumas they had engendered *one by one*: for each time singular, irreplaceable, unsubstitutable, vital relationships were destroyed. Victims were invited to testify to these very concrete destructions, and perpetrators had the duty to recognise these destructions (and not their generalised abstraction) as their responsibility.

Whether in Argentina, Chile, Algeria, Rwanda or elsewhere, amnesty is always a politics of singularities. It was so in South Africa, and from this perspective it was important that the floor be given to victims, that their testimonies be not only the first collected but also, additionally, the first heard *by all*. The order here made reparations from the start, since it consisted in breaking the dictatorship of silence by listening in the first place, in accordance with a new order of precedence, to those who had never before had the right. This rupture was not lip service. To liberate these buried stories, to give them a wide and public audience, to make it impossible for anyone to ignore them – beginning with Afrikaners – signalled to the criminals and their accomplices, to all who had consented to their crimes or who pretended not to know, to all who wanted to believe or make others believe they knew nothing, that they could no longer count on their victims' silence in order to hide their faces. And this is when the political strategy of amnesty (a 'deposing' of apartheid without a bloodbath) would take on an ethical dimension that is complementary and conditional. For the truth – brought forth by both sides together – to have this effect, for this attention not to be a sham or ultimately constitute the stumbling block for a new nation, if not the lever of its construction, *it had to be able to shame*.

Shame! How should such a requirement be understood? What was the meaning of the report and the joint injunction according to which truth should shame or should have shamed?

Above all else, this implied that truth's vocation was to make it impossible for any Afrikaner to attempt to dissociate him- or herself in good conscience from apartheid violences, whether they accepted, encouraged or perpetrated them. Shame was supposed to remind everyone that it was no longer possible to act as if, despite everything and even if unwittingly, they had not stood in solidarity with this criminal past. Shame confronts everyone with their own active or passive murderous consent. For this past was terrible, unbearable to hear! Words were lacking to relate the traumatic truth that the testimonies exhibited. Few accounts brought out the ensuing collective sorrow more clearly than that of the South African poet Antjie Krog. Listen to how *Country of My Skull* describes the trial [*l'épreuve*] of these hearings:

> I sit down on the steps and everything tears out of me. Flesh and blood can in the end only endure so much [. . .]. Every week we are stretched thinner and thinner over different pitches of grief [. . .]. How many people can one see crying, how much sorrow wrenched loose can one accommodate [. . .] and how does one get rid of the specific intonation of the words? It stays and stays. (Krog 2000: 65)

Later highlighting the extent to which the victims' narratives 'cut through class, language, persuasion', penetrating even 'the most frigid earhole of stone' (2000: 74), she adds:

> And hundreds of Afrikaners are walking this road – on their own with their own fears and shame and guilt. And some say it; most just live it. We are so utterly sorry. We are deeply ashamed and gripped with remorse. But hear us, we are from here. We will live it right – here – with you, for you. (2000: 125)

Nothing, however, was less certain than this effect of truth. If, in these circumstances, shame signified the impossibility of dissociating oneself from crimes of the past, it also implied, as a condition of this impossible distance, the will to free oneself from any partial and partisan, interested and consenting interpretation of the truth that, conversely, would have refused to recognise those crimes. Shame demanded thwarting the snares of belonging, since nothing is more contrary to accepting the truth than the deafness and blindness that these snares engender, as if proving oneself to be deaf and blind were a pledge of allegiance, as if admitting and publicly confessing the imputed crimes were a 'betrayal' of the linguistic, national, racial or religious community to which one 'belongs' or pretends to be faithful. It was the vocation of shame to thwart these pitfalls of identity and identifications, if not even to unmask them. It was up to shame to draw from the minds of Afrikaners a form of truth, no matter how painful, other than the form in which the lies of a complacent solidarity with past violations confined them. For the forces that shame collided against had the formidable power of denial and evasion, in all the forms they could take.

These denials occupy a considerable place in Krog's narratives, and they constitute no negligible part of the sorrowful character of her experience as a witness for the work of the TRC. The criminal strength of these denials comes from the fact that they constitute a resistance to both the truth and the shame that united by mutually supporting each other: one escapes shame by refusing to see truth, and one builds the fiction of a threatened society, thereby justifying recourse to violence, by rejecting the very idea that such a feeling was possible. One will have understood that this resistance was 'identarian' above all else. And if this resistance warns us about one thing, it is the ordinary regime in which community identity, always selective and regressive, is constructed. In the present case, this construction was selective because the 'identity of Afrikaners' assumed the establishment of an exclusive apparatus that supported no 'mixing', and the construction was regressive because it led to accepting violations by denying evidence of them. In this regard, Krog's report of Frederik de Klerk's deposition is significant. His lack of remorse was matched only by his evasion, which essentially consisted in maintaining that he did not know of all the abuses committed in the name of the National Party, that therefore in no case had these abuses been a constitutive element for the apartheid system or the object of a political decision. As a result, he insisted that not everything that could be considered criminal in his party's past was to be dismissed. If he was ready to admit that crimes were indeed committed, they should be attributed to the 'judgment clouded by [the] overzealousness or negligence' of their authors (Krog 2000: 136). This deposition was in fact consistent with the strategy of the National Party, which never ceased discrediting the work of the TRC. But this deposition also said something else. It pointed out that bringing forth the truth could not constitute a miracle cure; its vocation was not to ease tensions with the wave of a magic wand. How could it have done so? The deposition recalled that it would take time for the truth to impose itself, assimilate and begin producing these effects. This delay is precisely the time, safeguarded and protected from violence, that the Commission intended to create: a delay recognised and granted for a perilous and laborious transformation of hearts and minds, even though the emerging truth would imply, on both sides, increased vulnerability.

IV. The Nature of the Crimes:
Between Law, Ethics and Politics

However, the analysis must be pushed further. What needs to be understood, indeed, is the way in which, in the Commission's efforts to bring forth the truth, at stake was a complex articulation of ethics and politics on the preliminary background of their radical distinction. Reconciliation itself implied this articulation. Suppose the questions about it were: 'Why was it necessary?' 'Who would gain from it?' 'What would it or should it change in people's lives?' The answer, first, was political. It aimed to prevent a climate of vengeance from imposing the law of blood on both sides. It precluded this bloodthirst – the concern with which has hardly left us since the beginning of this book – by finding a derivative, a political solution that suspends the murderous effects of the negative passions of hatred and fear. However, neither passion had disappeared, and reconciliation had to reckon with their explosive ferment. This is why any preliminary and principal distinction between crimes and violations along party lines was excluded, even though the violences did not have the same meaning and could not be analysed in the same way, depending on whether they had been perpetrated in the name of apartheid or against its regime when, abandoning the principle of non-violence, the ANC had taken up armed action. Suspend the indissociably moral and political distinction between the crimes! This is the political act that conditioned the Commission's effectiveness, which is to say its equal – albeit minimal – recognition by all of the opposing forces. How else to keep some people from feeling wronged by others and, at the end of the day, the work from seeming like a game of dupes in which, under the mask of reconciliation, only revenge would have been at work? Tutu had to recall this firmly in paragraph 25 of his foreword:

> Some have criticised us because they believe we talk of some acts as morally justifiable and others not. Let us quickly state that the section of the Act relating to what constitutes a gross violation of human rights makes no moral distinction – it does not deal with morality. It deals with legality. A gross violation is a gross violation, whoever commits it and for whatever reason. There is thus legal equivalence between all perpetrators. Their political affiliation is irrelevant. If an ANC member tortures someone, that is a gross violation of the victim's rights. If a National Party member or a police officer tortures a prisoner, then that is a gross violation of the prisoner's rights.

There are two ways to understand Tutu's concern with highlighting the suspension of morality. The first consists in saying that the distinctions produced by morality ought to be put aside on account of their necessarily partial and interested character. The risk is that these distinctions would be contaminated by considerations of diverse orders that would compromise their impartiality. These distinctions, put otherwise, would never be clear and distinct enough to guarantee the equal treatment of everyone, and the criteria of good and evil, related to these categories, should be considered inappropriate since they would be assessed in various ways, depending on the situation, the strategic positioning, the armed camp of one side or another. Whatever else might be said of it, the invocation of morality will always be interested, partisan and thus impure. But does such a radical distrust of ethics align with the spirit that inspired the Commission's work? Nothing is less sure! Hence, there exists a second way to interpret the clarification offered by the Chairperson, whose activity as the head of the TRC, as we will see, was in reality inspired by more than one moral consideration. This second interpretation comes down to considering that, if morality must remain exterior to the legal assessment of facts, it is because evaluation of those facts stems from a necessary right that certainly has its political *raison d'être* – namely, to suspend the infernal cycle of vengeance – but should not therefore be confused in any way with the anticipated justice, even if it would be the condition of that justice. Assuming that the horizon of this justice is the indissociably moral and political constitution of the rainbow nation, which is to say the advent of a society that, finally rid of apartheid, forever invalidates all racial discrimination in everyone's hearts and minds by recognising that it belongs to radical evil, this means that it must pass through the legal process that remains *heterogenous* to this ultimate assessment of what is just and what is unjust, even though it is the condition of that assessment.

In reality, neither interpretation invalidates the other, and Tutu gives credence [*donne droit*] to both in the ensuing paragraphs of his foreword. In paragraphs 53 and 54, first of all, he highlights the ambivalence in the moral assessment of the acts by recalling that the perpetrators from the National Party had no justification for the horrible crimes of which they were guilty other than repeatedly invoking the war they were waging against evil and Communism, which they identified with an absolute evil. It was henceforth clear that the same act, according to the forces that assess it, could give rise to contradictory assessments. Did this mean all assessments took place on the same plane? From the outset, the Commission's Chairperson walks back any equalisation, any levelling that would lead to such a conclusion. 'A venerable tradition holds that those who use force to overthrow or even to oppose an unjust system occupy the moral high ground over those who use force to sustain that same system' (1998: 54).[10] It thus had to be recognised that their moral judgement was generally more legitimate than that of the agents and defenders of oppression. Undoubtedly, this did not justify any violation in principle [*en droit*], but it recalled that, despite an intractable concern for fairness, the TRC's work could not completely disregard 'a moral universe where right and wrong and justice and oppression matter' (1998: 54). Aware of the manoeuvres ceaselessly aiming to discredit the impartiality of this work, Tutu reaffirms this forcefully at the start of paragraph 56:

> We have sought to carry out our work to the best of our ability, without bias. I cannot, however, be asked to be neutral about apartheid. It is an intrinsically evil system. But I am even-handed in that I will let an apartheid supporter tell me what he or she sincerely believed moved him or her, and what his or her insights and perspectives were; and I will take these seriously into account in making my finding.

An 'evil system'! If the violations could not be distinguished on a strictly legal plane ('A gross violation is a gross violation'), they must be distinguished on another plane that was not exclusively one of political struggles either, depending on whether they served this system – encouraged, supported or maintained it – or whether they fought against it. In reality, three levels should be separated: the legal level that equalised crimes; the political level that did not abolish oppositions but prevented them from turning into a bloodbath by inscribing them into a democratic process; and, finally, the moral level that absolutely, without concession or reservation, condemns the apartheid regime. In his foreword, Tutu gives each of these three levels their due [*droit*]. He recalls both the legal impartiality of the process, a *sine qua non* of its effectiveness, and its democratic purpose: to spare the violence of a bloody transition *for everyone*. But it is at least as important to him to highlight the moral stakes in the recognition *by everyone* of apartheid as a crime against humanity. This double universality (*for everyone* and *by everyone*) constitutes the primary difficulty that confronts him. For his moral steering requires a conversion. He stipulates that, independently of any consideration of belonging, everyone *recognise* racism as a *radical evil* unconditionally and unequivocally.

Yet, this conversion is all the more difficult, laborious and perilous since, in South Africa, the roots of racism go much deeper than its systematic organisation in governmental policy. The Commission Chairperson recalls this in paragraph 65 of his foreword, which he presents as a condensed summary of the racist attacks on human dignity spanning South Africa's history, regardless of those – British or Boers – who were responsible:

> Racism came to South Africa in 1652; it has been part of the warp and woof of South African society since then. It was not the supporters of apartheid who gave this country the 1913 Land Act which ensured that the indigenous people of South Africa would effectively become hewers of wood and drawers of water for those with superior gun power from overseas. 1948 merely saw the beginning of a refinement and intensifying of repression, injustice and exploitation.

In other words, it was not merely a question of containing the violence in the short term within the framework of a democratic process for dispensing with apartheid, but also of bringing about in the long term a complete reconceptualisation of the country's history and the foundations of society. This resulted in a whole series of ineluctable ruptures. None of the conceptual and affective frameworks for defining belonging or the rules delimiting coexistence could remain the same. The story of Antjie Krog, who cannot forget that she herself grew up within an Afrikaner family, brings this difficult – and for many unacceptable – upheaval to light with all the force of a problematic identification. Undoubtedly, no society exists whose history is not marked, at one moment or another, by circumstantial crimes to which it consented either partially or totally. In each instance, sombre are the pages that stain its institutions for a determined stretch of time, remembered for the villainous laws and the violations they made possible: roundups, arbitrary detentions, displacements and deportations of entire populations, mass murders. And one knows that, when these criminal times subside, the society in question has not finished with these violences; it must organise reparation and assume responsibility for the memory of these violences through a political process that entails more than one decision. Yet, in the case of South Africa, like the case of the United States, the violence in question – a constitutive racism – cannot be considered circumstantial, much less accidental. At stake was not one page of history among others, with which it would be time to settle up, but rather a veritable culture. The author of *Country of My Skull* highlights this with the feeling of a contested and nonetheless implacable solidarity by evoking the strange familiarity she feels toward the perpetrators who belong to the world of her childhood: vocal intonations, postures, gestures, ways of speaking and thinking.

> What do I do with this? They are as familiar as my brothers, cousins, and school friends. Between us all distance is erased. Was there perhaps never a distance except the one I have built up with great effort within myself over the years? [. . .] From

the accents, I can guess where they buy their clothes, where they go on holiday, what car they drive, what music they listen to. What I have in common with them is a culture – and part of that culture over decades hatched the abominations for which they are responsible. In a sense, it is not these men but a culture that is asking for amnesty. (Krog 2000: 121)

As soon as this culture was stamped with the racist prejudices that overdetermined its reference points – beginning with the distribution of space, tasks and employment – one element dominated the culture, which we have already encountered through our earlier readings of Wright and King:[11] the presupposition, solidly rooted in hearts and minds, of hatred for the other. The most common conviction of white people, the common denominator of their culture that determined their way of living and thinking, pertained to the certainty that black people hated them. In Krog's narrative, this question recurs – and she highlights each time the contrast between the absence of manifest hatred in the victims of apartheid toward their oppressors and the hatred the latter project upon the former and anticipate like a coming explosion – with all the more fear in that the hatred seemed to be provisionally contained. They see it everywhere, imagine it where it is not. This hatred is the most durable part of their fantasies [fantasmes] and serves as their alibi for defying the entire process implemented by the Commission. Hence the 'white woman' in the Free State who tells the journalist that she does not to want to watch the televised broadcast of the TRC's work because she sees in it only a 'sea of hatred' (Krog 2000: 212). To which the latter responds with a decisive no, 'that is not true'; in all the hearings she has attended, 'there is really no hatred' (2000: 212).

V. The Language of Love

Avoiding violence is one thing. *Conquering hatred*, reversing the cultural presupposition of hatred into its opposite, is another. It is now time to come to the third level of analysis: the moral condition of exiting apartheid. It assumes clarification of the reconciliation that was presented as the primary objective – bringing forth the truth – in the Commission's work, but also the Ubuntu that defines (as much as the meaning of the word can be grasped) the 'community' it was supposed to engender. If racism imposed the language of hatred everywhere, this assumed first of all that another language, which Tutu unhesitatingly calls the language of 'love',[12] substitutes for the language of hatred. The expression deserves to be highlighted; it opens a whole series of questions, notably about the religious sources and inspiration for the Commission's Chairperson. To the degree that it was not only a matter of speaking the truth about the past, but also of doing this work in the language of 'love', one has the right, indeed, to wonder how this injunction should be understood. Who enjoins us to love whom? What relationship was there between this 'love', 'reconciliation' and Ubuntu? Finally, and above all, why did exiting apartheid necessitate and mobilise at this exact moment the invocation of particular spiritual, religious and moral resources by giving them the vocation of holding *for all* – all languages, all cultures, all 'origins' together – if it is true that the love in question had a dimension of this order?

However problematic, accepting such a language was nevertheless a precondition. 'Reconciliation' required bringing forth the truth, but hearing this same truth in itself assumed that one could hear it by first being freed from all prejudice and ulterior motive. How could one prevent the truth from producing excess wariness, resentment and anger through division? How can one even imagine that things could go otherwise when stories of the atrocities exceeded the imagination? Nothing was less obvious. A process could aim for reconciliation; reconciliation could not be decreed in the hearts and minds of each person. This is why Tutu could not sufficiently stress his 'amazement' at all the gestures and words of reconciliation coming largely from the victims – which is to say black people – who managed to contradict this apprehensiveness, but Tutu's 'amazement' also bespeaks his indignation at the reticence and manoeuvres by the leaders of the National Party in particular, who, inversely, had seemed to confirm it.

> We have been amazed at some almost breathtaking examples of reconciliation that have happened through the Commission. [. . .] On the whole we have been exhilarated by the magnanimity of those who should by rights be consumed by bitterness and a lust for revenge; who instead have time after time shown an astonishing magnanimity and willingness to forgive. [. . .] I have been saddened by what has appeared to be a mean-spiritedness in some of the leadership in the white community. They should be saying: 'How fortunate we are that these people do not want to treat us as we treated them. How fortunate that things have remained much the same for us except for the loss of some political power'. (1998: 71)

Krog's narrative also testifies to the different interpretations provoked by the very idea of 'reconciliation', the perplexity it inspires, the reticence it rouses. These different interpretations constitute the heart of *Country of My Skull*, the title of which in the French translation (*La Douleur des mots*),[13] while far from the original, at least has the merit of bespeaking the degree to which – everywhere in the world where this sort of process imposes itself as a double necessity (ethical and political) – reconciliation is a trial [*épreuve*] of language. It stipulates that, while nothing is less obvious, we trust the words spoken, that we give *credit* to what they manifest: the sorrow and forgiveness of victims, the remorse and the repentance of the perpetrators requesting amnesty. The challenge [*épreuve*] of reconciliation consists firstly in surmounting *its* own incredulity by making credible the incredible, by making imaginable what one barely dares to imagine, by making possible what the memory of the humiliations and violations, along with the confession of atrocities, would tend to make impossible. When all one's life one has been accustomed to 'speaking' and 'hearing' about others in the most contemptuous terms, when it was unthinkable to show them the slightest consideration, the slightest attention, when the use of language thoroughly reflected the division of society because language was itself contaminated from one end to another by the laws of exclusion and discrimination, when there were quite simply words that never crossed from some to others, how could one believe that another language was suddenly possible because it is desirable and desired?

What weight can one give words without being duped by circumstances? What sincerity to recognise in them when they went against these destructive language practices that, having paved the way for apartheid, had become a second nature, if not a sign of recognition, the token of belonging or an 'identity'? In *Country of My Skull*, the resultant suffering comes just as much from words conveying horror from the mouths of victims as from words – like forgiveness – that remain impossible to pronounce. But this suffering also comes from the mouths of the perpetrators through all the words that ring false and amount to denying wrongdoing, words that even redouble and maintain the wrongdoing by passing off reconciliation sometimes as a government ruse, sometimes as a comedy without consequence or wishful thinking. Significant in this respect are, among so many other things, the disillusioned indifference (he can do nothing about it), incredulity (he does not believe it), absence of compassion (he feels nothing before the child whose parents he killed) and inability to express remorse that Warrant Officer Paul van Vuuren displays throughout his interview with Krog:

> 'And they look at me and they think I am a monster . . . for sure I can feel it . . . their attitude and the way they look at me . . . I can actually say that I see the fear in their eyes as well as the hatred . . . The victim's lawyer says we must talk to them, but it is difficult . . . because every time we say we're sorry, they shake their heads and say they don't accept it . . . and that is also acceptable to me . . . You know, you say you're sorry, but on the other hand, it is also empty words . . . Do you understand what I'm trying to say? I mean here I walk up to a person I don't even know . . . and I say, "Listen here, I'm sorry". I mean isn't it just empty words?' (2000: 117)

This is why another language was necessary, a language that the elicited truth was not sufficient to define, but of which it was the precondition. And the first question concerned knowing how to describe this other language, how to understand in particular the 'love' that seems necessary to qualify it. The answer lies in the last paragraphs of the Chairperson's foreword, gathered under the title 'Reconciliation', and in the conclusion. These final reflections teach us that the expected result of bringing forth the truth was foremost the emergence of a consensus. Above all, perpetrators and victims had to agree that 'atrocious things happened on all sides' (Tutu 1998: 70). The first stone for the rainbow nation under construction demanded that establishing the facts cease to ferment division. Thus, amnesty was not an erasure but a restoration, and it restored not a lost unity – for a union had never existed in South Africa – but a double dignity. It allowed victims to see their suffering not only publicly recognised but also constitutive of a memory that would unify rather than divide. It would return to the perpetrators a bit of their lost humanity[14] and, along with it, the chance of integrating into a wider community freed from the criminal principles to which their prior conception of *their* identity had made them adhere. If a restoration was on the horizon, it was thus not the restoration of a past but, rather, of a future. This is what the expression 'the past is another country' means. It has as its counterpart the conviction that the future must also be 'another country'. This *consensus* about the past made possible the formation of this new 'we' that appears at the beginning of the Constitution.[15] It allowed society to rest, no longer upon several segregated 'identities' founded on racial distinctions, but rather upon only one and the same community that, in sharing the truth, exceeds those segregated identities. Tutu seems to say that there is at least one thing that should unite us: we know the cost of turning a blind eye to violence, of giving free rein to lies, torture and murder.

The truth was supposed to unify. Thus, how can the unification that the truth was called to produce be defined? This is where the overtly Christian dimension of reconciliation intervenes. For the Anglican Archbishop conceives this reconciled people, this people ready to celebrate its diversity in sharing one and the same truth and in the mutual refusal to see violences reproduced and divisions maintained, precisely as the 'family of God'. Paragraph 91 of his foreword should be read in detail:

Let us celebrate our diversity, our differences. God wants us as we are. South Africa wants and needs the Afrikaner, the English, the coloured, the Indian, the black. We are sisters and brothers in one family – God's family, the human family. [. . .] Let us move into the glorious future of a new kind of society where people count, not because of biological irrelevancies or other extraneous attributes, but because they are persons of infinite worth created in the image of God. Let that society be a new society – more compassionate, more caring, more gentle, more given to sharing [. . .].

Compassion, caring, gentleness, sharing: this is thus the language of love, and it is a language of Christianity! It first presents itself as a counterword opposed on all sides to the practices of the apartheid regime that Tutu unhesitatingly qualifies as a 'climate where moral standards have fallen disastrously' (1998: 70). No matter how particular and thus no matter how questionable the invoked virtues are, one must thus begin by recognising what they contradict. From the pen of he who had just spent months collecting testimonies from victims and perpetrators, these virtues take on their full sense when one thinks of the way in which these stories reminded him – and everyone who heard him – of the 'moral' signature of apartheid and every system of oppression and discrimination: a resilient refusal of compassion, a denial of charity, brutality understood as the ordinary mode for relating to others, an obsessive and unhealthy dread of all sharing. However, the imposing reference to Christian values inevitably became problematic in the effort to elicit adherence to a political process and to a social project in which Christians constituted only one part of the population concerned. Could the rainbow nation constitute itself by proclaiming moral and spiritual values that so visibly belonged to a determined fraction of the people called to unify? Once again, wasn't there something like a *commandeering of the universal*?

In a session of his seminar on pardon and perjury devoted to the processes of reconciliation underway in South Africa, Derrida did not fail to raise this point, recalling how the Preamble of the new Constitution invokes God in the following form: 'May God protect our people' (Constitution of the Republic South Africa 1996: 1). As soon as the constituted people defined themselves by their recognition of past injustices, by their will to 'heal the divisions of the past' and thereby establish 'a society based on democratic values, social justice and fundamental human rights' (Constitution 1996: 1), all these performative acts constitutive of an unprecedented 'we' found themselves placed under the protection of God.

Hence, the moment when the Constitution intended to found the existence of a new people no longer divided, a people united and reconciled, it anchored the people in the implicit recognition of a heritage that was foremost Christian: the Anglican, Protestant and above all Calvinist heritage of the Afrikaners. The very idea of reconciliation contributed to it since, as Derrida pointed out insistently, this concept with very Hegelian connotations came from [*relevait de*] Christian semantics. Finally, the issue grew still more complicated if one recalls that this reference to God had to be translated into more than one language: two African languages and the Afrikaner idiom. English hegemony, Christian semantic! The two went hand in hand, and they did not fail to rouse controversy. Here is how Derrida summarised the situation:

> Among all the complaints that have been made to this committee, presided over by the Anglican Bishop Desmond Tutu, who

played no small role in Christianising the language, even the spirit and the axiomatic, there was this one: taking for granted the translation of African idioms. These are not merely questions of language. It is a question of all the cultural and symbolic genealogies that work on words. He was therefore reproached for translating the eleven African idioms into the language that prevails, the English idiom, which is also to say, the Christian idiom. (2004: 116)

Nevertheless, the difficulty is not so much noting this as measuring its efficacy and necessity. If one closely follows the establishment of the process and the rhetoric accompanying it, the difficult question concerns the nature of this ultimate and in reality fundamental recourse to Christianity. On the one hand, it has been seen how exiting apartheid, which is first and foremost a political problem, also includes a moral dimension, given the nature of the deposed regime. This exiting assumes nothing less than a radical conversion, which amounts to recognising racism in all its manifestations – its language, gestures, crimes – as a radical evil. On the other hand, this dimension that engages all communities constituting the rainbow nation finds itself immediately bent to a culture (Christianity) that cannot be considered universal, from the point of view both of the language that this culture imposes on these communities (English) and the values it puts forth and with which it thereby ratifies its controversial vocation of universality (love, compassion, charity, sharing, forgiveness). The message and spirit of the Commission find themselves *forcefully* translated into a given semantic in which everyone – regardless of their language, culture, beliefs or history – is asked to recognise what is truly important *for the future nation*. The absence of consideration for 'colour, race, class, belief or sex' (Tutu 1998: 91) that defines its progression into the future is professed in the language of a particular religion. Everything thus happens as if *what is coming*, what must imperatively come to put an end to apartheid, *must* be Christian.

In this regard, can one speak of symbolic violence? Is there still something 'colonial' about this imposition, in the sense that, as Derrida maintains in *The Other Heading* (1992), the 'colonial' is the essence of all culture? Without a doubt! And yet, these values 'speak' *to all*, and they effectively have the sense of 'healing' *for all*, since they relate to the situation it is a matter of exiting: the 'disastrous' moral 'climate' of apartheid (Tutu 1998: 70). Indeed, nobody can deny that racism effectively excludes in principle compassion, charity, love and sharing, even in the Christian sense of the terms. Nobody can deny that this is precisely what all segregationist violence attacks first in the relationships it destroys. Nor, however, does anything say that this cannot be thought and expressed in another language and with other spiritual resources. The reference to Christianity is thus ambivalent. It is effective, but exclusive. This is why its necessity remains problematic. The question, in reality, is double and very similar to the one we already encountered while reading texts by King. Was it necessary to appeal to a moral doctrine of – once again – love in order to exit violence? And how can one explain that the Christian doctrine of love imposes itself?

Notes

1 This quotation from Mandela's statement at the Pretoria Trial was omitted from the abridged version printed in *In His Own Words* (2018), so this quotation is cited from the fuller version published online by the United Nations (see Mandela 1962). – Translators

2 'Even after 1949, the ANC remained determined to avoid violence' (Mandela 2018: 29). 'During the Defiance Campaign, the Public Safety Act and the Criminal Law Amendment Act were passed. [. . .] Despite this, the protests continued and the ANC adhered to its policy of non-violence' (2018: 29). 'The stay-at-home [the strike in 1960], in accordance with ANC policy, was to be a peaceful demonstration. Careful instructions were given to organisers and members to avoid any recourse to violence' (2018: 31).

3 'We of the ANC had always stood for a nonracial democracy, and we shrank from any action which might drive the races further apart than they already were' (Mandela 2018: 32).

4 See Part II, Chapter 4, 'The "Snares of Identity"'.

5 The 'double genitive' to which Crépon refers gets erased from the English translation of Derrida's essay when *Admiration de Nelson Mandela* appears as 'Nelson Mandela, in Admiration'. – Translators

6 In the sense that Derrida gives to this disjunction, this being 'out of joint', in *Specters of Marx* (2006).

7 See Part II, Chapters 1, 2, and 3.

8 See Part II, Chapter 4, 'The "Snares of Identity"', p. 145 ff.

9 For the scope Levinas gives to this expression, see Crépon, *The Vocation of Writing* (2018b).

10 Here and for the rest of this chapter, parenthetical citations of Tutu's foreword to the TRC report refer to standardised *paragraph* numbers rather than page numbers. – Translators

11 See Part II, Chapter 4, 'The "Snares of Identity"', p. 145 ff.

12 From paragraph 66 of the 'Foreword by Chairperson': 'To lift up racism and apartheid is not to gloat over or to humiliate the Afrikaner or the white community. Is it to try to speak the truth in love.'

13 A literal English translation of the French title of Krog's book would be something akin to *The Sorrow of Words*. – Translators

14 See the very beautiful testimony that Krog relates in *Country of My Skull*: '"This thing called reconciliation [. . .] if I am understanding it correctly [. . .] if it means this perpetrator, this man who has killed Christopher Piet, if it means he becomes human again, this man, so that I, so that all of us, get our humanity back [. . .] then I agree, then I support it all", declares Cynthia Ngewu, mother of Christopher Piet, one of the Guguletu Seven' (Krog 2000: 142).

15 The preamble of the Constitution of South African reads: 'We, the people of South Africa, recognise the injustices of our past [. . .]'. – Translators

6

On the Memory of a Genocide

I was mad with rage seeing all those heaps of dead bodies in Kigali. But you know all too well, after the genocide, life continued. They massacre people somewhere else, and we felt helpless. That's what's terrible: we can't do anything. It would take an entire lifetime. Our days are so short and the killers have so much more energy than decent people!
Boubacar Boris Diop (2016: 64)

I

When history or philosophy confront the memory of a genocide, like that of the Tutsis in Rwanda in 1994, they always seem to stumble over the abstraction of number. They quantify the violence, conflating the victims into an anonymous mass, even though every one of them should be remembered according to what constituted his or her absolute singularity. They unwittingly confirm the erasure of the eliminated lives, as singular lives irreducible to each other, which is the very essence of genocidal terror. In the novel by Boubacar Boris Diop, *Murambi, The Book of Bones*, which recounts the return to Rwanda of a man (Cornelius) whose father (the doctor Joseph Karekezi) had been one of the most ferocious organisers of the Tutsi massacre, a brief exchange between Cornelius and his guide during his visit to the Murambi Polytechnic School, that shrine of terror frozen in catacombs, recalls this risk with a particular intensity:

> He was satisfied to look, silent, horrified.
> 'Do you want to go on, sir?'
> The man must have noticed Cornelius's efforts to brave the nauseating stench of decomposing bodies.
> 'Yes. I want to see everything.'
> 'You'll see the same bodies everywhere.'
> 'No', said Cornelius dryly, 'I don't think so.'
> He was so furious with the unknown man that he almost asked him to leave him alone. This sudden bout of rage revealed to him his own suffering, much more profound than he had thought.
> The man said:
> 'Yes, you're right. I'm sorry.'
> Of course he was right. Each one of these corpses had had a life that was different from that of all the others, each one had dreamed and navigated between doubt and hope, between love and hate. (Diop 2016: 146–7)

Historical or conceptual, analysis is powerless to restore these singular lives, these dreams and navigations between doubt and hope, love and hate, that comprise the tissue of existence, when it reduces genocidal terror to the 'mass' of its victims. Whence the question that disturbs their certainties at the limits of representation. How to do justice to their singularity? How to respond to their 'call' from the other side? The hypothesis I would like to sustain in the present chapter holds that, if this is an inescapable dimension of the refusal of violence, literature *alone* is able confront it. In other words, the very words from Diop's book, *stories and testimonies must give flesh and figure back to bones.* However, in question is neither making the dead speak in an interminable prosopopoeia, nor of addressing them in an impossible dialogue from beyond the grave. Siméon Habineza, who stands out in the novel as the guardian of a bereaved memory that he keeps from descending into madness, warns Cornelius:

> 'There are no words to speak to the dead', said Siméon in a tense voice. 'They won't get up to answer you. What you'll learn there is that everything is quite over for the dead of Murambi. And maybe then you'll respect human life more.' (2016: 167–8)

In question is the possibility of restoring, in all their concreteness, individual lives, voices, bodies in movement, relationships, attachments, their history and their destiny, so as never to forget or confuse what genocide breaks and destroys. This is why the last part of *Murambi, The Book of Bones* is also perhaps its beginning. Everything happens as if precisely the haunted site of terror – the haunting of cadavers, skeletons, decomposing flesh and nameless corpses – called for the story. As if, in the space of a book, life needed to be recalled, as if some bodies needed to be revived for the genocide to escape its 'reasons', its 'justifications', its random 'explanations', like all those who will have invoked historical motives or attributed the genocide to ancestral hatred or irreducible ethnic tensions; as if life needed to be recalled and bodies revived for violence to be considered, contrary to all these masks, in the nakedness of its truth.

II

And yet, where ideologies weigh in, quibbles are not absent from the story. They punctuate the narrative as untruths, prejudices, simplifications that – put into perspective by Diop – redouble the violence they signify. They strengthen the violence insofar as they find 'good' reasons for it, one way or another, whether those reasons come from the murderers' strategies and their good conscience or from States' calculation, beginning with France, which was suspected of complicit passivity, indeed, the indifference of distant witnesses. Such are the two levels that ceaselessly interfere. On the one hand, *Murambi, The Book of Bones* represents the genocide. Assuming such an undertaking is possible, it reinscribes in readers' memory the genocide in all the cruelty of its planning and execution. On the other hand, the novel recalls all the false explanations or representations to which the genocide gave rise before, during and after all the words used, all the phrases constructed to avoid seeing and hearing what its horror meant in its most extreme brutality: millions of lives eliminated. Cornelius thus recalls his meeting with his girlfriend Zakya:

'From the first few days of our meeting, she wanted to know everything about Rwanda', he said to Jessica.

'Well, of course, she had the same old stereotypes in her head: two ethnic groups who've hated each other since time immemorial.'

'Of course. I tried to explain it to her patiently. I told her that it wasn't true and especially that the first massacres dated from 1959 and not from the beginning of time.'

[. . .] However, Zakya was not easy to convince. One day when we found her a little less reticent, he explained to her that there had never been any ethnic groups in Rwanda and that nothing distinguished the Twa, the Hutu, and the Tutsi. Straightaway a flash ran across Zakya's face. Worried that that meant she might be taking him for a liar, he threw himself into some rather chaotic explanations. (Diop 2016: 65–6)[1]

These ways of saying genocide without saying it, of announcing it, of commenting upon it and of finding explanations for it – whether they come from the mouths of killers, the governments and militaries involved, or the temporising chancelleries – all had in common that they eclipsed any consideration for life or, to put it once again in the words of Siméon Habineza, any 'respect' – *first* – for 'human life', in the unconditionality it must have (2016: 79). Such respect, indeed, cannot come *second* or *after the fact*. As soon as this respect ceases to constitute the precondition for action and thought, it is already ridiculed. Except with the most extreme hypocrisy, it cannot be invoked *a posteriori*, like a regret. This is why all these ways of saying presupposed a denial of the life of the living – the abyssal oblivion of what nevertheless should have attached each to the irreducible singularity of each of those lives *primarily*. These ways of saying contributed to the *banalisation* of genocidal violence in the sense in which Hannah Arendt, regarding Eichmann, spoke of the 'banality of evil'.[2]

Thus, the force of the novel – that of its characters, executioners and victims and of Cornelius, who, before his return, bore witness to their intersecting destinies – lies in opposing the multiple figures of this banalisation with a 'counter-representation', a relation to events that no longer considers violence to be banal or ordinary, justified or comprehensible in any way, as soon as it depicts concrete lives by recounting what genocide *makes* of the existence of those on both sides, by recounting what it destroys, which is always singular, and by reviving in the space of a few pages the world constituted by not only each victim but also each executioner.

It remains to be known exactly what one understands by banalisation. Alternating between scenes unfolding in the time of the genocide and, four years later, scenes corresponding to Cornelius's return and his 'visit' to the Ntamara parish, the Nyamata church and the Murambi Polytechnic School, the novel's temporal structure highlights its triple layers: the layer that comes from the murderers themselves (the Interahamwe militiamen and the massacre ideologues, like Cornelius's father), the layer that belongs to witnesses who are falsely neutral (but neutrality is here necessarily guilt), passive, or indifferent (the French army), and finally the layer that already comes from memory's selective and oriented conciliations.

Over the course of the story, the character Faustin Gasana first voices this 'banalisation'. He embodies the time of the genocide's preparation. And we discover that this preparation is always lingual, which is to say that it bears inevitably upon a double semantic: one used to designate the victims of the planned massacre with pejorative and insulting terms, and one that names the announced killing by minimising its scope and significance. The latter semantic consists in avoiding these terms (massacre, killing, genocide, mass murder) in favour of the much more neutral term 'work'. The term recurs like a leitmotif: 'I'm going to do my work properly' (2016: 19); '[n]o one will be able to stop our boys from drinking, from singing and dancing to give themselves the courage for their work' (2016: 20). And a few pages later, the broadcaster on Radio Télévision Libre des Mille Collines repeats the same antiphon: 'Have fun, my friends, but don't forget the work that's waiting for you!' (2016: 28).

Or again, this semantic consists in presenting the killing as a simple duty, an obligation imposed by war. Such is the fundamental tonality of the speech by doctor Joseph Karekezi, the orchestrator and director of the Murambi massacre. 'Come what may, I'll have done my duty. Duty. A simple word that I'm fond of' (2016: 100), he confesses to justify *a priori* the cruelty he expects from the killers he oversees. But also: 'We are at war, period. The sadistic way that things sometimes happen is just a detail' (2016: 102). These substitutions neutralise above all any reference to vulnerability and mortality as such. From such perspectives, to kill is not to destroy life; it is not to put an end to someone's existence, to extinguish once again the world that he or she alone singularly embodied and that made all of his or her freedom; it is to execute a task like any other, to finish necessary work. Yet, if all perception of the other as vulnerable and mortal can thus be erased, it is also because the systematic debasement and outrageous stigmatisation of the other have prepared minds long in advance to cease perceiving the other as a commonly mortal human being. Names, qualifiers, adjectives will never have been strong enough to qualify the targeted victim in advance and in such a way that nothing can recall a common belonging, no matter how it is defined. One thinks here of that other story of the Rwandan genocide, which plunges to the roots of stigmatisation of the Tutsis: *Cockroaches*, by Scholastique Mukasonga. Cockroaches! Here is something all genocides have in common: to plunge into the deepest regions of our animal phobias in order to extract the names of animals that inevitably arouse repulsion: vermin, cockroaches, rats! Thus the long monologue by the Interahamwe Aloys Ndasingwa, summarised by these few words: 'Those cockroaches will find out soon enough that you should never attribute good intentions to your enemy' (Diop 2016: 83).

I just stressed that there were three forms or three layers to the banalisation of genocidal violence. The first, as was seen, proceeds from the speech of murderers, since they announce, plan and present the killings as a simple job, a duty, an obligation imposed by war, even blood required by history. The second concerns the support they find, the complicity they arouse, the interests that encourage them. In the name of the strategies that justify them, the dead hardly matter. They are the price to pay for a higher State policy that barely bothers with principles like the respect for human life that Siméon Habineza professes. In the case of the Rwandan genocide, this support, this complicity, these interests are indissociable from the French government's criminal responsibilities. They appear in the novel in the state of affairs constituted by the interview held between the 'butcher of Murambi', recognised as such, and Colonel Perrin and in the proposal to leave the scene of the massacre under the protection of the French army. They are even more apparent in the story concerning the procrastination of the French authorities assigned to the 'Rwandan case' (2016: 120). For it then becomes apparent that blood does not have the same price when it flows on either side of the oceans and seas, and cruelty is not judged to be equally serious when it occurs in Europe or in Africa. Between the lines appear all the racial prejudices and survivals of a colonial spirit that never disappeared, according to which there are people who are naturally, if not essentially, carried to and destined for violence:

> The Parisian strategists kept scratching their heads: so, Doctor Karekezi or no? Some of them said: 'Alright, he's a real bastard. And afterwards? Had they forgotten that in Africa political questions get resolved everywhere with extreme cruelty?' 'Besides', they added, 'the survivors of this alleged genocide were soon going to forget this entire episode'. (2016: 120–1)

Still remaining is the third form of banalising genocidal violence, that of memory itself. If it is true that the false explanations given by the alleged weight of history, the supposed interethnic conflicts, and the alleged 'character' of peoples or races have their own violence, it is also true that they are inscribed in collective memory and obliterate it. They unwittingly sanction the victory of terror; they unwillingly provide support *a posteriori* for its most insidious strategy, since that strategy has no other objective than to erase its own meaning at the very moment it is exercised. As was shown above, makers of massacres always act *as if* these were not human lives they eliminate by the millions, relations they violate, worlds they make disappear. The erasure of names in the anonymous heaps of bodies, the oblivion, the confusion of faces in the mass of victims, the charnel houses, the mass graves of which there are so many in Ukraine still today, in fact, recount everywhere the same history, which is the will no longer to see *distinctly*, singularly, *one by one* the beings destroyed. There is no doubt that such a banalisation occupies a central role in *Murambi, The Book of Bones*, as if the novel itself, in its own construction, was one way of responding to banalisation or, even better, of opposing it with what could be called a counter-memory, like what was described elsewhere as a 'counterword'.[3] If Cornelius ultimately appears as the central character in the story, the phrase that summarises his return should be taken as an emblem of the book: 'He wanted to know, down to the very last detail, how his family had been massacred' (2016: 44). Thus, the memory of violence, the active memory that not only needs to hear stories and testimonies but also to see, to know *first-hand*, to go to the massacre sites, to confront – as is the case here – the last traces, which is to say the 'bones' that give the book its title, the scopic drive that painfully animates the 'return of Cornelius': all correspond to the quite vital attempt to snatch violence from its erasure – the last form of its banalisation – in order to reinscribe it in its proper order and return to it the sense that it does not recognise for itself. This attempt reveals cruelty *as* cruelty, mass murder *as* mass murder, and not as mere work or historical necessity.

III

Yet, when the memory [*mémoire*] of violences is identified with the recollection [*souvenir*] of the victims, when it amounts to taking on the burden of an impossible mourning, it has no other objective than restoring to their disappearance the sense that the executioners always seek to remove, which is, as Vasily Grossman (2006) recalls with regard to the Stalinist terror and the Shoah, the extinction of a life, of a freedom, of a world. Memory retraces not only violence but also its banalisation to that which it destroys in the domain of interhuman relations. As recalled earlier, to this destruction, regardless of the layer to which it belongs, I gave the name 'murderous consent'. When philosophy approaches the literary text, it runs the risk – and puts what it reads at risk – of erecting itself as a hermeneut, of imposing a reading grid, which the self-supporting work in truth never needs. This is why, in the reflections offered here, at stake is by no means an explanation, even less a clarification. And if, despite everything, one resolves to speak of 'interpretation', the need to do so proceeds more from philosophical reflection, there where the latter discovers its own limits, than from the novelistic work.

What do we learn from *Murambi, The Book of Bones*? That the mechanics of genocide rest on the stratified organisation of such 'consent': the voluntary or forced eclipse of the responsibility, of the political and ethical order, for which the vulnerability and mortality of the other call. This eclipse is everywhere in Diop's book; it is the novel's pain. Help, care and attention lack at every instant. They lack first in the blinded minds and in the grimacing mouths of the executioners, intoxicated by beer and slogans, misled by the bloodthirst of ideologues, deaf to all prayer and to all compassion:

> An old woman said to us, 'My children, let me pray one last time.' A little old lady, all wizened. It's crazy, the number of people who've asked to pray one last time since yesterday. Our commander answered the old woman with an air of false astonishment, 'Ah! Mama, didn't you know? We spent the night in heaven and we fought the God of the Tutsis there until dawn! We killed him and now it's your turn.' With a single stroke of his machete he sent her head to the devil. (2016: 84)

And this 'consent' is contagious! It takes hostage the Hutus who at first had been averse to the calls for blood and thought they could stay out of the massacres. The novel then describes how this 'lock' or this 'barricade' of humanity – which is the repulsion of crime, blood and cruelty – ends up exploding, restoring to the death drive its right over the life drive. This is the irresistible logic according to which murder encourages murder, the power with which the initial constraint imposed upon those for whom there was no choice but to kill, against their will if need be, ultimately reverts into an 'active consent'. The story of Marina Nkusi's father is exemplary on this point. He initially refuses to associate with the killings: 'Ah! I can't agree to do it, those people have never done anything to me! It's savagery!' (2016: 88). Then, he finally caves in to the pressure of the images and speeches that legitimised them: 'Then he screamed:

"Don't you watch the television? It's like all wars, you kill people and then it's over!'" (2016: 88). Finally, he shows himself to be the most intractable of murderers: 'He went to the barricades. They tell us that he handles his machete like a maniac over there' (2016: 88). 'Murderous consent' also applies to the men and women for whom the genocide helps satisfy their need for vengeance, like Valérie Rumiya, who pursues Rosa Karemera in hatred. It is also, and this is not the least of its manifestations, the attitude of foreign governments − beginning with the French authorities − passive witnesses to the genocide summarised in one sentence by the conversation between Jean-Marc Gaujean and Colonel Étienne Perrin:

> 'But, Jean-Marc, we did nothing to prevent the massacres. We were the only ones in the world who could have done it'. I slid my finger along my left arm and said, 'My dear Jean-Marc, we're in blood up to here in all of this'. That was the very evidence, he knew it. (2016: 124)

Finally, and this is not the least painful episode in the novel, it sometimes happens that, in order to save their own lives, potential victims are themselves forced to consent to murder. Even if every action in this sense had been doomed to failure, at the very moment they do nothing to try to prevent it because they do not have the means to do so, preferring to keep quiet or to hide, turning their back on those who need help, abandoning them to their programmed deaths, they know that in the space of an instant they are compromising the vital link, the essential link, that binds them to the rest of humanity. Like an essential element of its cruelty and its pleasure [jouissance], such is the effect of the fear from which genocidal terror wants no one to escape. Jessica, the friend of Cornelius and Stanley, has this terrible experience in the novel. At an identity checkpoint in the early hours of the massacres, she finds herself forced to refuse help to a woman who needs it, thus sending her to certain death:

> A woman they've wounded but are waiting to finish off a bit later comes toward me, the right part of her jaw and chest covered with blood. She swears that she's not a Tutsi and begs me to explain it to the man in charge of the barrier. I move away from her very quickly. She insists. I tell her dryly to leave me alone. Seeing this, the Interahamwe militiaman is convinced that I'm on his side. He blurts out in a joyful peal of laughter:
> 'Ah! You're hardhearted my sister, so you are! Come on, you should take pity on her!'
> Then he brutally pushes the woman back toward the throat slitters before checking ID cards again. (2016: 32)

IV

But consent to murder is not inevitable. This is why figures and voices that resist it also illuminate Diop's story. Jessica herself represents during and after the genocide, despite this episode with the memory of which she will have to accept to live, the will to oppose the snare that violence sets in the heart and soul of those who succumb to its evidence. And it is certainly no coincidence if, in the novel, it is up to her to bear the remarkable testimony of another woman, a Hutu nun named Félicité, who, opposed to all the logics of belonging, chooses her side clearly. In the brief chapter devoted to her, she appears, in an exemplary way, as the proof that all freedom can oppose genocidal terror, even if by sacrificing one's life, and thus break the double logic that comprises the essence of genocide: 'murderous identities' and fear. 'Let them come', she responds to her brother, who enjoins her to stop aiding the Tutsis by helping them cross the border and warns her of the Interahamwe's arrival. 'Let them come. I will keep on saving human lives' (2016: 109).

Notes

1 See also: "'And what do foreigners say when they're shown such things?' – 'Nothing, Jessica. The rare few who are interested are sincerely upset. They think that Hutus kill Tutsis and Tutsis kill Hutus, that's all.' – 'You should have explained it to them. [. . .] I tried, but very quickly you're overcome by their sympathetic smiles. You tell them: stop all your nonsense about hatred from time immemorial, it began in 1959! You can tell everything and they're happy to nod their heads somewhat skeptically' (Diop 2016: 71).

2 See Arendt, *Eichmann in Jerusalem* (2006).

3 See Crépon, *The Vocation of Writing* (2018b).

Conclusion:
Responding to Hatred and Violence

I

In the history of philosophy in the last century, marked by two world wars, with their procession of suffering, destruction and acts of ineradicable cruelty, there is a phrase – the first of a book familiar with all these traumas – that reverberates like a quasi-injunction. These words open *Totality and Infinity*, the major book by Emmanuel Levinas that appeared in 1961: 'Everyone will readily agree that it is of the highest importance to know whether we are not duped by morality' (1969: 21). When, how, on what occasions, under what circumstances are we so 'duped'? There are undoubtedly multiple ways to deceive oneself or to deceive others *in the name* of morality, which is to say, by invoking moral precepts and imposing them upon each other. But this deception is strongest when this invocation becomes an inextinguishable source of violence and cruelty. We are never as 'duped by morality' as when enjoyment [*jouissance*] of torturing bodies and minds accompanies the pleasure [*plaisir*] of laying claim to these precepts or rules. A dupe, then, is one who pretends to ignore it, anyone – in other words – who sees nothing and knows nothing or prefers to see nothing and know nothing of this violence, anyone in addition who gets lost in justifying this violence or strives to prove its disciplinary necessity in the name of this same morality, which is to say, allegedly for the good of the men and women on whom the violence is carried out.

From among a thousand and one examples, one need only recall the example that the director Michael Haneke developed a few years ago in a film that teaches us a lot about the ambivalence of moral sentiments when they are based on a doctrine of punishment: *The White Ribbon*. What, then, is this film about? A father who, in the name of the educational precepts that he applies with an implacable rigour, tortures his children's bodies and minds and, at the same time, sows throughout the village the seeds of an evil that the director has no trouble making the psychical origin of cruel acts that marked Germany's destiny during the first half of the twentieth century. Actually, the mechanism he describes is double. First, the rules handed down to this ruthless father, these words that are not his, this disembodied and mechanically reproduced language are in their own right the source of infinite refinements in the cruelty exercised against children. Next, their first effect, really their only effect, is to transform the children in turn – all the ambivalence of their education is summed up here – into cruel and insensible beings.

There are, then, two major ways to orient responses to the questions that arise with regard to this dupery. Either we start from the principle that this violence and cruelty belong to the very essence of morality, as Nietzsche says of Kant's categorical imperative. The education, discipline, strictures, surveillance and control in all morality would imply the pleasure of psychologically or physically torturing and making the other suffer. Methods might vary from one era to another; nevertheless, the pyres of the Inquisition, the dungeons of disciplinary institutions, mortifications and privations would best express the essence of morality. Or – and this is another possibility – we try 'to rescue morality' by taking precautions not to be duped by it any longer, for example by spelling out the conditions of its universality or unconditionality in the hope that, if it applies to everyone as the principle of a universal legislation, morality can no longer be suspected of being motivated by any cruelty whatsoever; it will be exempt from all particular enjoyment [*jouissance*] and all singular pleasure [*plaisir*] in causing and seeing someone suffer. Such a perspective, which still wants to believe in the possibility of an irreproachable and universal morality, amounts to maintaining that all violence or every act of cruelty that would find its justification and legitimacy in the catechism, precepts or quibbles of a particular morality must be held as a perversion that turns morality against itself.

Unable to cite, read and analyse here all the treatises, catechisms and instruction manuals that would perfectly illustrate this violence lodged in the heart of moral prescriptions and the codified punishments that sanction any infraction of their rules, I will limit myself to recalling the way this violence haunts, for example, Ingmar Bergman's films, which offer infinite variations on the perversion of relationships that morally bind a man and a woman, a father and his children, a teacher and his or her students, brothers and sisters. At stake each time, indeed, is a rupture in the ties that bind beings together, a rupture in the minimal solidarity that *holds* us together and makes that attachment vital. Yet, the characters in each film – like those in, for example, *Scenes from a Marriage* or *Saraband* – also have a thousand and one reasons, each more moral than the next, to break these ties and take real pleasure in doing so. All the heritage, and all the educational, moral and religious capital behind which they hide, no longer save or protect the relationships but, rather, make them fragile and end up devastating them. For these same relationships, such heritage and capital become – like all 'rigid and constraining moral education' threatens to become – a source of insecurity.

II

But I will not orient this book's concluding reflections in this direction. Regretfully leaving aside the intimate and private forms of violence that destroy lives behind closed doors and shutters, away from prying eyes, I will instead focus on the field of prescriptions, injunctions and imperatives that accompanied the preceding chapters – namely, those commandments that engage the articulation of morality and politics for which Levinas's recommendation takes on a particular resonance. Indeed, whether we formulate them ourselves while calling for their intervention or political leaders, their advisors and supporters who put them forth to justify this or that decision and action, what is the status of these 'moral rules' of which politics is reminded? Are we not 'duped by morality' when a war's industrial, economic and geopolitical interests are disguised as a 'crusade against evil'? Isn't this the case every time, aiming to hold onto power or to perpetuate a *de facto* domination, military or police actions don the rags of morality with a good conscience that aspires to universality and is always indignant if not shared by all? And what is one to say when, in the name of this same morality, torture gets justified in defence of the good? Finally – and this is perhaps the most difficult question – are we not again and always duped by morality whenever, here or there, we look away from what we elsewhere condemn in the name of this same morality, which thus constitutes the pedestal upon which rest both a geometrically variable perception of evil and an entirely random and partial condemnation of cruelty? Is this not the very sense of the ambivalence that, for example, partisan uses of the concept of 'barbarism' will have always concealed?

And yet, as we have seen, we cannot renounce the necessity of such injunctions lightly. Can political decisions dispense with 'moral principles', especially when these decisions relate to life and death, vulnerability and mortality, and more generally whenever there is a risk of violence and threats of cruelty? What happens when we consider that politics *laughs* at morality and deals with morality only when calculating its own interests? What occurs, at the end of the day, if not something like a 'generalised consent to violence', the acceptance – resigned or rejoiceful – of all the means that seem necessary to the ends of a politics in pursuit of its objectives, no matter how exclusive, discriminatory, unequal, unjust and contrary to the most elementary principles of a shared solidarity they might be? The question of knowing whether one is or is not duped by morality confronts us with the following dilemma. Either we consider that any invocation of morality in politics – especially a particular, communitarian or denominational morality – is the alibi of a manifest or hidden violence, and we call for strict separation of morality and politics, for their radical separation, as an imperative condition to stop being duped. Or we pretend to ignore this effective or potential violence; we buttress ourselves with the principles of a particular morality in which we believe or pretend to believe, even though its supposed or claimed universality, proselytisation and messianism are only a supplementary alibi for the exactions, acts of cruelty and infringements of the refusal to murder that it tolerates, legitimises or encourages.

In the first case, one forbids oneself all 'moral' condemnation of violence, limiting oneself to measurements of its efficacy, cost and benefit but in no case its 'moral value'. Nothing then forbids the crime, and the risk becomes an absolute nihilism according to which there is nothing to say or do, no protest, no critical indignation, no solidary revolt, no outburst of unsolicited kindness, no sense of shared shame that holds up with regard to political exigencies. Cruelty itself, in very determined circumstances, becomes acceptable when it is the price to pay to obtain a political result, as the advocates of terror and terrorism hold on all continents and with good conscience. In the second case, in the name of its principles, morality is perverted into the partial justification of the partisan violence it supports. By making exceptions to its refusal and to its condemnation of decisions, speeches and actions that make fragile the lives on all sides and that bend the demand for universal solidarity, morality discredits itself, making those who invoke it the dupes of the credit they give it. This credit, moreover, might itself always be an illusion. Perhaps the thurifers of a murderous intervention in the name of moral principles, in the name of 'good' and 'evil', only pretend to believe in it! What if the articulation of morality and politics were nothing other than a universe of false pretences! What if it always came down to grandiloquent words![1] This is what would discredit the importance given to morality from the outset, as if all belief in its principles were, at the end of the day, only ever a fool's errand [*jeu de dupes*]! One can see that the alternative, the major traits of which I have just outlined, is hardly comforting because, on both sides, the result is the same: violence and cruelty still always emerge victorious. Should we then resign ourselves to the fact that nothing can eradicate them and recognise that it is vain, biased, self-interested and, at the same time, often suspect to condemn them?

How to escape the snare of such an alternative? This is the whole question. After having heard all the voices I have solicited, if what I will try to describe in conclusion has any meaning, it pertains entirely to the need to leave this pitfall in which, as Camus already foresaw, the *nihilism* of our time and its *misology* are concentrated – a *misology* that means not only hatred of language and reason, as the word's etymology indicates, but also the absence of confidence in the capacity of language and reason to stem violence, to ward off barbarism, to substitute the inevitability of war with a principle of solidarity and a desire for peace. If it is true that violence always amounts to suspending discourse, to interrupting it or turning verbal exchange into a destructive weapon, then one expects language to constitute a helpful recourse, to bring peace or preserve it, to calm the conflicts or remove the spectre of it. This is why the credibility of ethics and the credibility of language within which it utters its injunctions and commandments go hand in hand, for (this is what we learn from the memory of wars!) the bankruptcy of one (ethics) is always at the same time the bankruptcy of the other (language). This is how the possibility for a few protective words to conserve a minimum of meaning comes into play. How can we continue to speak of 'hospitality', 'forgiveness' and 'solidarity', as well as 'goodness', 'generosity' and 'humanity' itself, if invocation of them is the objective of a calculation, which is to say, if their usage, the recourse they constitute and the help they give are always self-interested and partisan and if they refuse to others what they claim for some? Language is certainly the element of ethics, but it is just as much the element of moral perversion or the turning of morality against itself, for this is perhaps the essence of nihilism: in the vindictive and vengeful discourses to which morality sometimes caves in and in what it then does with the words of language, even by manipulating partisan and complacent images, morality can get caught in the snare of renewing violence. One thus grasps the stakes of this articulation of ethics and politics toward which the reflections of the previous chapters are directed: at stake is the possibility of restoring a meaning to 'lost words' like humanity, generosity, goodness, solidarity, shame. At stake is not restoring a forgotten language but, rather, analysing the conditions under which these words could become, simply and minimally, audible and credible so as to oppose violence. This is the question upon which the foregoing reflections converge: what dimension of existence must one recognise to be able to appeal, still today, to these moral sentiments?

III

Violence is linked to vulnerability and mortality, ours and that of others. What makes violence possible, what makes it *always* possible, what makes it perhaps one of our ownmost possibilities, whether we suffer or inflict it, pertains to the fact that we are and we live among *vulnerable* and *mortal* beings. It is therefore easier to understand what ethics and politics have in common. They both have to do with this vulnerability and mortality. For the *institutions* of politics, indeed, must be understood as the collective and shared implementation of a *being-against-death* in solidarity. As I recalled at the onset, politics exists because life is exposed to multiple forms of insecurity, and nothing *alone* can ensure its protection. Everyone needs the help, assistance and attention to their security that only institutions guaranteed by law are able to assure them. However, nothing is so simple, as I said, for politics is also distinguished by its capacity to distort that same solidarity. Regardless of how it unfolds between institutions, the *being-against-death* with which politics arms society is, indeed, not only *exclusive* and *selective* but also, for this or that community of individuals, prone to turn into its opposite. Thus, the security that this defence against death is supposed to ensure always threatens to swerve into insecurity. Consequently, the essence of politics pertains both to the protection it guarantees against death, by way of the law in particular, and to the multiple exceptions it allows and the arrangements it makes with this protective principle. Truth be told, politics does not stop making these arrangements, not only when it declares war and exposes to death those it sends into combat while at the same time, albeit within certain limits, giving them a licence to kill, but also each time it closes the borders and refuses entry into its territory to those from elsewhere whom violence and poverty have forced to seek asylum. Put otherwise, this constitutes the essence of politics: by the simple fact that it is limited to a territory not identical to the totality of the world, the *being-toward-death* for which politics assumes responsibility is essentially particular, relative and always − above all − *reversible*. Thus, for entire categories of the population, for communities united by this or that feeling of belonging, the laws of their country − far from protecting them − can become a threat to their lives. From the laws in Nuremberg to those of the French State and including those of Marshal Antonescu in Romania, the history of State anti-Semitism would suffice, among many other examples, to remind ourselves of this. To say nothing of the impunity enjoyed still today in certain countries – like Russia – by ultraviolent gangs, militias and other small groups whose regressive xenophobia targets, in the most murderous way, all those they judge to be undesirable.

This is obviously not the case with ethics. Ethics is also concerned with vulnerability and mortality, but it is concerned with the vulnerability and mortality of *every other* [tout autre], and the resulting responsibility brooks no exception. Here we touch upon a decisive point. The difference between ethics and politics pertains to the fact that the former, unlike the latter, cannot enclose within (or fold over) a territory circumscribed in advance the responsibility called for *everywhere* by the care, help and attention that the vulnerability and mortality of the other demand. The logic of borders can be defended politically, if need be, since it responds to calculations involving interests that are always particular. This is the reason why it lends itself to all possible and imaginable productions of discriminatory discourses, relying on photomontages and partisan frameworks that serve its objectives. War too, as we know, can have its own necessities – and it is not the last to request and control these montages and frameworks. The fact remains that neither murderous war nor the unjust logic of borders will ever find any ethical foundation behind which to shelter the decisions associated with them. Except by making those who would claim such a foundation the 'dupes' – here we are – of the principles they would advance, except by wishing to be deceived and to deceive everyone in advancing such principles: the combatants, their families, passive and active witnesses, agents. Indeed, ethics cannot tolerate enjoining here what it condemns elsewhere. Once it serves a particular political interest, ethics cannot make the refusal of violence and murder an absolute principle and reject *a priori* – *as it should* – every act of barbarism and cruelty and all compromise with this same principle.

Is this to say there is no 'just war'? Put otherwise, what do we do from the perspective of such a convenient distinction between 'just wars' and 'unjust wars'? Two remarks impose themselves here. The first is that a distinction of this order remains necessary. Not all wars are equal, and we must remember how they differ according to their motives, their finality and the means they implement. It is therefore not forbidden to assume that a war can have 'just motives' that make it necessary, just like acts of resistance to all aggression or any intervention that would come to the aid of a people massacred by their leaders. However, one must also emphasise that the purity of these motives can never be fully guaranteed. No war's reasons are entirely ethical and *uncontaminated* by interests and calculations of a completely different order. This impurity is already in itself a reason to doubt the pertinence of the concept of 'just war', if one makes its 'justness' an ethical principle. Indeed, what is an impure principle if not a rule that threatens to turn against itself at any moment? The second remark pertains to the following fact. Assuming that war is *just*, in its principle, what it does never is. Put otherwise, 'ethical' reasons for waging war might exist, but no ethical reasons exist for *doing* what war *commands*: to destroy, to take life. Nothing can abolish this contradiction. It is what all veterans of all wars know they have to live with and deal with when the memory of past battles returns to haunt them.

Before any possible articulation of ethics and politics, what appears is their *opposition*. On the one hand, politics never stops its dealings with regard to the principle that would eliminate all limits to the care that politics extends to the vulnerability and mortality of others, to the attention it gives and the help it provides. If the foundation of politics is the implementation of 'being-against-death' in common and in solidarity, as we just recalled, it never stops applying new *conditions* to it. First, it selects the forms of existential insecurity that seem to call for decisions and action. Next, it circumscribes the circle of its beneficiaries or its victims, determining itself the modalities for expanding or contracting this circle. Lastly, it grants itself the right to suspend the principle by imposing, in the name of security, new forms of insecurity upon everyone. The proof is that the variety, if not the variation, of political regimes – that which, in other words, is supposed to comprise the difference between democracies, authoritarian regimes, theocracies and other military dictatorships – is directly linked to the distinction and extent of these restrictions. Thus, in non-democratic regimes, the benefit of the *being-against-death* guaranteed by the State is subject to the condition of absolute submission to the dictator, to the civil, military or religious despot who holds the reins of power. In theocracies, the condition is denominational. Elsewhere, it is linked to the nation, ethnicity or race. For all the others, for those who do not meet these conditions of allegiance or belonging to an idealised community or to its phantasm, the State offers less protection, if any, when it does not constitute a threat. *Being-against-death* thus divides the population as much as it brings the population together: this is the essence of politics.

On the one hand, then, there is this division. On the other, there is its impossibility in principle. If, indeed, one does not want to be 'duped by morality', one must recognise that responsibility for the attention, care and help for which the vulnerability and mortality of others calls applies *to everyone* and makes itself heard *everywhere*. That it 'applies to everyone' signifies not only that, *de jure*, it cannot posit any exception, but also that the resulting principle (the demand to aid) applies *to all*. That it is heard *everywhere* means, in a word, that ethics knows no borders. What is it? In fact, at stake is an impossible decision. Ethics cannot decide or try to be indifferent *a priori* to the vulnerability and mortality of any determined set of individuals, however they are circumscribed. Ethics cannot make this a question of law or principle without nullifying itself. Or, to put it differently still, when a call of this nature reaches it – and this happens everywhere and all the time – ethics cannot close its eyes in good conscience or acquiescence and resign itself to a tacit consent to the order and state of the world, along with its procession of injustices and inequalities, poverty, violence and cruelty. A morality that accepts this, accommodates itself to it or justifies it, is not a morality, or else it is a morality that 'dupes' anyone who pretends to believe in it, to believe in it without truly believing in it.

IV

Yet, we live precisely in this contradiction. For, over the course of our lives, we never stop making exceptions, accommodating ourselves, compromising with the impossible principle of this responsibility I just recalled. We never stop differentiating, making distinctions that have their own reasons. We cannot, we say, 'take in all the misery of the world'. These compromises and exceptions are obviously of various orders, and they cannot all be put on the same level. It is nevertheless important to describe them and understand what they have in common. War provokes the first among them and, as we saw in the opening chapters of this book, does so in at least two ways. First, with all the means at its disposal, war imposes what I will call a 'geography of vulnerability and mortality'. The psychological motivation for an armed conflict that makes people believe in its 'necessity', indeed, pertains essentially to the division of this attention, care and help. For the violence inherent in any conflict to be supported by the people, the wounded and the dead must not have the same price, and States must mobilise all their media power to persuade the people at war of this. Put otherwise, the prohibition against murder must be lifted, which cannot happen without producing a faultline in the ethical principle of the responsibility called for by the vulnerability and mortality of others, which is to say, without eclipsing this responsibility itself. The prohibition needs to be lifted so that the 'putting to death' of the 'enemy', however surgical the killing purports to be, and the suffering inflicted upon civilian populations as 'collateral damage' do not provoke feelings of revolt and shame, which is the first, most ordinary and common movement of our 'being-against-death'. Whether we want this or not, war always presupposes a legitimation of violence that suspends or erases this responsibility. And even if military-statist rhetoric carefully avoids calling the physical elimination of the enemy 'murder', the line [*frontière*] between these different ways of 'taking lives' [*donner la mort*][2] blurs in every conflict, which never completely escapes the acts of cruelty and barbarism that ethics nevertheless commands us to condemn. But war does not limit itself to authorising death or at least making it possible, if not probable. War entirely upsets our attitude toward death. In a word, which – as we already saw[3] – constitutes a whole problem on its own, war makes the *sacrifice* of a generation of men and women a collective demand. Moreover, this is how the essence of the sovereign decision that declares war should be thought most accurately: it turns *being-against-death* into its opposite. It substitutes the protective measures that ordinarily define its action, in the name of this same protection, with the obligation and the risk of an exposure to death. It asks families, fathers, mothers and wives to consent to sacrificing their children, husbands and brothers; in the name of principles with strong moral connotations, like love of the fatherland or 'defence of good against the axis of evil', it condemns those who would still find the strength to protest.

But war is not the only compromise we make with the ethical principle of responsibility for the attention, care and help called for *everywhere* and *for everyone* by the vulnerability and mortality of the other. Indeed, these compromises belong more generally to the ordinary course of existence. Indeed, it is not as an exception that we fracture this solidaristic *being-against-death*, which is alone capable of giving an ethical meaning to our belonging to the world. The knowledge, if not the experience, we might have of the injustices that divide the world – like the unequal access to medical care that condemns to death here millions of men and women who could be cured elsewhere, the absence of communicating vessels between endemic famine striking the poorest populations in the world and the food surpluses of the richest countries, the regimes of terror that directly threaten the lives of those who try to oppose it – is constitutive of the feeling we can have of this belonging. And, at the same time, the attention we pay to each of these phenomena is secondary at best and non-existent for many, dominated as it is by a feeling of helplessness and inevitability. We know without knowing, we see without seeing, we move on to something else, busy as we are, consumed day after day with the course of life. Such is the law of our relation to the world: our 'care' for it is necessarily partial and partisan, and the responsibility for which it calls is aporetic. It has no solution, no way out. When we are not the criminal agents or the victims of states of violence in the world and the acts of cruelty they engender, these states and these acts make us their powerless spectators, resigned by the force of things to live with.[4] No way to think our 'humanity' otherwise!

To this aporia, constitutive of our 'being-in-the-world' in the ethical and political sense of the term, I have chosen to give the difficult name 'murderous consent'. The name is difficult because it first provokes an inevitable feeling of revolt. How can we *consent* to that *against which* we can do nothing? If our powerlessness is at stake, does that not outright exclude all forms of 'consent'? Being unable to do anything, and thus doing nothing, does not mean 'to acquiesce'. Yet, there can be no consent without acquiescence. Only partisans of violence 'consent': those who encourage it, those who order it and those who commit acts called 'violent'. Granted! This burst of revolt has its legitimacy. But, as we know, these distinctions are fragile and porous. The border that separates acquiescence from resignation is not established once and for all. And who could calmly claim that this border is not the alibi of a good conscience all the more certain of its values and feelings (of 'humanity', of 'solidarity', etc.) in that they do not disrupt or influence in the slightest the course of one's existence? As for acquiescence, it does not necessarily give way to grand declarations. It does not always equal an immediately perceptible act of the will. Not wanting to see or hear, pretending not to see or hear, not being revolted in any way by the human condition, renouncing critique, restraining all outbursts of kindness and no longer even being ashamed by what people inflict upon each other – does this not, despite everything, amount to an acquiescence? This is why the notion of murderous consent immediately calls for two clarifications. It takes its ethical radicality from the fact that this consent can be just as much of the order of approbation and active participation as of the order of indifference or passive resignation. One can consent to violent death, to murder and even to acts of cruelty as an agent or a supporter by wishing for them and upholding them in thought and in action, but one can also consent by looking away through weariness or cowardice, by pretending not to know, with the certainty that nothing can be done about it, that this is how things are, that society, the State, the world, etc., 'are made that way'. One certainly must distinguish these different forms of consent – and we will never do so sufficiently – but, as a prerequisite for any discussion concerning the articulation of ethics and politics, it is also important to bring these different forms together under a single concept so as to designate this dimension of our belonging to the world.

For this is the second clarification that imposes itself: no one escapes this murderous consent. The world does not divide between those it would concern and others who might persuade themselves that, as far as they are concerned, this is not the case because they are 'good' people certain of their moral precepts. Uncovering murderous consent does not in any case constitute a tribunal; nor does it designate culprits or exempt the innocent. It stands short of these questions of judgement and guilt. What is at stake, then? Recall Levinas's phrase, with which I began this chapter some time ago now: 'Everyone will readily agree that it is of the highest importance to know whether we are not duped by morality'. Supposing therefore that one wonders about the conditions under which it is actually possible to escape this dupery, the above allows us to provide the first element of a response: one is not duped by morality when one recognises 'murderous consent' as an irreducible dimension of our belonging to the world – a dimension one must nevertheless attempt to reduce, aporetically, as one endeavours to make the impossible possible. For example, imagine that, in the name of moral principles, politicians are required to intervene to put an end to a state of violence in the world; we must know that this demand, no matter how legitimate it might be, nevertheless comes from an *exclusive* and *discriminatory being-against-death*. It condemns here – it cannot do otherwise – what it tolerates elsewhere. It divides the world's population between those who urgently need help and those who will still have to wait, when it does not find some legitimacy and justification for the violence they suffer, which has been the case so often and everywhere in the history of the last two centuries. Moreover, this observation does not detract in any way from the urgency of intervention or prohibit any assistance. It only means that we should not pay lip service to ethics when an intervention of this order, which always obeys political motives, dresses itself in the rags of morality. In other words, one does not get out of this contradiction so easily. In reality, one gets out of it even less when one claims or *believes* one gets out of it, when one imagines oneself to have gotten out scot-free and to incarnate goodness, freedom or justice.

V

If we want to rethink something like an articulation of ethics and politics, we thus have to relaunch from murderous consent – once again, namely, with the infringements of the responsibility for the attention, care and help called for *everywhere* and *for everyone* by the vulnerability and mortality of the other. Since this consent *each time* signifies a faultline in belonging to the world, care for the world comes to insert itself between ethics and politics as the aporetic site of their relation. In other words, because the recognition of murderous consent, understood as an incontrovertible dimension of all existence, constitutes the condition of such a relation, this relation must be thought as *ethi-cosmo-political* [éthi-cosmo-politique]. Divided with two hyphens, however, this portmanteau signifies even more – or, as it were, supports two complementary theses. It first recalls that cosmopolitanism – a politics of solidarity that would claim, if not to free itself from national interests, at least to take into account in its calculations a belonging or a connection that surpasses them, in other words, to adopt the point of view of the world – needs *ethics* to operate this surpassing. Politics undoubtedly suffices to determine and valorise solidarities or alliances limited by and to regional interests. Yet, to undo the double logic of sovereignty and the necessarily limited union or federation of sovereign States through pacts and treaties in order to rise to the point of view of the world, politics needs a principle heterogenous to any *Realpolitik*, a principle that perhaps – this is, in any case, what the portmanteau suggests – ethics alone is capable of providing politics. If we now admit that ethics defends the principle of a universal 'being-against-death', the notion of ethicosmopolitics supports the idea that ethics can legitimately address its injunctions to politics only by *holding* [tenant] – in the strongest sense of the term, as one takes a position – the point of view of the world. It *must* not compromise; it *cannot* bend to the imperatives of a partisan, communal, denominational and/or identity politics. Each time ethics transgresses this law, each time it is compromised in partisan support for particular interests, it makes those who let themselves be taken in by it the dupes of morality. And thus the principles that they defend, intend to promote and sometimes even make respected, even if by violence, self-destruct on their own.

The articulation of ethics and politics thus presupposes the point of view of the world. But how should we understand the world itself? What is the concept such that this articulation calls for it? To respond to this question, we must remember how this point of view irrupted in the preceding analyses. It was linked to two questions: borders and morality. These questions interrogated the meaning of our belonging to the world together with the sense of mortality, morality understood minimally as the common property that transcends all particular belonging (local, regional, national and others), but they still left in the dark the sense of their conjunction. One must relaunch from this conjunction insofar as it conjugates two concepts of the world *into one*. The first, easy to understand, is *extensive* and *negative*. The world is what we have in common beyond all borders. If everyone derives his or her singularity from the bundle of relations that link it, possibly, with everyone else and from which no link is therefore excluded *a priori*, then the world designates the totality of possible relations. *De jure*, it extends *for everyone* to *all beings, living and non-living*. But then here, in the facts, as everyone knows, there are no two *extensions* that are equal. None of us is identical to others by the same cluster of relations. Every relation is thus unique, singular and irreplaceable for everyone. The result is an intensive concept of the world: it concentrates on the fact that everyone is on their own *intensely* alone – unsubstitutable, irreplaceable.

Whence, ultimately, the principle that makes attention, care and help the object of an infinite responsibility *extended* to every other. Because the unicity and totality of the world are at stake each time – and because each death signifies, in its very singularity, the disappearance of the world – something like an 'ethicosmopolitics' imposes itself as a necessity. Because the world repeats in everyone in an absolutely singular way, in other words, the only point of view that holds when ethics mixes with politics is one that does justice to the infinite variety of singularities that produce this repetition. At once sombre, luminous and incandescent, one page I will borrow from Vasily Grossman's masterpiece *Life and Fate* suffices to clarify this point of view. Haunted by the memory of the death camps and the Gulag, as is known, this vast novelistic fresco brings to light the convergence of the two major totalitarian systems of the twentieth century through a whole gallery of characters caught up in the turmoil of history and, in particular, the Battle of Stalingrad. The following passage, on which I would like to comment briefly as a final word, follows the account of the slow progression that leads Sofya Osipovna and little David from the train's arrival in the Auschwitz station to the gas chamber, as if the proposed meditation was called up from the depths of horror by the memory of each victim in what, despite the erasures in the mass murder, must give his or her death its proper singularity. At stake is a reflexive pause, a stop – one almost wants to say a freezeframe: the image of smoke exiting the crematoria ovens – because this meditation cannot be detached from the pages that precede it. This meditation is the bridge that connects to *Murderous Consent* (2019) and *The Vocation of Writing* (2018b):

> When a person dies, they cross over from the realm of freedom to the realm of slavery. Life is freedom, and dying is a gradual denial of freedom. Consciousness first weakens and then disappears. The life-processes – respiration, the metabolism, the circulation – continue for some time, but an irrevocable move has been made toward slavery; consciousness, the flame of freedom, has died out.

The stars have disappeared from the night sky; the Milky Way has vanished; the sun has gone out; Venus, Mars and Jupiter have been extinguished; millions of leaves have died; the wind and the oceans have faded away; flowers have lost their colour and fragrance; bread has vanished; water has vanished; even the air itself, the sometimes cool, sometimes sultry air, has vanished. The universe inside a person has ceased to exist. This universe is astonishingly similar to the universe that exists outside people. It is astonishingly similar to the universe still reflected within the skulls of millions of living people. But still more astonishing is the fact that this universe had something in it that distinguished the sound of its ocean, the smell of its flowers, the rustle of its leaves, the hues of its granite and the sadness of its autumn field both from those of every other universe that exists and ever has existed within people, and from those of the universe that exists eternally outside people. What constitutes the freedom, the soul of an individual life, is its uniqueness. The reflection of the universe in someone's consciousness is the foundation of his or her power, but life only becomes happiness, is only endowed with freedom and meaning when someone exists as a whole world that has never been repeated in all eternity. Only then can they experience the joy of freedom and kindness, finding in others what they have already found in themselves. (Grossman 2006: 555)

Since the beginning, we have been searching for an ethical foundation for the condemnation and refusal of violence and hatred. We would like to know how to avoid being duped by the principles we invoke and the precepts we proclaim in such circumstances. Finally, if we believe we can find such a foundation, irreducible to all kinds of political manipulations and to moral compromises on the responsibility for the attention, care and help called for *everywhere* and *for everyone* by the vulnerability and mortality of the other, we legitimately wonder about the origins of this *responsibility*. Why, after all, should it extend to the totality of the world? What prevents us from being content with a salutary withdrawal while looking out for the interest of a restricted community? And here the voice of doubt and despair clears a path all the way to us. What if the very idea of a cosmopolitan conscience enjoining the refusal of all violence were nothing but a posture, a dream or an illusion? This is when Grossman's response makes itself heard, clearly and imperatively, to allay our doubts and to quell our hesitations. We understand nothing about violence, he tells us, and we know nothing about the cruelty of the gas chambers, of all the extermination sites, of all the camps throughout the world where we kill or let die, as long as we have not grasped what these mortiferous devices extinguish or try to extinguish in each life, what they make disappear or want to make disappear, what they try to erase each time, namely, *the world*. This is the loss! This is what all destruction signifies! And this is why the only way to restore meaning to such diffuse and confused notions as 'humanity' or 'solidarity', 'goodness' and 'generosity', in opposition to hatred, consists in recognising in ethics the radicality of its responsibility: a responsibility for the attention, care and help called for by the vulnerability and mortality of the other. Such thinking denies enumeration of victims all relevance for describing that vulnerability and mortality. For as Romain Rolland, Gandhi, Martin Luther King, Jr and so many others who accompanied us knew, victims must always be counted one by one. Exception is henceforth impossible: *each* world is *the* world, and all murderous consent *consents* to its end.

Notes

1 All the questions of 'hyperbolic ethics' to which Jacques Derrida devoted his teaching – hospitality, testimony, forgiveness, etc. – can be understood as an attempt to escape the grandiloquence of conditions – conditional hospitality, conditional pardon – via the hyperbole of the unconditional: if one does not want to pay lip service by appealing to hospitality, forgiveness, etc., then one must recognise that only unconditional hospitality or unconditional forgiveness conforms to a principle of justice. Inversely, one must recognise that – by essence partisan – all institutional, legal and political production of conditions compromises with this principle that is nevertheless the only one that can claim to be ethical: the absolute absence of conditions.

2 Crépon's phrase *donner la mort* is clearly a reference to Derrida's text of the same name, which appears in English as *The Gift of Death*. In the context of Crépon's sentence, we chose to translate as 'taking lives' rather than 'giving death' or 'gifting death' because it is idiomatic, has the same meaning and keeps the give-and-take economy. This translation decision loses the explicit reference to death, though, so we glossed the French phrase to draw the connection directly to Derrida. – Translators

3 See Part II, Chapter 1, 'The Fatherland, a Murderous Idol?', and Chapter 2, 'Of Hatred'.

4 The phrase *vivre avec* – literally 'to live with' – here refers to Crépon's book *Vivre avec: la pensée de la mort et la mémoire des guerres*, which has been translated into English by its subtitle alone: *The Thought of Death and the Memory of War* (2013). – Translators

Bibliography

Alain. 1930. *Mars; or, The Truth about War*, trans. Doris Mudie and Elizabeth Hill. New York: J. Cape & H. Smith.

——. 1960. *Mars ou la guerre jugée*. In *Les Passions et la Sagesse*, ed. Georges Bénézé. Paris: Gallimard.

Arendt, Hannah. 2006. *Eichmann in Jerusalem: A Report on the Banality of Evil*. New York: Penguin.

Baldwin, James. 1998a. The American Dream and the American Negro. In *Collected Essays*, ed. Toni Morrison, 714–19. New York: Library of America.

——. 1998b. *Another Country*. In *Early Novels & Stories*, ed. Toni Morrison, 361–756. New York: Library of America.

——. 1998c. Talk to Teachers. In *Collected Essays*, ed. Toni Morrison, 678–86. New York: Library of America.

——. 1998d. They Can't Turn Back. In *Collected Essays*, ed. Toni Morrison, 622–37. New York: Library of America.

Becker, Jean-Jacques. 1988. *La France en guerre (1914–1918). La grande mutation*. Brussels: Éditions complexe.

Bloch, Marc. 2006. *L'Histoire, la guerre, la résistance*. Paris: Gallimard.

——. 2013. Reflections of a Historian on the False News of the War, trans. James P. Holoka, *Michigan War Studies Review*, 51: 1–11.

Camus, Albert. 1975. *The Plague*, trans. Stuart Gilbert. New York: Vintage.

Constitution of the Republic South Africa, 1996. As Adopted on 8 May 1996 and Amended on 11 October 1996 by the Constitutional Assembly. Department of Justice and Constitutional Development. <www.justice.gov.za/legislation/constitution/SAConstitution-web-eng.pdf>. Accessed 8 November 2020.

Crépon, Marc. 2006. *Altérités de l'Europe*. Paris: Galilée.

—. 2008. *La Culture de la peur, Vol. I: Démocratie, identité, sécurité*. Paris: Galilée.

—. 2010. *La Guerre des civilisations*. Paris: Galilée.

—. 2012. *Le Consentement meurtrier*. Paris: Éditions du Cerf.

—. 2013. *The Thought of Death and the Memory of War*, trans. Michael Loriaux. Minneapolis: University of Minnesota Press.

—. 2018a. *Inhumaines conditions*. Paris: Odile Jacob Publishing.

—. 2018b. *The Vocation of Writing: Literature, Philosophy, and the Test of Violence*, trans. D. J. S. Cross and Tyler M. Williams. Albany: SUNY Press.

—. 2019. *Murderous Consent: On the Accommodation of Violent Death*, trans. Michael Loriaux and Jacob Levi. New York: Fordham.

—. 2020. *La Société à l'épreuve des affaires de mœurs*. Paris: Rivages.

Derrida, Jacques. 1992. *The Other Heading: Reflections on Today's Europe*, trans. Pascale-Anne Brault and Michael B. Naas. Bloomington: Indiana University Press.

—. 1998. *Monolingualism of the Other, or The Prosthesis of Origin*, trans. Patrick Mensah. Stanford: Stanford University Press.

—. 2004. Versöhnung, Ubuntu, Pardon, quel genre? In *Vérité, réconciliation, réparation*, ed. Barbara Cassin, Olivier Cayla and Philippe Joseph Salazar, 111–56. Paris: Seuil.

—. 2006. *Specters of Marx: The State of Debt, the Work of Mourning and the New International*, trans. Peggy Kamuf. New York: Routledge.

—. 2008. The Laws of Reflection: Nelson Mandela, in Admiration, trans. Mary Ann Caws and Isabelle Lorenz. In *Psyche: Inventions of the Other*, ed. Peggy Kamuf and Elizabeth Rottenberg, vol. 2, 63–86. Stanford: Stanford University Press.

Diop, Boubacar Boris. 2016. *Murambi, The Book of Bones*, trans. Fiona McLaughlin. Bloomington: Indiana University Press.

Duclert, Vincent. 2013. *Jean Jaurès. Combattre la guerre, penser la guerre*. Paris: Fondation Jean Jaurès.

Figes, Orlando. 2017. *The Whisperers: Private Life in Stalin's Russia*. New York: Picador.

Freud, Sigmund. 1918. *Reflections on War and Death*, trans. A. A. Brill and Alfred B. Kuttner. New York: Moffat, Yard & Co.

Grossman, Vasily. 2006. *Life and Fate*, trans. Robert Chandler. New York: New York Review of Books.

Héritier, Françoise. 1996. *De la violence*. Paris: Odile Jacob.

Hervé, Gustave. 1901. Au conseil général de l'Yonne. *Cahiers de la quinzaine* 3(5): 55–8.

—. 1921. *My Country, Right or Wrong*, trans. G. Bowman. London: Jonathan Cape.

Hirsch, Martin and Sylvaine Villeneuve. 2006. *La Pauvreté en héritage. 2 millions d'enfants pauvres en France.* Paris: Robert Laffont.

Jaurès, Jean. 1915. *L'Armée nouvelle.* Paris: L'Humanité.

—. 1916. *Democracy and Military Service,* trans. G. G. Coulton. London: Simpkin, Marshall, & Co.

—. 2009. *L'intégrale des articles de 1887 à 1914 publiés dans La Dépêche.* Toulouse: Éditions privat.

Jouve, Pierre Jean. 1920. *Romain Rolland vivant. 1914–1919.* Paris: Ollendorff.

Kant, Immanuel. 1970. *Political Writings,* ed. H. S. Reiss, trans. H. B. Nisbet. Cambridge: Cambridge University Press.

Kepel, Gilles. 2015. *Terreur dans l'Hexagone. Genèse du djihad français.* Paris: Gallimard.

King, Jr, Martin Luther. 1991. Nonviolence and Racial Justice. In *Testament of Hope: The Essential Writing and Speeches of Martin Luther King Jr.,* ed. James Melvin Washington. 5–9. New York: Harper Collins.

—. 2000. Letter from Birmingham Jail. In *Why We Can't Wait.* 85–112. New York: Signet.

—. 2010. Loving Your Enemies. In *Strength to Love.* 43–52. Minneapolis: Fortress.

Krog, Antjie. 2000. *Country of My Skull: Guilt, Sorrow, and the Limits of Forgiveness in the New South Africa.* New York: Three Rivers.

Laurent, Sylvie. 2015. *Martin Luther King. Une biographie.* Paris: Seuil.

Levinas, Emmanuel. 1969. *Totality and Infinity: An Essay on Exteriority,* trans. Alphonso Lingis. Pittsburgh: Duquesne University Press.

Mandela, Nelson. 1962. 'Black Man in a White Court': Nelson Mandela's First Court Statement. United Nations. <www.un.org/en/events/mandeladay/court_statement_1962.shtml>. Accessed 8 November 2020.

—. 2018. *In His Own Words.* New York: Back Bay.

Marx, Karl and Friedrich Engels. 2010. *Collected Works, Vol. VI: Marx and Engels 1845–1848.* London: Lawrence & Wishart.

Rolland, Romain. 1915. *Les Allemands destructeurs de cathédrales et de trésors du passé, mémoire relatif aux bombardements de Reims, Arras, Senlis, Louvain, Soisson, etc., accompagné de photographies et pieces justificatives.* Paris: Hachette.

—. 1916. *Above the Battle,* trans. C. K. Ogden. Chicago: Open Court.

—. 1920a. *Clérambault: Histoire d'une conscience libre pendant la guerre.* Paris: Albin Michel.

—. 1920b. Declaration of the Independence of the Mind. In *The Forerunners,* trans. Eden and Cedar Paul. New York: Harcourt, Brace, and Howe.

—. 1935. *Quinze ans de combat (1919–1934).* Paris: Rieder.

—. 1937. *Par la révolution la paix*. Paris: Éditions sociales internationales.

—. 1948. *Mahatma Gandhi: The Man Who Became One with the Universal Being*, trans. Catherine D. Groth. Agra: Shiva Lal Agarwala.

—. 1967. *Un beau visage à tous sens. Choix des lettres de Romain Rolland (1886–1944)*. Cahiers Romain Rolland. Cahier 17. Paris: Albin Michel.

—. 1992. *Voyage à Moscou, juin–juillet 1935*. Paris: Albin Michel.

— and Jean-Richard Bloch. 2019. *Correspondance (1919–1944)*, ed. Roland Roudil and Antoinette Blum. Dijon: Éditions Universitaires de Dijon.

— and Gandhi. 1976. *Romain Rolland and Gandhi Correspondence: Letters, Diary Extracts, Articles, etc*. New Delhi: Ministry of Information and Broadcasting Government of India.

— and Stefan Zweig. 2014a. *Correspondance 1910–1919*, ed. Jean-Yves Brancy, trans. Siegrun Barat. Paris: Albin Michel.

— and — 2014b. *Von Welt zu Welt. Briefe einer Freundschaft 1914–1918*. Berlin: Aufbau Verlag.

Salazar, Philippe-Joseph. 2017. *Words Are Weapons: Inside ISIS's Rhetoric of Terror*, trans. Dorna Khazeni. New Haven: Yale University Press.

Tutu, Desmond. 1998. Foreword by Chairperson. *Truth and Reconciliation Commission of South Africa Report*, vol. 1. Department of Justice and Constitutional Development. <www.justice.gov.za/trc/report/finalreport/Volume%201.pdf>. Accessed 3 November 2020.

Wright, Richard. 1991. *Black Boy*. New York: Harper Perennial.

X, Malcolm. 1990a. The Ballot or the Bullet. In *Malcolm X Speaks: Selected Speeches and Statements*, ed. George Breitman, 23–44. New York: Grove.

—. 1990b. Message to the Grass Roots. In *Malcolm X Speaks: Selected Speeches and Statements*, ed. George Breitman, 3–17. New York: Grove.

Index